"*Women in Church Ministries: Reform Movements in Ecumenism* offers renewed hope to the enduring question of women's sacramental equality, too often stifled behind 'closed doors.' Through skillful ecumenical analysis, this collection not only affirms women as protagonists of Christianity but demands ecclesiological innovation to realize the fullness of women's ministries. This collection boldly models the dialogue a living church so desperately needs to free itself from harmful paradigms to more deeply embody our baptismal equality."

—Kate McElwee
Executive Director, Women's Ordination Conference

"For decades, women, more than half the global Christian community, have asked repeatedly to participate in, contribute to, and function at all levels of ecclesial membership, consultation, decision-making, leadership, and ministry. Most poignantly these arguments have been grounded in a theology of baptism. The astute, incisive, and accessible essays gathered here extend, deepen, and sharpen that argument. These historians, theologians, scholars, and pastoral ministers insist on 'true equality between all with regard to the dignity and to the activity which is common to all the faithful in the building up of the Body of Christ' (LG 32)."

—M. Shawn Copeland
Professor of Systematic Theology *Emerita*, Boston College

"'What's behind the door?' This brilliant and multi-faceted discussion of women in church ministry is a must-read as we continue to walk the path toward visible Christian unity. Anyone interested in the potential of women for church leadership, both lay and ordained, will find in this volume a wide array of stimulating insights and questions. This courageous and scholarly collection of essays will challenge its readers to look beyond the answers of yesteryear to discover new and vital perspectives."

—Rita Ferrone, author of *Liturgy:* Sacrosanctum Concilium

"*Women in Church Ministries* provides scientific evidence that there is a very old tradition of women's participation in different church ministries and offices. This is an extremely important book because it gives back the debate on the role of women in the church to theological arguments in an ecumenical and global framework and with a pastoral perspective. It is both possible and urgent to talk about women in church ministries theologically, without resorting to arguments of cultural politics."

—Massimo Faggioli
Villanova University

"*Women in Church Ministries* systematically dismantles the arguments—theological and otherwise—used to justify the exclusion of women from ordination in the Catholic Church. This is an excellent resource for those committed to the women's diaconate and for those interested in carving out a larger place for women in the Catholic Church. These pages invite conversation partners as they explore alternative pathways forward for women and provide inspiring examples of women who redefine the boundaries of their role within the church."

—Sarah Kohles, OSF, author of *In Our Own Words: Religious Life in a Changing World*

Women in Church Ministries

Reform Movements in Ecumenism

Edited by Margit Eckholt, Dorothea Sattler,
Ulrike Link-Wieczorek, and Andrea Strübind

LP
A

LITURGICAL PRESS
ACADEMIC

Collegeville, Minnesota
www.litpress.org

Cover design by Monica Bokinskie. Cover photo courtesy of Ally Kateusz. A stone sarcophagus front from Hagia Sophia in Constantinople, Istanbul Archaeological Museum.

Originally published as Frauen in kirchlichen Ämtern. Reformbewegungen in der Ökumene, edited by Margit Eckholt / Ulrike Link-Wieczorek / Dorothea Sattler / Andrea Strübind © 2018 Verlag Herder GmbH, Freiburg im Breisgau.

1 2 3 4 5 6 7 8 9

Library of Congress Cataloging-in-Publication Data

Names: Eckholt, Margit, 1960– editor. | Sattler, Dorothea, 1961– editor. | Link-Wieczorek, Ulrike, editor. | Strübind, Andrea, 1963– editor.

Title: Women in church ministries : reform movements in ecumenism / edited by Margit Eckholt, Dorothea Sattler, Ulrike Link-Wieczorek, and Andrea Strübind.

Other titles: Frauen in kirchlichen Ämtern. English.

Description: Collegeville, Minnesota : Liturgical Press Academic, [2021] | "Originally published as Frauen in kirchlichen Amtern. Reformbewegungen in der Okumene, edited by Margit Eckholt / Ulrike Link-Wieczorek / Dorothea Sattler / Andrea Strübind © 2018 Verlag Herder GmbH, Freiburg im Breisgau." | Includes bibliographical references. | Summary: "Women in Church Ministries documents the ecumenical congress that took place in Osnabrück in December 2017 and the "Osnabrück theses," arguing for the participation of women in all church offices and ministries"— Provided by publisher.

Identifiers: LCCN 2020033974 (print) | LCCN 2020033975 (ebook) | ISBN 9780814685136 (paperback) | ISBN 9780814685389 (epub) | ISBN 9780814685389 (mobi) | ISBN 9780814685389 (pdf)

Subjects: LCSH: Ordination of women—Congresses. | Women and Christian union—Congresses. | Christian leadership—Congresses.

Classification: LCC BV676 .F75513 2021 (print) | LCC BV676 (ebook) | DDC 262/.14082—dc23

LC record available at https://lccn.loc.gov/2020033974

LC ebook record available at https://lccn.loc.gov/2020033975

Contents

III. Women's Diaconate: Ecumenical Perspectives

IV. The Debate on the Admission of Women to Ministry: From the Perspective of Systematic Theology and Canon Law

V. Broadening the Horizon: Pastoral Perspectives

Osnabrück Theses

A scientific congress under the title "Women in Church Ministries. Reform Movements in Ecumenism" was held in Osnabrück, Germany from December 6 to 9, 2017, as a joint ecumenical cooperation between theological institutions of the Universities of Osnabrück, Oldenburg, and Münster, together with German Roman Catholic and Protestant associations and institutions. After lectures, discussions, and intensive consultations, a majority of over 120 participants to the congress, who came from multilateral ecumenical contexts in Germany and other countries, adopted the following theses:

(1)

The declared goal of the ecumenical movement, the visible unity of the churches, cannot be achieved without an agreement on the presence of women in all ecclesiastical ministries.

(2)

Women in church ministries make a profound difference to the way each religious community is perceived by itself and by others.

(3)

It is necessary to find reasons not for women's access to offices and ministries of the church, but rather for their exclusion.

(4)

The discussion can and must remain open as to whether God has given an immutable instruction as to how and by whom he/she is to be witnessed through the church's ministry.

(5)

The distinction between specific offices within the one (sacramental) ministry (episcopate, priesthood, and diaconate) has developed historically and can be further developed in an ecumenical perspective. All forms of office should be opened for women. It is important to ensure that no gender-specific determination is made.

(6)

Critical inquiries into the church's teaching on the exclusion of women from church offices and ministries are a manifestation of women's readiness to exercise their vocation to serve the proclamation of the Gospel in word and deed.

(7)

The Spirit of Jesus Christ obliges us always to approach the various theological convictions regarding ecclesiastical ministries with argumentative cooperation, appreciation, and readiness to reconciliation.

Self-commitment

(1)

We will ensure that gender equality in the assumption and exercise of ecclesiastical ministries is the touchstone for credibility in the proclamation of the Gospel. This is indispensable for the apostolic mission of the churches. Beyond the question of the ordination of women, other forms of insensitivity toward gender equality in the churches should be recognized and overcome.

(2)

We will continue the theological discussions on the presence of women in all ecclesiastical ministries with the goal of reaching an understanding in the remaining controversies. Depending on the denominational situation, we will not shun critical discussion with the responsible church leaders about all forms of ordained ministry. In ecumenical fellowship, we strive for the ordination of women as deaconesses, presbyters (pastors, priests), and bishops.

(3)

We will continue to make theological contributions to the necessary differentiation between the opening to women of the diaconate and of other ministries within the one (sacramental) *ordo*. As a ministry for men and women, the diaconate strengthens the basic diaconal orientation of the church.

(4)

Within the bounds of our responsibility, we will strive for the increasing participation of women in leadership positions and ministries. We seek a culture of partnership in all churches.

Introduction by the Editors

This publication grew out of the Ecumenical Congress on Women in Church Ministries: Reform Movements in Ecumenism held at the University of Osnabrück December 6–9, 2017, which was organized and hosted by the Roman Catholic theologians Margit Eckholt, Institute of Catholic Theology, University of Osnabrück, and Dorothea Sattler, Faculty of Catholic Theology, University of Münster, together with the Protestant theologians Ulrike Link-Wieczorek and Andrea Strübind, both of the Institute of Protestant Theology, University of Oldenburg. At this conference, arguments were scientifically examined that, long after the reformation of churches began in the sixteenth century, led to an opening with regard to the participation of women in all church offices and ministries in the twentieth century.

In most churches of the Reformation the ordination of women is possible, and the Orthodox Patriarchates of Alexandria and Jerusalem reintroduced the ordination of deaconesses in 2017. In the Catholic Church, the doctrine is held that the church does not have the mandate to ordain women; this doctrine has high magisterial authority and was reaffirmed by Luis Ladaria, Prefect of the Congregation for the Doctrine of the Faith, in an article in May 2018.[1] The scientific presentations during the ecumenical

1. Cf. Luis Ladaria, Il carattere definitivo della dottrina di "Ordinatio sacerdotalis." A proposito di alcuni dubbi, in: *L'Osservatore Romano*, May 29, 2018, http://www.vatican.va/roman_curia/congregations/cfaith/ladaria-ferrer/documents/rc_con_cfaith_doc_20180529_caratteredefinitivo-ordinatiosacerdotalis_it.html; Joshua J. McElwee, Vatican's doctrinal prefect reaffirms ban on women priests, calls teaching "definitive," in: *National Catholic Reporter*, May 29, 2018, https://www.ncronline.org/news/vatican/vaticans-doctrinal-prefect-reaffirms-ban-women-priests-calls-teaching-definitive.

congress were encouraging and carried by a great spiritual depth; they made clear that there is a very old tradition of women's participation in different church ministries and offices. Deaconesses were ordained in the first millennium with prayer and the laying on of hands. The change in this practice, which led to the exclusion of women from church ministries, needs to be justified. There have always been innovations in the history of the church. In accordance with the equal dignity of woman and man, which is established in the texts of Scripture, one of the central results of the congress is to criticize tradition and call for the adoption of what scientific discourses have found. Belonging to Jesus Christ through baptism overcomes the socially or religiously founded boundaries between Jews and Greeks, slaves and free, man and woman (cf. Gal 3:28).

In autumn 2018, Herder Verlag published the conference proceedings under the title *Frauen in kirchlichen Ämtern: Reformbewegungen in der Ökumene* (Women in Church Offices: Reform Movements in Ecumenism). Central contributions to this publication have been included in this English-language publication. We would like to thank Herder Verlag and its literary editor Dr. Stephan Weber for the opportunity to publish a selection of these contributions in English with Liturgical Press, as well as Mr. Hans Christoffersen for accompanying us in this English book project on behalf of Liturgical Press. Above all, however, we thank Mr. Neville Williamson, Kassel, who translated the majority of the contributions into English. We would also like to thank the Thyssen Foundation for subsidizing the costs of translating the book.

The editors hope that this publication will help to set into motion a debate about ministries and services in the church that has been stagnant for a long time, and that it will become clear that these questions can only be answered together—by men and women—from now on.

At the end of the congress the participants endorsed the modified theses that had been worked out in an ecumenical exchange by the initiators beforehand. These "Osnabrück Theses" are placed in front of this volume and then again at the end of this book with explanatory notes. They are meant to serve the future ecumenical conversation and further discussion about the questions of women in church offices, including in the international context. These questions also need to be incorporated into priestly formation and theological teaching and training. Ecumenical support will be particularly helpful with these questions in the future. It is necessary to continue the joint efforts in these questions, because without a thematization of the question of women's ordination there will be no way to achieve the visible unity of the churches.

The editors would like to thank Bishop Dr. Franz-Josef Bode, Local Ordinary of the Diocese of Osnabrück and chairman of the Pastoral Commission of the German Bishops' Conference as well as the Sub-Commission for Women in Church and Society, for his openness and support in preparing and hosting the congress, which dealt with a topic that is still explosive in the Catholic Church.

It was and is clear in all this: God's Spirit works in history and opens closed doors; they cannot be kept closed on the church's path into the future. This also applies to the question of women in church offices.

Osnabrück, Münster, Oldenburg, February 28, 2020

Margit Eckholt, Osnabrück
Dorothea Sattler, Münster
Ulrike Link-Wieczorek, Oldenburg
Andrea Strübind, Oldenburg

I

Between Tradition and Innovation

Broadening the Horizon for the Question of Women in Church Ministries

Tradition, Criticism of Tradition, and Innovation

On the Road to Gender Equitable Structures of Ministry in the Roman Catholic Church

Eva-Maria Faber

1. Justice for Women in the Church: A Victim of the Overextension of the Magisterium

"This door is closed." This remark, made in an interview during a flight,[1] is often used as evidence that Pope Francis is also following the well-known doctrinal position on the ordination of women to the priesthood. But wait: what is the status of such an interview statement? Whoever calls "Stop!" here will have to repeat the same call many more times. As Johanna Rahner recently remarked, the question of women's ordination is "slowly but surely becoming a classic of post-conciliar dogma hermeneutics."[2]

It is a problem that the doctrinal authorities quote their own statements, thereby intensifying the tradition in order to be able to refer back to it.[3]

1. "E, con riferimento all'ordinazione delle donne, la Chiesa ha parlato e dice: 'No.' L'ha detto Giovanni Paolo II, ma con una formulazione definitiva. Quella è chiusa, quella porta": Conferenza stampa del Santo Padre Francesco durante il volo di ritorno, July 28, 2013, in: http://w2.vatican.va/content/francesco/it/speeches/2013/july/documents/papa-francesco_20130728_gmg-conferenza-stampa.html (21.12.2017).

2. J. Rahner, Eine Frage der Theologie. Wie definitiv ist das Verbot der Frauenordination?, in: *Herder Korrespondenz* 71 (2017) 48–51, 48.

3. Cf. P. Walter, Was heißt und zu welchem Ende studiert man Theologiegeschichte? Eine akademische Abschiedsrede, in: *Freiburger Universitätsblätter* 54 (2015) 53–65, 54.

It is a problem when attempts are made to treat texts of the ordinary magisterium inaccurately as texts of the extraordinary magisterium.[4]

It is also a problem, as one should recall, that the report of the Pontifical Biblical Commission of 1976 was ignored, which considered that there was no solution to the question of women's access to the presbyterate on the basis of the New Testament alone.[5] This investigation need never have been commissioned if the doctrine had already been clarified at that time or had been regarded as firmly taught"[6] and "set forth infallibly."[7] By ignoring this report in the context of the 1976 Congregation for the Doctrine of the Faith's Declaration *Inter Insigniores* on the Question of the Admission of Women to the Ministerial Priesthood, the magisterium neglected its moral duty to "diligently strive to

4. "In the curial interpretation, the corresponding passages in texts of the ordinary Magisterium are intentionally treated as texts of the extraordinary Magisterium": O. Fuchs, *"Ihr aber seid ein priesterliches Volk." Ein pastoraltheologischer Zwischenruf zu Firmung und Ordination* (Ostfildern, 2017) 210. From a formal point of view, canon law expert Jean-Pierre Torrell criticizes the quality of the magisterial procedure, for instance "the impression of a rather summary argumentation," in *Ordinatio sacerdotalis*, the claim to a "definite" binding character in spite of the lack of final infallibility, as well as inconsistencies in the response of 1995: "We were accustomed to more clarity and coherence in the earlier documents": J.-P. Torrell, Die Verbindlichkeit von *Ordinatio sacerdotalis*. Zur Hermeneutik lehramtlicher Dokumente, in: G. L. Müller (ed.), *Frauen in der Kirche. Eigensein und Mitverantwortung* (Würzburg, 1999) 357–79, 369, 370, 376.

5. Cf. on this: W. Groß, Bericht der Päpstlichen Bibelkommission, 1976, in: Groß (ed.), *Frauenordination. Stand der Diskussion in der katholischen Kirche* (Munich, 1996) 25–31, 26; 31. Furthermore, there seems to have been a majority vote that the reasons derived from Scripture are not sufficient to exclude the possibility of ordination of women, and conversely that the church has the authority "to entrust women with the ministries of the Eucharist and reconciliation without going against Christ's original intentions" (31).

6. Pope John Paul II, Apostolic Letter *Ordinatio Sacerdotalis* to the Bishops of the Catholic Church on Reserving Priestly Ordination to Men Alone, May 22 1994, par. 4: https://w2.vatican.va/content/john-paul-ii/en/apost_letters/1994/documents/hf_jp-ii_apl_19940522_ordinatio-sacerdotalis.html.

7. Congregation for the Doctrine of the Faith, Responsum ad Propositum Dubium concerning the Teaching Contained in *Ordinatio Sacerdotalis*, October 28, 1995: http://www.vatican.va/roman_curia/congregations/cfaith/documents/rc_con_cfaith_doc_19951028_dubium-ordinatio-sac_en.html.

inquire properly" into revelation and "to give apt expression to its contents" (LG 25).[8]

With these opening remarks I do not intend to reduce the theme of the conference whose lectures are to be found in this book purely to the issue of the presbyteral ordination of women. I want to start by making it crystal clear how much effort some people in the Roman Catholic Church are investing in order to ensure that this door is heavily protected. The door is closed, and no one should even dream of asking whether a key exists, or why there is a door there at all. The barriers that have been set up in front of the door are so wide that it is not even possible to recognize any other doors nearby.

2. Desideratum: Church with Women—on All Levels

So let us forget the door; let us ask about the room behind it. Certainly it is not a good thing to stretch metaphors too far, but it is obviously interesting to find out what is to be found behind this closed door. Looking at it from this angle, the main problem is not that women are excluded from ordination. The main problem is that for them a whole realm within the church has been closed off,[9] not least the area of high-level consultations, decision-making, and leadership. There are two levels to this problem.

2.1 Deficits in Opportunities for Synodal Participation

One of the crucial statements made by the Second Vatican Council concerns the "true equality between all with regard to the dignity and to the activity which is common to all the faithful in the building up of the

8. The report is echoed in the defensive formulations of the second section of the declaration: Congregation for the Doctrine of the Faith, Declaration on the Question of the Admission of Women to the Priesthood *Inter Insigniores,* October 15, 1976, par. 2: http://www.vatican.va/roman_curia/congregations/cfaith/documents/rc_con_cfaith_doc_19761015_inter-insigniores_en.html: "It is true that these facts do not make the matter immediately obvious. This is no surprise, for the questions that the Word of God brings before us go beyond the obvious. In order to reach the ultimate meaning of the mission of Jesus and the ultimate meaning of Scripture, a purely historical exegesis of the texts cannot suffice."

9. In the following, the term "church" usually refers to the Roman Catholic Church unless the context indicates otherwise.

Body of Christ" (LG 32).[10] This equality precedes all differentiations and is based on the participation of all the baptized in the priestly, prophetic, and royal ministry of Jesus Christ (cf. LG 10:12). The Holy Spirit gives gifts to all believers and makes them "fit and ready to undertake the various tasks and offices which contribute toward the renewal and building up of the Church" (LG 12).

However, these charisms cannot be employed sufficiently, because the structures for participation in the Roman Catholic Church are underdeveloped.[11] Both men and women are affected by this deficit. The Roman Catholic Church lags behind all other churches in the development of synodal structures.

2.2 Ministerial Structures Largely Closed to Women

Notwithstanding such synodal structures, the church needs offices that are "constituted in a stable manner by divine or ecclesiastical ordinance." According to CIC/1983 can. 145 §1 and can. 228 §1, such offices are not in principle bound to ordination. But women are also underrepresented in offices that are accessible to lay people.[12] At least some local churches have, in the meantime, succeeded in assigning women to offices that, at the same time, enable them to participate in local church advisory and decision-making processes. The contribution by Bishop Franz-Josef Bode has thankfully combined a survey of this situation with a clear appeal to continue in this direction. In the church as a whole, the development is lagging behind, so that it already causes a stir when a woman is appointed to the position of an undersecretary in the Vatican.

Corresponding efforts encounter legal and dogmatic limits at all levels insofar as, according to present understanding, "the full care of souls . . . for whose fulfillment the exercise of the priestly order is required" (CIC/1983 can. 150), the administration of the sacraments and the power

10. Second Vatican Council, Dogmatic Constitution on the Church (*Lumen Gentium*), in *Vatican Council II: The Conciliar and Postconciliar Documents*, new rev. ed., Austin Flannery, OP, ed. (Collegeville, 2014) 389.

11. Cf., e.g., S. Demel, Beteiligungsrechte der Laien und Frauen in der katholischen Kirche. Grundlagen und Grenzen im CIC/1983, in: *Jahrbuch für christliche Sozialwissenschaften* 55 (2014) 179–98.

12. Cf. A. Qualbrink, Frauen in kirchlichen Leitungspositionen. Hemmnisse, Herausforderungen und Perspektiven, in: *Theologisch-praktische Quartalschrift* 165 (2017) 245–55.

of governance (cf. CIC/1983 can. 129) are largely reserved for ordained persons. Does this mean that these areas are closed to women in principle? But can it be possible that the Roman Catholic Church deprives itself of women's charisms in all these fields? Half of the members of the Roman Catholic Church are marginalized in this way; the consequences must be borne by all its members.[13]

In view of such dimensions, one would normally expect the problem to be dealt with in a prompt and determined fashion. But the gaze is fixed on the locked door of presbyteral ordination for women and on the worry that someone might lay a hand on it. This leads to paralysis and inhibition. The topic of women is dangerous, because someone (a man or a woman) could get near this door. As a result, not everyone in this church is doing everything possible to keep moving on the path to gender equitable structures in the church and the ministry.

On the one hand, dealing with the problem would imply that all possibilities of the present church order are exploited that might allow forms of synodal participation and nonordained women's ministries as well as participation in leadership authority.

On the other hand, dealing with the problem would have to address pressing tasks in connection with tradition, criticism of tradition, and innovation in order to look for doors, and even to take a closer look at the door that is so comprehensively protected. The following considerations focus on these aspects of dealing with the problem.

3. Sounding Out Scripture and Tradition

A church that is seriously interested in being a church with women would have to take the highest conceivable care to investigate the testimonies of apostolic and ecclesiastical tradition regarding the church ministries and roles that were occupied by women. In this way one would be able to find points of reference for the urgently needed development of church structures today.

13. P. Hünermann explains that through the exclusion of social groups from responsible leadership functions "the entire group is denied recognition as equal, morally responsible partners": "The church also needs . . . women in church offices," in: M. Heimbach-Steins, G. Kruip, S. Wendel, eds., *Kirche 2011. Ein notwendiger Aufbruch. Argumente zum Memorandum* (Freiburg i.Br., 2011) 189–97, 191, with reference to analyses by A. Honneth.

Many theologians have undertaken this task, but their research was not really taken up by the church. It must suffice here to name a few examples.

The aforementioned report by the Pontifical Biblical Commission in 1976 might today possibly have turned out to be even more explicit, since the female apostle (formerly male "Junias") may once again be called Junia, and the deaconess Phoebe as well as other women named by Paul in his greetings have achieved further exegetical recognition.[14]

For a long time, official ecclesial and theological discussions have been devoted to the question of how to understand the sources on the deaconesses of the early church. I take this opportunity to express my regret that, more than twenty years ago, I myself wrote an article on historical assessments that can no longer be maintained.[15] In the early church and long after, there were deaconesses whose ministry took place in what was then understood as an "Order" (see, for example, the studies of Ute Eisen,[16] Gary Macy,[17] Dorothea Reininger,[18] and Cipriano Vagaggini, as well as Phyllis Zagano[19]).

14. Cf. E. Schüssler Fiorenza, *Zu ihrem Gedächtnis. Eine feministisch-theologische Rekonstruktion der christlichen Ursprünge* (Mainz/Munich, 1988); M. Gielen, Die Wahrnehmung gemeindlicher Leitungsfunktionen durch Frauen im Spiegel der Paulusbriefe, in: Th. Schmeller, M. Ebner, R. Hoppe, eds., *Neutestamentliche Ämtermodelle im Kontext* (Freiburg i.Br., 2010) 129–65; E. Schüssler Fiorenza, Frauen als Diakone in paulinischen Gemeinden, in: D.W. Winkler, ed., *Diakonat der Frau. Befunde aus biblischer, patristischer, ostkirchlicher, liturgischer und systematisch-theologischer Perspektive* (Vienna, 2012) 11–40; H. Scherer, Die Mühe der Frauen. "Charismatische Gemeindeleitung" in Röm 6,6.12, in: *Biblische Zeitschrift* 60 (2016) 264–76.

15. Cf. E.-M. Faber, Art. Diakon. II. Historisch-theologisch, in: LThK3, vol. 3 (1995) 179–81.

16. U. Eisen, *Amtsträgerinnen im frühen Christentum. Epigraphische und literarische Studien* (Göttingen, 1996).

17. See G. Macy, *The Hidden History of Women's Ordination. Female Clergy in the Medieval West* (New York, 2008); Macy, Die Bedeutung der Ordination im ersten Jahrtausend des Christentums, in: *Theologische Quartalschrift* 192 (2012) 329–41, 336–40.

18. D. Reininger, *Diakonat der Frau in der einen Kirche. Diskussionen, Entscheidungen und pastoral-praktische Erfahrungen in der christlichen Ökumene und ihr Beitrag zur römisch-katholischen Diskussion* (Ostfildern, 1999).

19. C. Vagaggini, *Ordination of Women to the Diaconate in the Eastern Churches* (Collegeville, 2013); Ph. Zagano, Gerechtigkeit für das Leben der Pfarrgemeinde: Frauen wieder zur Diakonatsweihe zulassen, in: *Concilium* 53 (2017) 232–39.

A church that is willing to take a step in the direction of offices for women would find adequate criteria in the tradition resolutely followed by other churches.

An ecumenical attitude that regards the perspectives and spiritual practices of other churches as an enrichment of one's own church[20] should also pay attention to the ecumenical relevance of the living tradition of other churches that ordain women. It is unfortunate that usually the Roman Catholic Church only mentions the ordination of women practiced in other churches as an additional obstacle, without acknowledging the unresolved issues of better, equal participation of women in its own area. This contravenes the injunction formulated in the Second Vatican Council's Decree on Ecumenism that the primary duty should be "to make a careful and honest appraisal of whatever needs to be renewed and done in the Catholic household itself" (UR 4). The lively experiences and traditions of other churches are helpful for this.

These brief indications may suffice to show that tradition as such does not pose a problem for allowing women to participate in responsible structures of the church, namely, as ordained ministers. To refer to the historical existence of tradition while at the same time rejecting the significance of historical evidence, as does the *Inter Insigniores* statement,[21] is contradictory. What is lacking is a bold approach to those traditions that now call for reception.

What is also missing is a bold criticism of tradition.

4. Criticism of Tradition

Dealing with tradition creates problems not only if its abundance is not received, but also if one is not prepared to get to grips with the deficits of tradition.

20. "Nor should we forget that anything wrought by the grace of the Holy Spirit in the hearts of our separated brethren can contribute to our own edification" (UR 4); in Second Vatican Council, Decree on Ecumenism (*Unitatis Redintegratio*), in *Vatican Council II: The Conciliar and Postconciliar Documents*, new rev. ed., Austin Flannery, OP, ed. (Collegeville, 2014) 459. The fact that just at this point in the document, as is customary in council texts, only the "brethren" are mentioned can be taken as an indication of the learning process that lies before us.

21. Cf. note 8 above.

The tradition of the church includes highly problematic anthropological statements about women.[22] They range from philosophically inspired statements on women's deficient humanity to culturally shared beliefs regarding women's inabilities (such as their unsuitability for public office) and specifically theological reservations on their creation in the image of God (which have been maintained until recently[23]).

The conglomerate of such discriminatory statements forms a broad stream of tradition.

It is not only shocking that such a tradition exists. It is also shocking to see that hardly anyone complains about the contempt for women expressed in such theological statements. Their significance is all too quickly played down.

Pope John Paul II's Universal Prayer of March 12, 2000 did indeed contain a confession of sins against the dignity of women and the unity of the human race.[24] In his letter to women in 1995, this pope had already stated that it was time "to assign responsibility where it is due."[25] It is often the case, however, that the inner-church problem is touched up. The *Inter Insigniores* Declaration of 1976 mentions social discrimination against women and then states: "In the life of the Church herself, as history shows us, women have played a decisive role and accomplished tasks of outstanding value." But women did that in society as well. It would be necessary to compare the virulent discrimination in both cases.

The document of the Congregation for the Doctrine of the Faith of 2004 on the collaboration of men and women in the church and in the

22. Cf. the groundbreaking work by I. Raming, *Der Ausschluss der Frau vom priesterlichen Amt. Gottgewollte Tradition oder Diskriminierung? Eine rechtshistorisch-dogmatische Untersuchung der Grundlagen von can. 968 §1 des Codex Iuris Canonici* (Cologne, 1973; new edition 2002 entitled *Priesteramt der Frau. Geschenk Gottes für eine erneuerte Kirche*); G. Macy, *History*, 111–27.

23. Cf. E.-M. Faber, Zur Lehre von der Gottebenbildlichkeit der Frau bei Matthias Joseph Scheeben, in: B. Jeggle-Merz, A. Kaupp, U. Nothelle-Wildfeuer, eds., *Frauen bewegen Theologie. Die Präsenz von Frauen in der theologischen Wissenschaft am Beispiel der Theologischen Fakultät der Albert-Ludwigs-Universität* (Freiburg i.Br./Leipzig, 2007) 117–39.

24. See http://www.vatican.va/news_services/liturgy/documents/ns_lit_doc_20000312_prayer-day-pardon_en.html.

25. Pope John Paul II, Letter to Women, June 29, 1995, par. 3: http://w2.vatican.va/content/john-paul-ii/en/letters/1995/documents/hf_jp-ii_let_29061995_women.html.

world shows a similar imbalance. It uses the term "structures of sin" with reference to relations between the sexes in order to identify a situation that is "potentially conflictual." Such structures of sin were "inscribed in culture."[26] In culture, and not in the church?[27]

Apart from this strange combination of admitting to the problem and denying their own involvement, official church voices underestimate the historical impact of misogynist views. For the two most important reference points of tradition—patristics and scholasticism—*Inter Insigniores* admits that there one finds "the undeniable influence of prejudices unfavourable to woman" (for the church fathers), as well as arguments that "modern thought would have difficulty in admitting, or would even rightly reject" (for scholasticism). Nevertheless, this tradition is considered "firm" in terms of its rejection of women's ordination.

Criticizing tradition and owning up to deficits in anthropology and creation theology does not lead to consequences when critics of tradition question ecclesiology. It is not just amazing that there is no willingness to examine the validity of the reasons for the exclusion of women from ordination. Criticism of tradition also shows no regret in face of the many centuries of church history in which women were excluded from formal and undiminished participation in consultation and decision-making processes on the basis of questionable beliefs concerning the subordination of women and their inability to hold public office. Tradition is in urgent need of criticism, and the consequential processes of reversal are overdue.

The aim of such processes cannot be achieved simply on the basis of the abundance of tradition and the criticism of tradition. This cannot work without innovation.

26. Congregation for the Doctrine of the Faith, Letter to the Bishops of the Catholic Church on Collaboration between Men and Women in the Church and in the World, May 31, 2004, par. 8: http://www.vatican.va/roman_curia/congregations/cfaith/documents/rc_con_cfaith_doc_20040731_collaboration_en.html.

27. See also the statement in Pope John Paul II, Apostolic Letter *Mulieris Dignitatem*, August 15, 1988, par. 27: https://w2.vatican.va/content/john-paul-ii/en/apost_letters/1988/documents/hf_jp-ii_apl_19880815_mulieris-dignitatem.html: "The witness and the achievements of Christian women have had a significant impact on the life of the Church as well as of society. Even in the face of serious social discrimination [!], holy women have acted 'freely,' strengthened by their union with Christ."

5. Innovation

5.1 The Relationship between Tradition and Innovation

The relationship between tradition and innovation has aroused lively interest in recent years. Publications before 2013 slaved away at the flood of relevant statements by Pope Benedict XVI on the relationship between continuity, reform, and discontinuity. After 2013, publications sought to explore the scope for the dynamics of reform that had been set in motion again by Pope Francis. In terms of tradition theory, it can hardly be denied that a living tradition depends on innovation if it is not to wither or stagnate. Historically, it should be noted that many things that may appear to be discontinuities in the present are in continuity with old traditions and may have to remedy earlier discontinuities. To put it in a nutshell: anyone who nowadays considers the introduction of a women's diaconate as an inadmissible discontinuity would be obliged to provide explanations for other discontinuities. In that case, why did the women disappear from ecclesial greeting lists, why were deaconesses ousted, why were the abbesses deprived of jurisdictional powers?

But in fact, alongside innovations that merely correct discontinuities, genuine innovation is required: the Church's response to new insights, new needs, to the signs of the times.[28]

The much quoted sentence from Galatians is a thorn: "There is no longer Jew or Greek, there is no longer slave or free, there is no longer male and female; for all of you are one in Christ Jesus" (Gal 3:28).[29] Paul here takes a firm stance on the necessary and apparently unquestionable consequences of faith in Jesus Christ. However, none of the consequences named here was smoothly implemented in the history of the church. The early frictions between Jews and Greeks are already unpleasantly described in the New Testament. The consequent effects cost the lives of countless Jews. It was not until the twentieth century that the Christians of Gentile origin and the churches were prepared to relate to Jews in a respectful and friendly way.

28. Cf. M. Eckholt, *Ohne die Frauen ist keine Kirche zu machen. Der Aufbruch des Konzils und die Zeichen der Zeit* (Ostfildern, 2012).

29. See, e.g., J. Kügler, Gal 3,26–28 und die vielen Geschlechter der Glaubenden. Impuls für eine christliche Geschlechtsrollenpastoral jenseits von "Sex and Gender," in: M. E. Aigner, J. Pock, eds., *Geschlecht quer gedacht. Widerstandspotenziale und Gestaltungsmöglichkeiten in kirchlicher Praxis* (Münster, 2009) 53–70.

The idea that there is no longer slave or free was not prevalent in the Roman Catholic Church until the nineteenth century.[30] For centuries, it approved of slavery and practiced it. There were only a few who called for a different position; these were the marginalized traditions within the richness of tradition for which one is nowadays grateful. Quakers and Methodists understood at an early stage that slavery contradicted the Christian image of humankind. The Roman Church could have learned early from other Christian believers and churches. But it was not until 1839 that a fundamental condemnation of slavery was made by the magisterium (cf. DH[31] 2745f.). Beyond that, and what is this other than innovation, Pope John Paul II qualified slavery as one of the acts that are "*intrinsically evil" (intrinsece malum)*, thus "*always and per se*, in other words, on account of their very object, and quite apart from the ulterior intentions of the one acting and the circumstances."[32]

In one of his most emphatic statements on the subject, Pope Francis criticized the *servidumbre* (servitude) of women in the church that he perceived.[33] When will the church learn that there is no difference be-

30. The connection between the struggle to abolish slavery and the liberation of women was already described by Elizabeth Cady Stanton: cf. M.-Th. Wacker, Geschichtliche, hermeneutische und methodologische Grundlagen, in: L. Schottroff, S. Schroer, M.-Th. Wacker, *Feministische Exegese. Forschungserträge zur Bibel aus der Perspektive von Frauen* (Darmstadt, 1995) 1–79, 3–7.

31. *Enchiridion symbolorum definitionum et declarationum de rebus fidei et morum (Kompendium der Glaubensbekenntnisse und kirchlichen Lehrentscheidungen)* by Heinrich Denziger, trans. Peter Hünermann with Helmut Hoping (Freiburg im Breisgau u.a., 2017).

32. Pope John Paul II, Encyclical *Veritatis Splendor*, August 6, 1993, par. 80: http://www.vatican.va/content/john-paul-ii/en/encyclicals/documents/hf_jp-ii_enc_06081993_veritatis-splendor.html. The same pope draws a parallel to the relationship between man and woman in *Mulieris Dignitatem*: "Saint Paul not only wrote: 'In Christ Jesus . . . there is no more man or woman,' but also wrote: 'There is no more slave or freeman.' Yet how many generations were needed for such a principle to be realized in the history of humanity through the abolition of slavery! And what is one to say of the many forms of slavery to which individuals and peoples are subjected, which have not yet disappeared from history?" (24). See J. T. Noonan, *A Church That Can and Cannot Change. The Development of Catholic Moral Teaching* (Notre Dame, 2005) 15–123.

33. Pope Francis, address to the participants in a seminar organized by the Pontifical Council for the Laity on the 25th anniversary of the Apostolic Letter *Mulieris*

tween male and female in the church, either with respect to dignity or to participation in responsibility? What is needed here is a rethink analogous to the about-turn in the attitude toward slavery.

5.2 Innovation as Consistent Realization of Tradition

This is an important insight: innovation does not happen by chance. In the church, innovative processes take place when a faith insight comes to bear in areas that had not yet been covered by it. This means that innovation is a (more) consistent realization of the traditions passed down.

What are the insights that so far were unable to have an innovative effect on the position of women in the church?

5.3 Insights of Creation Theology

First and foremost is the fundamental insight that the equal dignity of all human beings, whether male or female, which has been formulated in creation theology and in anthropology, must take effect in ecclesiology and in the theology of ministry. This applies not least in view of the fact that Gal 3:28 uses christological reasoning to aim directly at the formation of relations in the church community.

5.4 Insights of ministerial theology

Insights gained from the ministerial orders of the Old Church can be of value for innovation. The main question is not whether a direct line leads from the deaconesses of the early church to a diaconate for women today. Today it is, in fact, not necessary to conduct the same ministry as that of the early church deaconesses. However, the diversity of early church practice loosens the fixation on a particular, narrowly defined office. When comparing the different ordinances of the early church (not just concerning the deaconesses, but including them), one can recognize precisely "the room for manoeuvre which the congregations of the 2nd to 4th centuries made use of."[34]

Dignitatem: http://w2.vatican.va/content/francesco/de/speeches/2013/october/documents/papa-francesco_20131012_seminario-xxv-mulieris-dignitatem.html.

34. F. Dünzl, Die Diakonin in altchristlichen Kirchenordnungen oder: Der Spielraum der Kirche, in: Th. Franz, H. Sauer, eds., *Glaube in der Welt von heute. Theologie und Kirche nach dem Zweiten Vatikanischen Konzil*, vol. 2, *Diskursfelder* (Würzburg, 2006) 169–187.

At the same time, the criteria to be applied to ecclesial offices are highlighted. The relativizing statement that the deaconesses of the early church were "only" or "primarily" appointed for reasons of decency mistakes the weight of this statement. The church was guided by *pastoral necessities* that were *culturally* conditioned by attitudes toward decency. The necessities of church practice and cultural perceptions of decency have now changed. In *church* practice, desiderata (often formulated by women, but not infrequently also by men) are expressed, hoping to experience women serving in preaching and pastoral care or to be able to talk with women about intimate matters of guilt and reconciliation.[35] For their part, it is particularly in the area of leadership that the *cultural* plausibilities run contrary to the position of women in the Roman Catholic Church. For many contemporaries, this may well have had something to do with decency.[36]

5.5 Insights of Ecclesiology on the Subjectivity of the Church

For the challenge of applying existent insights in an innovative fashion, it may well be helpful to follow a train of thought developed by Hermann Josef Pottmeyer in connection with the relationship between the First and Second Vatican Councils. Instead of describing a discontinuity, as is usual, Pottmeyer demonstrates that there was a continuity, since both councils were reacting to the dynamics of a *growing subject consciousness* of the church. Within this framework, both councils were inescapably confronted with the question of the concrete subjects who act historically in the Church and for the Church. However, they gave different answers. While the First Vatican Council identified "the Pope as the only subject," the Second Vatican Council determined that the Church is collegially and communally subject, including "the bishops, priests and the laity as subjects of the Church."[37]

The question that demands further innovations is: how do women act as subjects within the subject church? How are they also subjects when

35. The significance of the pastoral role of women in counseling at the sickbed is not very far removed from the situation in the early church.

36. See R. Radlbeck-Ossmann, Das Argument von der Einheit des Ordo. Fundament für die Ablehnung eines Diakonats der Frau?, in: Winkler, ed., *Diakonat*, 119–134, 121.

37. H. J. Pottmeyer, Kontinuität und Innovation in der Ekklesiologie des II. Vatikanums, in: G. Alberigo, ed., *Kirche im Wandel. Eine kritische Zwischenbilanz nach dem Zweiten Vatikanum* (Düsseldorf, 1982) 89–110, 105.

the church acts, advises, and decides officially? It is imperative for their dignity as humans and in the church that women be treated as human beings and responsibly involved in this area, and it is urgently necessary to open a door for this.

In his explanations, Pottmeyer emphasizes that there is a challenge to assume active responsibility resulting from the increasing awareness of the church as subject. This confirms the aforementioned conviction with respect to the authority of the church in organizing the ministerial order. If the church very strongly claims to be subject and authority in various matters, it is questionable when this "power of decision and innovation"[38] is then abruptly restricted by the highly disputable claim that Jesus was gender-oriented in his actions. In any case, the diagnosis of Elmar Klinger applies: "The statement that the Church does not consider itself competent by no means answers the question whether it is not in truth competent to do so, in spite of its own assessment."[39]

5.6 Women as Subjects of the Pending Advisory and Decision-Making Processes

When Pope Francis met the Superiors General in May 2016, they expressed their wish, their desire, even their right, to be included in the assemblies of their congregation: "How is it possible that we are quite often forgotten and not included as participants . . . ? Can the Church afford to continue speaking about us, instead of speaking with us?" The answer of Pope Francis was clear: "You must be present in the Assembly!" and at the same time honest: "I did not imagine such separation."[40] In fact, it may not have been clear or important to many church leaders what it means for women to be simply excluded at so many levels. But the longer a lack of awareness of this deficit in the life of the church lasts, the more it becomes a disconcerting ignorance. Insight demands more than mere declarations of intent.[41] Despite all appreciation for and relief

38. Pottmeyer, Kontinuität und Innovation, 106.

39. E. Klinger, *Christologie im Feminismus. Eine Herausforderung der Tradition* (Regensburg, 2001) 235.

40. Pope Francis, Address to the International Union of Superiors General, May 12, 2016: https://w2.vatican.va/content/francesco/en/speeches/2016/may/documents/papa-francesco_20160512_uisg.html.

41. Papal declarations of intent have existed since Pope Paul VI, whom Pope John Paul II quoted at the beginning of his letter *Mulieris Dignitatem* (1). In 1996, in his

over the pontificate of Pope Francis, it is for me personally the greatest disappointment that he did not appoint any women to the reform body he created, although there were no legal stipulations whatsoever—no closed doors.

The desideratum of women's participation in counseling and decision-making processes cannot be postponed. If necessary, provisional forms could be found. That is why the Swiss project "Kirche mit* den Frauen"[42] focuses on this one point: women must be able to take part in consultation and decision-making, and that must be before the course is set for further structural and official integration of women.[43] The next decisions, especially about the way women participate in counseling and leadership in the church, should not be made by men, but by women and men together.

Pope Francis clearly stated this at the meeting with the Superiors General mentioned above: "It is true that women are excluded from the decision-making processes in the Church: not excluded, but the integration of women there, in the decision-making processes, is very weak. We must move forward."[44]

(Translation from German by Neville Williamson)

Post-Synodal Apostolic Exhortation *Vita Consecrata.* On the Consecrated Life and Its Mission in the Church and in the World, March 25, 1996, Pope John Paul II underlined the urgency of concrete action: "It is therefore urgently necessary to take certain concrete steps, beginning by *providing room for women to participate* in different fields and at all levels, including decision-making processes, above all in matters which concern women themselves" (58): http://w2.vatican.va/content/john-paul-ii/de/apost_exhortations/documents/hf_jp-ii_exh_25031996_vita-consecrata.html.

42. Cf. www.kirche-mit.ch.

43. Even under the premise that the offices of presbyter and bishop are not open to women, structures should be developed to enable women at all levels to assume responsibility in the processes of consultation, decision-making, and leadership. Cf. the thought experiment of J. Kügler, who wants to see the priesthood "stripped of all functions of power," while "*everything* in the Church that has to do with leadership, organisation, finances, legislation and discipline, life and education is accessible to baptised men and women equally. And this must apply on the levels of full-time, part-time and honorary work": Gal 3:26-28 (M. Eckholt, *Ohne die Frauen*, 66). Such a thought experiment raises the question of where the greater continuities or discontinuities lie: in extending the possibilities for nonordained ministries or changing the practice of admission.

44. Pope Francis, Address to the International Union of Superiors General.

II

Women in Church Ministries

Biblical and Historical Perspectives

Apostolicity and Power

Who Is in Charge? Or, On the Ambivalent Role of Women in the New Testament (Together with a Proposal for the Feast of the Apostle Mary Magdalene)

Michael Theobald

The theme presented to me by the organizers of the Congress, with its connection between "apostolicity" and "power," does not obscure the hermeneutic location of answers expected from the New Testament. The current situation of the Roman Catholic Church nourishes the ideology-critical suspicion that alleged constructs of apostolicity are also concerned with power. Apostolicity is not only *attributed to* the church and ministry; those in ministerial office also *lay claim to it*. It can be distorted in a great variety of ways, by rivalry and power struggles in church politics, or by individuals by the disastrous exercise of their office. Even the unwavering continuation of authoritatively high-ranking concepts of apostolicity[1] is now suspected of being ideologically motivated.

Theological discourses on apostolicity are no longer "artless," given the historical-critical insights into the genesis of the church that have

1. The most recent normative concept is presented in the third chapter of the Dogmatic Constitution *Lumen Gentium* passed by the Second Vatican Council: "On the hierarchical structure of the Church and in particular on the episcopate," and there above all pars. 19–21. Insights and analyses from the history of theology and systematics are to be found in T. Schneider, Das Amt in der frühen Kirche, in *Ursprünge und Wandlungen*, vol. 2 of D. Sattler, G. Wenz, eds., *Das kirchliche Amt in apostolischer Nachfolge* (Freiburg i.Br., 2004/2006/2008).

been communicated for many years. They find themselves confronted with the question of "power" and "renunciation of power," which is not marginal but central for a church invoking Jesus of Nazareth (cf. Mark 10:42-44). The thesis that I would like to elucidate here in three New Testament contexts has two aspects that state that: (a) New Testament concepts of the apostolate are guided by interests; they resonate with certain expectations and set their theological accents accordingly; (b) this affects the role of women in the foundation and building of the church, which can be ignored, obscured, or minimized. This has consequences for a hermeneutically reflected approach to the New Testament texts.

1. On Terminology

The New Testament very often uses ἀποστέλλω = "send,"[2] also the verbal adjective ἀπόστολος = "envoy" derived from it,[3] and finally ἀποστολή = "mission"/"apostleship" (the latter especially in Paul[4]). The word usage is always related to concrete events or persons or groups of persons; an attributional expression such as ἀποστολική = "apostolic" does not yet occur. The later confessional reference to the "apostolic church" can indeed be connected with a statement such as Eph 2:20: "You are built upon the foundation of the apostles and prophets, with Christ Jesus himself as the cornerstone." The metaphor of a building used here contains *in nuce* a concept of an apostolic church.[5] From the second half of the second century the adjective ἀποστολική = "apostolic"[6] is to be found. The term "apostolicity," as it is used nowadays in systematics, "goes back

2. One hundred thirty-three times in the entire New Testament; see J. Roloff, F. Mildenberger, Art. Apostel/Apostolat (A. I and III), in: *TRE*, vol. 3 (1978) 430–45; 466–77.

3. Altogether seventy-nine times in the entire New Testament (Gospels 10x; Acts 28x; Pauline Epistles 34x [Heb only 1x: Christ = Apostolos]; the Catholic Epistles 4x; Rev 3x).

4. Rom 1:5; 1 Cor 9:2; Gal 2:8; also Acts 1:25.

5. Cf. M. Theobald, *Mit den Augen des Herzens sehen. Der Epheserbrief als Leitfaden für Spiritualität und Kirche* (Würzburg, 2000) 96–98 and elsewhere. See also 1 Cor 3:10-18.

6. Ignatius, Tr inscr.: ἐν ἀποστολικῇ χαρακτῆρι; MPol 16,2: διδάσκαλος ἀποστολικὸς καὶ προφητικός; before that Papias fr. 2,12: τὰς ἀποστολικὰς διηγήσεις = "the reports of the apostles."

via the adjective 'apostolic' to the title 'apostle' and denotes agreement with the apostles or origin or derivation from the apostles."[7] On the basis of the Niceno-Constantinopolitan Creed (DH 150), the apostolicity of the *church* (besides its unity, holiness, and catholicity, the other *notae ecclesiae*) is the confessional content of all churches. Over and above that, the Roman Catholic approach also defines apostolicity as the legitimate succession to office (*successio apostolica*)[8] going back to the apostles via the college of bishops. The Reformation approach declares that the Gospel is the only criterion of apostolicity. The Catholic concept, which depends on *person,* does not have so much freedom in putting the gender issue unconditionally when it comes to ministerial office. When the New Testament speaks of "the (male) apostles," everything else seems to follow as a matter of course.

Coming from the canonical tradition, one may quickly build a bridge between the concept of "apostolicity" and the second concept of our title, "power" or "force" (*potestas*).[9] In the New Testament there is a broad and polyvalent range of concepts and terms for power.[10] One term that stands out is ἐξουσία, which is very often used in a christological

7. W. Härle, Art. Apostolizität (Apostolicity), in: RGG4, 1 (1998) 653f., 653.

8. Vat. II: DH 4119.4144.4207-4211; LG 20,2: *per successionem ab initio decurrentem*; W. Beinert, Art. Apostolizität der Kirche (Apostolicity of the Church), in: LThK3, vol. 1 (1993) 881f., 881: "Vatican II. shows the A. as a quality of the universal Church (LG 13, 17, 31, 35), provided that it proclaims the Gospel to the whole human race as a universal sacrament of salvation (LG 1); it therefore also includes the mission of the laity (AA 1f.). The A. as the original unity is preserved by the pneumatological combination of Scripture, tradition and office (DV 7f.; 10) and sensus fidelium (LG 12)"; cf. Beinert, Die Apostolizität der Kirche als Kategorie der Theologie, in: *Theologie und Philosophie* 52 (1977) 161–81.

9. Cf. Conf. Aug. XXVIII (De potestate ecclesiastica): Sic autem sentiunt, *potestatem clavium* eu *potestatem episcoporum* iuxta evangelium *potestatem* esse seu mandatum Dei praedicandi evangeliii, remittendi et retinendi peccata et administrandi sacramenta (BESLK 121); CIC (1983) can. 381 §1: Episcopo dioecesano in dioecesi ipsi commissa omnis competit *potestas ordinaria*, propria et immediata, quae ad exercitium eius muneris pastoralis requiritur.

10. Cf. H. Schlier, *Mächte und Gewalten im Neuen Testament* (Freiburg, 1958); otherwise cf. the relevant encyclopedia articles on ἀρχαι, ἐξουσίαι in: G. Kittel, G. Friedrich, eds., *Theologisches Wörterbuch zum Neuen Testament* (Stuttgart 1933–1979). Still significant, also because of his far-sighted diagnosis of modernity, which is still valid: R. Guardini, *Die Macht, Versuch einer Wegweisung*, 5th ed. (Würzburg, 1960).

context.[11] Here, it is interesting to see how apostolate and power overlap. Such overlapping can be seen in the early Jewish legal model, according to which the emissary is equal to and represents the one who has sent him.[12] This is the model that forms the background to New Testament commissions such as Luke 10:16: "whoever listens to you listens to me."[13] In 1 Cor 9 Paul links his "apostleship" (v.2) with possible areas in which he is authorized to claim "rights" (ἐξουσία: v.4-6)[14] that he voluntarily refuses to make use of for himself. Jesus demands a radical rejection of the exercise of power from those who "lead" and bear responsibility in the church (Mark 10:42-45; par. Matt 20:24-28; Luke 22:24-27)—in sharp contrast to the exercise of power in the Roman Empire.[15]

2. The Authority of Men and the Invisibility of Women. Three New Testament Ways of Speaking of the "Apostles"

In the next section we shall look into three ways of speaking of "the apostles" (2.1 and 2.2) or of "the apostle" Paul (2.3) in order to see what

11. K. Scholtissek, *Die Vollmacht Jesus. Traditions—und redaktionsgeschichtliche Analysen zu einem Leitmotiv markinischer Christologie* (Münster, 1992); M. Ebner, Die Rede von der "Vollmacht" Jesu im MkEv—und die realpolitischen Implikationen (2013), in: Ebner, *Inkarnation der Botschaft. Kultureller Horizont und theologischer Anspruch neutestamentlicher Texte* (Stuttgart, 2015) 364–83; H. Blatz, *Die Semantik der Macht. Eine zeit—und religionsgeschichtliche Studie zu den markinischen Wundererzählungen* (Münster, 2016).

12. J.-A. Bühner, *Der Gesandte und sein Weg im 4. Evangelium. Die kultur—und religionsgeschichtlichen Grundlagen der johanneischen Sendungschristologie sowie ihre traditionsgeschichtliche Entwicklung* (Tübingen, 1977).

13. This is emphatically applied by LG 20 to the bishops. See also 2 Cor 5:20: "So we are ambassadors for Christ, since God is making his appeal through us."

14. The Vulgate translates all three occurrences of ἐξουσία with *potestas*. See also 1 Cor 9:12.

15. Mark 10:42-45: "You know that among the Gentiles those whom they recognize as their rulers lord it over them, and their great ones are tyrants over them. But it is not so among you; but whoever wishes to become great among you must be your servant, and whoever wishes to be first among you must be slave of all. For the Son of Man came not to be served but to serve, and to give his life as a ransom for many." Cf. P. Hoffmann, Herrschaftsverzicht: Befreite und befreiende Menschlichkeit, in: Hoffmann, *Studien zur Frühgeschichte der Jesus-Bewegung* (Stuttgart, 1994) 139–70; Ebner, "Vollmacht," 364–83.

effect they have on the visibility or invisibility of women in the respective image of the church.

2.1 The Resurrection "Appearance Formulas" (1 Cor 15:5 etc.) as Apostolic "Legitimation Formulas"

"Appearance formulas" were used for the first time in 1 Cor 15:3-9 in the context of the catechetical belief formula handed down by Paul,[16] and that in four different versions:

> For I handed on to you as of first importance
> what I in turn had received:
> that Christ died for our sins in accordance with the scriptures,
> and that he was buried,
> and that he was raised on the third day in accordance with the scriptures,
> and that he appeared [ὤφθη] to Cephas [cf. Luke 24:34],
> then to the twelve [cf. Luke 24:36ff.; Matt 28; John 20].
> Then he appeared [ὤφθη] to more than five hundred brothers and sisters at one time,
> most of whom are still alive,
> though some have died.
> Then he appeared [ὤφθη] to James,
> then to all the apostles.
> Last of all, as to one untimely born, he appeared also to me.
> For I am the least of the apostles,
> unfit to be called an apostle,
> because I persecuted the church of God. . . .

The meaning of the "appearance formulas," consisting of the verbal statement "he appeared" + dative of those who witnessed the appearance,[17] is illuminated by the (Greek) Bible. There it is the phrase used to designate God's theophany in the form of his messengers as well as his self-revelation to the patriarchs, to Moses and Solomon. Gen 12:7^LXX^, for example, says: "The Lord appeared to Abram (καὶ ὤφθη κύριος τῷ

16. On this see M. Theobald, Angefochtener Osterglaube—im Neuen Testament und heute, in: *Theologische Quartalschrift* 193 (2013) 4–31, 12–23.

17. The aorist pass. of ὁράω + dative has intransitive meaning "to appear to someone," "to be seen." Cf. A. Lindemann, *Der erste Korintherbrief* (Tübingen, 2000) 332.

Αβραμ) and said . . ." Exod 3:2^LXX says of Moses: "There the angel of the Lord appeared to him (ὤφθη δὲ αὐτῷ ἄγγελος) in a flame of fire out of a bush." This is followed by YHWH's commission to him to lead the people out of Egypt (Exod 3:10).[18] His appearance to Moses is therefore an act of legitimation. The same applies to the New Testament appearance formulas,[19] as becomes clear by their order in 1 Cor 15, showing how the belief formula developed historically: it starts with the authorization of Cephas as a witness to the resurrection; that leads to the authorization of the Twelve. V.7 was appended secondarily to the original fourfold belief formula (= 3c-5b)[20]: "He appeared to James, then to all the apostles." After the departure of Cephas from Jerusalem, James the brother of the Lord took charge, so that the development in v.7 reflects the history of the early Jerusalem congregation. The talk of "*all* the apostles" goes beyond the twelve mentioned in v.5b[21] and at the same time calls into question the "unique position of the Twelve," as it appears in the original version of the belief formula.[22] If the Twelve are now also reckoned, from the perspective of v.7, to be among the apostles, then there are more of them,

18. Cf. Gen 17:1; 18:1; 26:2, 24; 35:9f.; also 1 Kgs 3:5; 9:2f. Jer 31:2 (LXX: 38:3).

19. On the "appearance words" as "legitimation words" see U. Wilckens, *Auferstehung. Das biblische Auferstehungszeugnis historisch untersucht und erklärt* (3rd ed., Gütersloh, 1981) 21; "In the tradition, the reason for recording the appearances is that through them the first Christian leaders received their legitimation, their calling and their position of authority from heaven"; H.-J. Eckstein, Die Wirklichkeit der Auferstehung Jesu. Lukas 24,34 als Beispiel früher formelhafter Zeugnisse, in Eckstein, *Der aus Glauben Gerechte wird leben. Beiträge zur Theologie des Neuen Testaments* (Münster, 2003) 171f.; 176.

20. Marked by quotation marks in the text above.

21. It is not necessary here to go deeper into the historically important dissociation between the Twelve chosen by Jesus and the postresurrection circle of apostles, which is evident in this text. It also goes without saying that the prophetically significant number "Twelve," symbolising the twelve tribes of Israel and the twelve patriarchs, could naturally only function for the men among Jesus' followers, so that any reference to the "Twelve Apostles" is completely irrelevant when it comes to the exclusion of women from offices in the church. The Roman pronouncements on this subject are either completely uninformed or deliberately deny recent research.

22. D.-A. Koch, Zwölferkreis und Gottesvolk (1995), in: Koch, *Hellenistisches Christentum. Schriftverständnis—Ekklesiologie—Geschichte*, ed. F. W. Horn (Göttingen, 2008) 111–25, 113f.

and they are included. The exact number is not important, only the fact that those falling under the description πάντες ἀπόστολοι enjoy special authority, because they were witnesses to the appearance of the risen Christ. When Paul, at the very end of the text passage, also uses the same appearance formula when speaking of his own vocation on the road to Damascus and thus declares it to be the climax of the foregoing list of appearances, it is evidently intended to legitimize not only testimony, but also authority and power of leadership.[23] Although Paul emphasizes at the end in v.11 that all "proclaim" the same thing, the order of the phrases and the way each one outdoes the preceding ones proves that there were competitive claims and disputes. Paul had to fight for his authority.[24]

When examining the appearance formulas within the broader context of the Easter narratives in the gospels, two things may be observed:

(1) Where these formulas mention by name people who experienced these appearances, they are only men: Cephas, James, and Paul; otherwise only the Twelve. The gospels only mention the Twelve in connection with the reports on appearances, not Peter or James. Thus, when in Luke the Emmaus disciples return to Jerusalem, the Eleven greet them with the news: "The Lord (ὁ κύριος) has risen indeed, and he has *appeared to Simon* (ὤφθη Σίμωνι)" (Luke 24:34), but this is a story that the reader has not heard.

(2) The claim that Peter was the witness of the Easter protophany (meaning the first appearance), made in 1 Cor 15:5a and Luke 24:34[25] is

23. This function of the phrases is also confirmed by the fact that they forgo all other auxiliary information, such as naming the place where the respective appearance took place or reporting the words allegedly spoken to the witnesses at the appearance.

24. J. Becker, *Die Auferstehung Jesu Christi nach dem Neuen Testament. Ostererfahrung und Osterverständnis im Urchristentum* (Tübingen, 2007), remains cautious about the "suggestion that the list reveals competition between Peter and James. It is true that James took over the leadership of the Jerusalem community from Peter, and this may have been in connection with problems. But one cannot cite this enumeration to justify this, for it was drawn up by Paul in order to emphasise the unanimity of all witnesses with regard to Jesus' resurrection" (117).

25. The tradition of the Emmaus disciples implies that *they* were the first to whom the risen Christ appeared. Luke, who seems to know about the protophany to Peter, seeks to find a compromise by letting the Eleven greet the returning Emmaus disciples with the words of Luke 24:34, which is "indeterminate enough to allow

in contradiction to the Gospels of both Matthew and John, whereby the latter also explicitly doubts whether Peter was the first to be called by Jesus at the Sea of Galilee as the Synoptics claim (cf. Mark 1:16; Matt 4:18; 10:2; Luke 5:3,4-11), seeing him called in *third* place *after* Andrew and an anonymous person (John 1:41f.).[26] The honor of protophany is attributed to Mary Magdalene, who was commissioned by the risen Christ in John 20:17 to announce the Easter message to the disciples as *apostola apostolorum*.[27] An old tradition that is independent of that can be found in Matt 28:9f. Here the resurrected Jesus "meets" Mary Magdalene and the "other Mary" immediately after the women have found the empty tomb and commands them to go and tell his "brothers." In the final literary form of the gospels, however, the protophany of Mary Magdalene and the other women is overshadowed by the quasi-"official" epiphany in the presence of the Twelve (Matt 28; John 20), or has been mitigated by the editors of the Fourth Gospel, in which the Beloved Disciple takes priority before Mary Magdalene as the first Easter believer—also a consequence of church "politics."[28] The so-called secondary conclusion of the Gospel of Mark from the early second century, which the Council of Trent declared to be part of the New Testament canon according to

readers to imagine that Jesus appeared to Peter before the Emmaus disciples. The undetermined time between v. 12 and v. 13 is also long enough to allow this" (M. Wolter, *Das Lukasevangelium* [Tübingen, 2008] 786). The double expression—combining the phrases of resurrection and appearance—is certainly traditional; it is also to be found in Lucan language in Acts 10:40f. ("But God raised him on the third day and allowed him to appear [ἔδωκεν αὐτὸν ἐμφανῆ γενέσθαι], not to all the people but to us who were chosen by God as witnesses, and who ate and drank with him after he rose from the dead") and 13:30f. ("But God raised him from the dead; and for many days he appeared [ὤφθη] to those who came up with him from Galilee to Jerusalem, and they are now his witnesses to the people").

26. Cf. M. Theobald, *Das Johannesevangelium. Kapitel 1–12* (Regensburg, 2009) 181–83.

27. Many works on Mary Magdalene have appeared in recent years; here we can mention: S. Ruschmann, *Maria von Magdala im Johannesevangelium. Jüngerin—Zeugin—Lebensbotin* (Münster, 2002); A. Taschl-Erber, *Maria von Magdala—erste Apostolin? Joh 20,1–18: Tradition und Relecture* (Freiburg i.Br., 2007).

28. Cf. M. Theobald, Der Jünger, den Jesus liebte. Beobachtungen zum narrativen Konzept der johanneischen Redaktion, in: Theobald, *Studien zum Corpus Iohanneum* (Tübingen, 2010) 493–533.

the Vulgate,[29] explicitly attributes the protophany—in this case by use of the appearance formula—to Mary Magdalene,[30] even if the emphasis in the series of the three appearances listed lies on the last one, in which the Eleven receive their official commission.[31]

There are plausible reasons to believe that the tradition of the protophany to the women is based on reliable old historical recollections.[32] Then the question arises why the so-called "appearance formulas" do not mention women anywhere and why they are eclipsed by the Easter stories in the gospels. The answer is given by the generic definition of the "appearance formulas" as legitimation formulas: since they serve to offer legitimization over against the authorities in the early church, they make

29. *Decretum de canonicis Scripturis* of April 8, 1546, DH 1504: "But if any one receive not, as sacred and canonical, the said books entire with all their parts, as they have been used to be read in the Catholic Church, and as they are contained in the old Latin vulgate edition; . . . let him be anathema." The preamble of the decree alludes to the end of Mark's Gospel: [Evangelium] per suos Apostolos . . . *omni creaturae praedicari iussit* (DH 1501); cf. Mk 16:15. On questions of textual history, cf. K. Aland, Der Schluss des Markusevangeliums, in: Aland, *Neutestamentliche Entwürfe* (Munich, 1979) 246–83.

30. Mark 16:9-11: "[9]Now after he rose early on the first day of the week, *he appeared first to Mary Magdalene*, from whom he had cast out seven demons. [10]She went out and told those who had been with him, while they were mourning and weeping. [11]But when they heard that he was alive and had been seen by her, they would not believe it." The appearances before the disciples of Emmaus and the Eleven follow, the latter accompanied by a detailed discourse by the risen Jesus. The conclusion forms a brief reference to Jesus' ascension into heaven and a notification that "they went out and proclaimed the good news everywhere, while the Lord worked with them and confirmed the message by the signs that accompanied it" (v. 20).

31. R. Pesch, *Das Markusevangelium. 2. Teil* (Freiburg i.Br., 1977) 549. Cf. also Becker, *Auferstehung*, 85–91.

32. P. Benoit, Marie-Madeleine et les disciples au tombeau selon Joh 20,1–18, in: W. Eltester, ed., *Judentum, Urchristentum, Kirche* (Berlin, 1960) 141–52; M. Hengel, Maria Magdalena und die Frauen als Zeugen, in: O. Betz, ed., *Abraham unser Vater. Juden und Christen im Gespräch über die Bibel* (Leiden/Cologne, 1963) 243–56; cf. also F. Schleritt, Der Jüngling im Grab als Epigone des Auferstandenen. Zum Verhältnis der Geschichte vom Grabbesuch der Frauen zur Überlieferung von der Erscheinung Jesu vor Maria Magdalena, in: M. Janßen et al., eds., *Frühes Christentum und Religionsgeschichtliche Schule* (Göttingen, 2011) 83–95.

allowances for social expectations that are only prepared to believe men in the case of such momentous claims. It is revealing, for example, how Josephus in his *Antiquities* comments on the law concerning witnesses in Deut 19:15: "But let not a single witness be credited, but three, or two at the least, and those such whose testimony is confirmed by their good lives. But let not the testimony of women be admitted, on account of the levity and boldness of their sex" (*Ant.* IV ch. 8/no. 15). Josephus is not alone in this view.[33] A socially established mentality becomes visible that only permits men to be official witnesses in public. It can be assumed that this is the exact reason for the findings mentioned above. And there is an additional further observation.

Just as the mention of "five hundred brothers" in 1 Cor 15:6 is very probably to be understood inclusively, so is that also the case for the πάντες ἀπόστολοι in v.5b. Ἀπόστολος is a) a verbal adjective of the compound ἀπο-Ἀπόστολος and not yet a *terminus technicus* in the New Testament,[34] and b) there are only two endings for verbal adjectives of compounds (-ος; -ον), which means that they do not have a feminine form.[35] Consequently, to refer to "all the apostles" (as long as they are not identified as the Twelve) says nothing about the sex of individual members of this group. On the question of who belonged to it, Wolfgang Schrage explains in his commentary on 1 Corinthians: "All the apostles in a group which obviously appears to be no longer capable of extension, although we are unable to say who belongs to it and at what point it was considered to be closed, are witnesses of the resurrection, but not all witnesses of the resurrection are apostles. The most likely persons to come into question are the apostles of [1 Cor] 9:5f. or Gal 1:17.19 and similar passages, and according to Rom 16:7 this will also include women."[36] In the conclusion of his Epistle to the Romans Paul explains, as is well known, that the married couple Andronicus and Junia, who

33. Cf. the documents in Theobald, *Osterglaube*, 17 n. 47.

34. F. Hahn, Art. Apostel i. Neues Testament, in: RGG4, vol. 1 (1998) 636–638, 636.

35. A. Kaegi, *Kurzgefasste Griechische Schulgrammatik* (6th ed., Berlin, 1961) (provided by E. Bornemann), 180 (§213).

36. W. Schrage, *Der erste Brief an die Korinther (1 Cor 15:1-16,24)* (Düsseldorf et al., 2001) 60, with reference in note 221 to Wyclif, *Sermones* III 387: potest intelligi mixtim de viris et feminis.

were beloved to him, were "prominent among the apostles"—a remark that was misunderstood for centuries and only came into its own in the German language in the Bible revisions of the Catholic *Einheitsübersetzung* (Unity Translation) and Luther's translation 2016/2017.[37]

We can draw this conclusion: in spite of attempts to push aside Rom 16:7 during the present dispute on the participation of women in the ministry of the church,[38] the exegetical discourse shows that the question of gender is not trivial but central, because it affects the correct interpretation of the creed in 1 Cor 15, which Paul confirms in Gal 3:28: "There is no longer male and female; for all of you are one in Christ Jesus."

2.2 The Concept of Apostolic Continuity in Acts

Because the author of the Acts of the Apostles sees himself as a historian and has collected valuable traditions, his work provides us with invaluable insights into the early history of the ekklesia, especially with regard to the role of women in its development. Fortunately, it provides a great deal of complementary information on equivalent clues in the Pauline corpus.[39] Luke mentions women by name, thus rescuing them from anonymity; apart from *Mary*, the "mother of Jesus," who is already known from Luke's Gospel (1:14), these are in the order of their appearance: *Sapphira*, the wife of Ananias (5:1-11), *Tabitha*, meaning (Dorcas) Gazelle (9:36), *Mary*, "the mother of John, whose other name was Mark" (12:12), *Rhoda*, a maid in the "house of Mary" (12:13), *Lydia*

37. For the history of the sex change of Junia into a man named Junias cf. E. J. Epp, *Junia. The First Woman Apostle* (Minneapolis, 2005).

38. In ignorance of the state of discussion in text criticism, this is what W. Kasper does in *Katholische Kirche. Wesen, Wirklichkeit, Sendung* (Freiburg, 2011) 534f. n. 183. On his meandering comments on the issue of the admission of women to ecclesiastical office, cf. M. Theobald, Phoebe und Junia. Zwei biblische Frauen—ohne Heimatrecht in der römisch-katholischen Kirche?, in: Theobald, *Jesus, Kirche und das Heil der Anderen* (Stuttgart, 2013) 163–69, 163 n. 1; 166f. n. 5; 168f. n. 11.

39. Cf. A. Weiser, Die Rolle der Frau in der urchristlichen Mission, in: G. Dautzenberg et al., eds., *Die Frau im Urchristentum* (Freiburg i.Br., 1983) 158–81; G. Dautzenberg, *Zur Stellung der Frauen in den paulinischen Gemeinden*, in *Die Frau im Urchristentum*,182–224; M. Gielen, Frauen in leitender Funktion, in: Gielen, J. Kügler, *Papst Franziskus und die Zukunft der Kirche. Neutestamentliche Orientierungsangebote* (Berlin, 2014) 101–77. Cf. also L. H. Cohick, *Women in the World of the Earliest Christians. Illuminating Ancient Ways of Life* (Grand Rapids, 2009).

from Thyatira (16:14f., 40),[40] *Damaris* from Athens (17:34), *Priscilla*, the wife of Aquila (18:2, 18, 26),[41] the Jewess *Drusilla*, the wife of the Governor Felix (24:24), *Bernice*, the wife of King Agrippa (25:13, 23, 30).[42] Particularly revealing are the references to the "house of Mary" (12:12) in Jerusalem—obviously the meeting place of the ekklesia there[43]—and that of Lydia in Philippi, who lets Paul baptize her and her household and who opens her home to the young congregation (16:40: "the brothers") in the city, possibly as the leader.[44]

Now these are only locally limited episodes in Luke's historical review. The men have the say, be it in groups—for example, the "apostles" connected with Jerusalem,[45] the so-called "seven" in and beyond Je-

40. Lydia would be a *nomen gentilicium*: "the (woman) from Lydia"—according to 16:13f. Lydia is one of several women who used to visit the synagogue outside the city: "On the sabbath day we went outside the gate by the river, where we supposed there was a προσευχή (= synagogue); and we sat down and spoke to the women who had gathered there. A woman named Lydia . . ." The usual literal translation of προσευχή with "place of prayer" is misleading, because it makes us think of a place in the open air by the river. προσευχή is, however, a widespread designation for synagogue. (M. Hengel, Proseuche und Synagoge. Jüdische Gemeinde, Gotteshaus und Gottesdienst in der Diaspora und in Palästina, in: Hengel, *Judaica et Hellenistica. Kleine Schriften*, vol. 1 [Tübingen, 1996] 171–95). Thus the women belong to the synagogue community.

41. Paul calls her Prisca: Rom 16:3, 1 Cor 16:19. Cf. also 2 Tim 4:19.

42. Some remain anonymous: Timothy's mother, "a Jewish woman who was a believer" (16:1; 2 Tim 1:5 provides her name: Eunikē); "a slave-girl who had a spirit of divination" (16:16-18); the four daughters of the evangelist Philip, "who had the gift of prophecy" (21:9); Paul's sister (23:16).

43. Weiser, *Rolle*, 173 n. 37: "The mention of the outer gate (πυλών) and the maid Rhoda indicates an imposing property and a certain degree of prosperity. Given that this information is locally anchored, it is probably one of the oldest elements in the story and is likely to be historically correct."

44. L. Schottroff, Lydia, in: K. Walter, ed., *Zwischen Ohnmacht und Befreiung. Biblische Frauengestalten* (Freiburg i.Br., 1988) 148–54; Schottroff, *Lydias ungeduldige Schwestern. Feministische Sozialgeschichte des frühen Christentums* (Gütersloh, 1992).

45. The verbal adjective ἀπόστολοι occurs twenty-eight times altogether in Acts, always in the plural; on Luke (there ten times) see T. Frauenlob, *Die Gestalt der Zwölf-Apostel im Lukasevangelium. Israel, Jesus und die Zwölf-Apostel im ersten Teil des lukanischen Doppelwerks* (Würzburg, 2015).

rusalem (6:5), the "elders" there (15), the "prophets and teachers" in Antioch (13:1)[46]—or be it individuals such as Peter, John, the Lord's brother James, Barnabas, and Paul. In the narrative these figures have the important function of repeatedly taking up the thread of the overall story between the individual episodes and narrative cycles. In the first major section of Acts it is the group of "apostles," with Peter and John at their head, which is of outstanding importance, while it is Paul in the second major section. Whenever Luke identifies "the apostles" with the group of "Twelve," then it is clear that they are male (cf. Luke 6:13), and this identification provides the answer to the question of why it is so important for his theological construct.

"The apostles" are bodily witnesses to continuity in the history of salvation, not only in the crucial period between Jesus' lifetime and the time when the church was founded, but also critical turning points of its further growth.[47] Selected by Jesus from among his disciples (Luke 6:13), they remain in Jerusalem after his crucifixion (Luke 24:49; Acts 1:4, 13), they "eat and drink" with the resurrected Christ in the period between Easter and Ascension (Acts 10:41; cf. 1:4), and do not leave the Holy City after Pentecost, even in the worst persecution (8:1); they sanction Philip's independent mission in Samaria by giving the Spirit to those he had baptized there by prayer and the laying on of hands (8:14-17), receive and approve Peter's report after the conversion of the first "Gentile" Cornelius in Caesarea (11:1-18), organize the supervision of the newly founded church in Antioch by sending Barnabas there (11:22f.), and finally, after hearing from "Barnabas and Paul"[48] at the "Apostles' Council," set the course for the future of the ekklesia together with the "elders" under the leadership of James in collegial unanimity with their spokesman, Peter, together with the whole assembly (Acts 15; 16:4). After that, they leave the field to Paul on the one hand, who now becomes the main protagonist of the narrative, and on the other hand to the Jerusalem "elders" under James's leadership.

46. Five men are mentioned by name, but no woman.

47. For Luke, this continuity is guaranteed by the "Holy Spirit," who also secures the identity of the existing ecclesia: cf. J. Roloff, *Die Kirche im Neuen Testament* (Göttingen, 1993) 207–9 ("Kirche unter der Leitung des Geistes"); G. K. A. Bonnah, *The Holy Spirit. A Narrative Factor in the Acts of the Apostles* (Stuttgart, 2007).

48. In that order, cf. Acts 15:12.

The central role of the "apostles" as it is thus outlined is that, having been commissioned by Jesus (Luke 24:44-49) and led by the Spirit (Acts 2:15), they shape the salvific "kerygma" in accordance with the life of Jesus from his teaching to his resurrection, ascension, and promise of the Spirit, thus enabling the ekklesia to be securely oriented toward the "teaching of the apostles" (2:42). This kerygma guarantees the identity of the church. Above all, two elements portrayed by Luke in this picture ensure that it is impossible to suspect that "the apostles" are something akin to a central church "authority":

On the one hand, in different conflict situations such as that of providing for the widows in the Jerusalem ekklesia (Acts 6) or the issue of circumcision in the mission to the Gentiles, Luke depicts exemplary strategies of conflict resolution that are brought into play by the "apostles" in a synodal fashion.[49] On the other hand, from the very outset he paints the picture of a core congregation of brothers and sisters exemplifying what Peter emphasized on the day of Pentecost by quoting Joel 2:28-29, namely, that the Spirit of God is poured out "upon *all* flesh," "your sons *and* your daughters," "male *and* female slaves," and so forth.[50] This means that there is a noteworthy line leading, in the sense of the continuity from Jesus to the church, from the highly remarkable statement in Luke 8:1-3 ("the twelve were with him as well as some women"[51]) via 23:49 ("acquaintances" of Jesus at the cross together with the women "who had followed him from Galilee"), 24:10 (the women are the first to proclaim to the apostles the message that Jesus is alive[52]), 24:33 ("the eleven and their companions"[53]) to Acts 1:13-14, where Luke describes the inner circle of the church waiting for the Spirit in the "upstairs room" of a Jerusalem house: "All these [the twelve previously named] were constantly

49. The conflict solutions in Acts 6:1-7 and 15:1-35 are of exemplary and forward-looking significance.

50. On the astonishing early Christian effect of Joel 3^{LXX} see Dautzenberg, *Stellung*, 192 with note 192.

51. Luke lists the women by name: Mary, "called Magdalene," Joanna, "wife of Herod's steward Chuza," Susanna. The first two meet later again in Luke 24:10 (cf. the next note).

52. These are: Mary Magdalene, Joanna and Mary the mother of James, and the other women with them.

53. The women of 23:49 and 24:10 must also be among the unnamed.

devoting themselves to prayer, *together with certain women,* including Mary the mother of Jesus, as well as his brothers."[54]

Seeing how often Luke speaks explicitly of "men *and* women" (Acts 8:3, 12; 9:2; 17:12; 21:5; cf. also 13:49) and takes care to treat them equally in contrasting episodes in his Gospel and in Acts,[55] one should be wary of using his construct of "the apostles" as an argument for excluding women from offices in the church.[56] Such a bold approach is thwarted, above all, by the insight into the *function* of the narrative figure, namely, to serve the Lucan model of continuity and the strengthening of church identity. Similarly to the androcentrically expressed "appearance formulas," the narrative figure of "the apostles" in Luke's two-volume work is co-dictated by patterns of cultural expectation.[57]

2.3 Successio Paulina *in the Pastoral Epistles—Means of "Domesticating" Women*

It is well known that the Pastoral Epistles (1 Tim, 2 Tim, and Tit) were not written by Paul, but are a much later interpretation of his views from the second quarter of the second century.[58] Purporting to come from "Paul," they use legal language[59] to forbid women to "teach" (1 Tim

54. The keyword "brothers" recalls, in particular, James, who will play a decisive role in the later chapters of the book (see 2.1 above).

55. Cf. Luke 13:18-21 (parables of the mustard seed and the yeast); 15:3-7/8-10 (parables of the lost sheep and the lost coin); Acts 9:32-35 (Aeneas), 36-43 (Dorcas/Gazelle).

56. Luke opens a window on the *factual* shape of church leadership at his time in Paul's farewell message sent from Miletus to the elders in Ephesus, Acts 20:17-35. Cf. A. Weiser, Gemeinde und Amt nach dem Zeugnis der Apostelgeschichte, in: Weiser, *Studien zu Christsein und Kirche* (Stuttgart, 1990) 305–20.

57. Also made clear by Luke 24:10f., where it says: "They [the women] told this to the apostles. But these words seemed to them an idle tale, and they did not believe them."

58. M. Theobald, *Israel-Vergessenheit in den Pastoralbriefen. Ein neuer Vorschlag zu ihrer historischen-theologischen Verortung im 2. Jahrhundert n.Chr. unter besonderer Berücksichtigung der Ignatius-Briefe* (Stuttgart, 2016).

59. M. Theobald, Vom Werden des Rechts in der Kirche. Beobachtungen zur Sprachform von Weisungen im Corpus Pastorale und bei Paulus, in: *Zeitschrift für die neutestamentliche Wissenschaft und die Kunde der Älteren Kirche* 106 (2015) 65–95.

2:12),[60] thus excluding them from public office in the ekklesia, which is also incidentally the case in the secondary gloss 1 Cor 14:34-36, originating from the same milieu. The author of the Pastoral Epistles makes a direct connection between his view of the role of women and the apostle's authority, assuming that ministry in the church is a "teaching office" reserved only for men. He claims the authority of the apostle in such a way as to construct a kind of *successio paulina*, when his "Paul" admonishes "Timothy" in 2 Tim 2:1f.: "You then, my child, be strong in the grace that is in Christ Jesus; and what you have heard from me through many witnesses entrust to faithful people who will be able to teach others as well." *The apostle* (1) admonishes the *disciple of the apostle* (2) to entrust what he has heard through witnesses to *faithful people* (3), so that they in turn may be able to teach *"others"* (4). Here we can recognize four stations of a chain of a juridical nature.

By reference to "Paul," women are officially excluded from this chain. They do not occur in the existing circle of "elders," which is per se male-determined as *patres familiae* representing the individual house churches in the local ekklesia, and they are most certainly not eligible for the episcopal ministry, which the author of the Pastoral Epistles wishes to promote as the office of a *primus inter pares* within the circle of "elders" to improve the organization of the ekklesia. The author insists that the Episcopus, who must have proved himself in managing his household and as a good father of his children, should also be particularly qualified "to preach with sound doctrine" (Tit 1:9; 1 Tim 3:2). He also expects the older women to be able to "teach what is good," to be καλοδιδάσκαλος, but in this case he is not referring to an official teaching office but to their years of experience, which enable them to pass on their worldly wisdom to the young women for their household tasks (Tit 2:3f.). The fact that women hold the office of deacons according to 1 Tim 3:11 does not contradict the teaching prohibition, because the Pastoral Epistles understand that "deacons" are (1) not involved in the teaching ministry of the ekklesia and therefore not ordained and (2) intended to fulfill, under the

60. Dautzenberg, *Stellung*, 197–201, offers revealing parallels to the "commandment of silence" (secondarily also inserted in 1 Cor 14:34) from the Greek Hellenistic and Jewish literature, but also hints that it was disputed "in view of the increasing emancipation of women from the Hellenistic period" (198, following K. Thraede, Art. Frau, in: RAC, vol. 6 [1966] 197–267).

responsibility of the episcopate, social and charitable duties for which men *and* women are required, if they are gender-specific.[61]

The instructions regarding the order of widows in 1 Tim 5:3-16 are revealing. First, they show that the limitation of female competence to the "household" actually serves the purpose of their "domestication"; second, they show that this tendency is directed against an alternative understanding of the role of women, which is oriented toward Paul himself and his program expressed in Gal 3:28, but here branded heterodox by the author. Thus it is ultimately a question of who (more) rightfully claims the authentic Paul for himself: the author of the Pastoral Epistles or his "opponents." It concerns a struggle for the apostolic heritage, a "conflict of interpretation." In this dispute, the question of the role of women is only *one* point of contention.

The hallmark of the opposing milieu was probably an asceticism derived from 1 Cor 7. Women followed the Pauline ideal of religiously motivated virginity, which they associated with emancipatory tendencies in comparison to the social roles of contemporary households but wished to put into practice in the service of the Christian community. When the author of the Pastoral Epistles polemicizes against young widows, it should be remembered that he uses the Greek word χῆραι, which can also stand for παρθένοι = "unmarried women."[62] He was trying to bring the order of widows as it existed—"young women" took a vow, did social service in the congregation, and were supported by it financially—into line with the strict legal stipulation that only women who were at least sixty years old and had no relatives were allowed to be enrolled. He feared that the order of widows as it had been practiced so far would become a breeding ground for heterodoxy.

When assessing the tangible and historically most effective success of the Pastoral Epistles in excluding women from ecclesiastical ministry by reference to the apostle Paul, it is only of minor significance that these pseudepigraphic texts do not originate from him. (They are in the canon and therefore part of his normative testimony.) More important is the insight into the ulterior intention of locating the ekklesia within the recognized social structure of "households" and thus taking over

61. M. Theobald, *Eucharistie als Quelle sozialen Handelns. Eine biblisch-frühkirchliche Besinnung* (2nd ed., Neukirchen-Vluyn, 2014) 172–77.

62. Theobald, *Werden des Rechts*, 81–88.

the corresponding roles. For the first time in the history of theology, the author explicitly designates the public sphere of the polis as a criterion for inculturation, the adoption of recognized social and ethical standards. Although the inculturation of the gospel and the church is still considered to be desirable and decisive today, the concrete implementation of this model offered by the Pastoral Epistles can on no account be written in stone for all time. These three epistles are to be evaluated critically with reference to the testimony of Jesus and Paul.

3. From the *Officium* to *Ministerium*: A proposal for the Feast of the Apostle Mary Magdalene on July 22

In the context of our topic, it is good to remember the many women in the Old and New Testaments who play a prominent role among the people of God: the prophetesses Miriam (Exod 15:20), Deborah (Judg 4:4), Abigail, wife of Nabal (1 Sam 25), Huldah (2 Kgs 22:14-20; 2 Chr 34:22-28), and Noadiah (Neh 6:14), but also Judith (Jdt) and Esther (Esth), Mary Magdalene, Priscilla, Lydia, Phoebe, and all the others. But it is better, and closer to the heart of the matter, to confront the opposition to the fully valid inclusion of women in ecclesiastical office at the point where it is apparently the most invulnerable: in personalized constructions of apostolicity. It is obsolete to continue to follow New Testament concepts blindly without taking historical-critical objections into consideration. If it is clear that in the ancient world only men were taken seriously as witnesses, and that this is the reason why women are not mentioned in formulas testifying to the Christian faith, then a reflected handling of these formulas, as of other New Testament texts, will make it imperative to criticize ideology and resist their instrumentalization for the exclusion of women from church office.

This is the point at which those in office should exercise self-reflection regarding the handling of ecclesiastical power and dominance; renunciation of such authority, as Jesus intended, does not result in a disavowal of claims to truth[63] but in the admission that the questions arising can

63. Guardini, *Die Macht*, 38: "Jesus' whole existence is the translation of power into humility. Actively speaking, in obedience to the Father's will as expressed in each specific situation; but this situation, both overall and in singular events, is such that it demands constant 'self-emptying.' For Jesus, obedience is not something secondary, an auxiliary, but forms the core of his being."

only be answered in synodal processes and at the height of contemporary socioethical standards. It not only means that the incumbents of offices should examine their conscience and turn back; before that, there should be critical reflection on the process of the sacralization of power in the church in general.[64] In their sphere of influence, the claims of the office appear to be unassailable, and a taboo is imposed upon the construction of chains of male successors within the framework of apostolicity in the context of a lifestyle sanctified by celibacy. In this way the carpet for far-reaching structural debates is pulled away.

I would like to conclude with a proposal. In June 2016, Pope Francis declared July 22, the annual commemoration of Mary Magdalene, to be the feast of the *apostola apostolorum,* thus putting it on an equal footing with the feasts of other apostles in the liturgical calendar.[65] This decision does not appear to be very spectacular at first sight, but on looking closer one can see considerable consequences. Should the feast of the apostle from Magdala, in accordance with the decree of June 3, 2016, be a celebration of her as the first witness of the Easter message to the Apostles and therefore as "model of women's role in the church," then it could serve as an opportunity for the Roman Catholic Church to reflect on the implications of its concept of apostolic succession for the role of women. The official Latin preface for the feast[66] speaks only of Mary

64. H. Joas, *Die Macht des Heiligen. Eine Alternative zur Geschichte von der Entzauberung* (Berlin, 2017), treats the sacred in the context of a theory of power and points to the danger of (collective) self-sacralization in connection with the experience of sacredness. The sacred is always interwoven with power. Cf. in particular 419–88 ("Das Heilige und die Macht. Kollektive Selbstsakralisierung und ihre Überwindung").

65. By decree of the Congregation for Divine Worship of June 3, 2016. In *Mulieris Dignitatem*, John Paul II described Mary Magdalene as the first witness of the Resurrection: "Mary Magdalene was the first eyewitness of the Risen Christ, and for this reason she was also *the first to bear witness to him before the Apostles*" (16).

66. It reads: "Vere dignum et iustum est, / æquum et salutare, / nos te, Pater omnipotens, / cuius non minor est misericordia quam potestas, / in omnibus prædicare per Christum Dominum nostrum. / Qui in hortu manifestus appáruit Mariæ Magdalenæ, / quippe quae eum dilexerat viventem, / in cruce viderat morientem, / quæsierat in sepulcro iacentem, / ac prima adoraverat a mortuis resurgentem, / et *eam apostolatus officio coram apostolis honoravit* / ut bonum novæ vitæ nuntium / ad mundi fines perveniret. / Unde et nos, Domine, cum Angelis et Sanctis universis / tibi confitemur, in exsultatione dicentes: Sanctus, Sanctus, Sanctus . . ."

Magdalene's "task of being Apostle" (*officium apostolatus*), which she exercised toward the apostles according to John 20:18.[67] But if the feast is to *remind* us of her in a sense that is relevant for today, this *remembrance* of Mary's *officium* must take the form that the *expectation* of the church's future potential represented by her will be redeemed. The recollection of the *officium* must lead to a transformed *ministerium* of the church, a "(ministerial) office" exercised by men and women on an equal footing. Let us therefore celebrate July 22 as a special day of the apostolic mission of women in our church, as an admonition to open the ecclesial *ministerium* to women, as a day on which the Holy Spirit will renew the structure of our church out of its abundant resources.

(Translation from German by Neville Williamson)

67. John 20:18: "Mary Magdalene went and announced to the disciples, 'I have seen the Lord.' And she told them that he had said these things to her."

Neither Male nor Female

Gregory of Nyssa and the Equality of Men and Women[1]

Sr. Makrina Finlay, OSB

In recent years, much has been written about Gregory of Nyssa's image of St. Macrina. Many articles rightly show that Gregory's portrait of his sister does not correspond with current gender stereotypes.[2] Although

1. The following considerations were written for the workshop "Consecration of Women in Historical and International Perspective" organized by AGENDA—Forum of Catholic Women Theologians e.V. (Prof. Dr. Margit Eckholt) at the Ecumenical Congress "Women in Church Offices; Reform Movements in Ecumenism" on December 7, 2017.

2. Cf. P. Rousseau, *Basil of Caesarea* (Berkeley, 1998), esp. 3–11; R. Van Dam, *Families and Friends in late Roman Cappadocia* (Philadelphia, 2003), esp. 104; F. Cardmann, *Whose Life Is It? The Vita Macrinae of Gregory of Nyssa* (Leuven, 1999) 413–30; E. Clark, Holy Women, Holy Words. Early Christian Women, Social History and the Linguistic Turn, in: *Journal of Early Christian Studies* 6 (1998) 413–30, 424–46; and, The Lady Vanishes. Dilemmas of a Feminist Historian after the Linguistic Turn, in: *Church History* 67 (1998) 25–30; V. Burrus, Is Macrina a Woman? Gregory of Nyssa's Dialogue on the Soul and Resurrection, in: Graham Ward, ed., *The Blackwell Companion to Postmodern Theology* (Oxford, 2005) 249–64. The works of M. Laird, *Gregory of Nyssa and the Grasp of Faith* (Oxford, 2007) and Silvas are more differentiated. See especially Silvas, *Macrina the Younger, Philosopher of God* (Turnhout, 2008), and *The Asketikon of St. Basil the Great* (Oxford, 2007). J. Warren Smith shows Macrina's role as the intermediary of health and hope in his article: A Just and Reasonable Grief, in: *Journal of Early Christian Studies* 12 (2004) 57–84. Gregory's "anagogical" approach, that is, his preference to look at subjects in a spiritual light, is considered by H. Boersma in: *Embodiment and*

some modern researchers wish for a sharper separation, Gregory does not apologize when he brings together—and even confuses—the historical and the spiritual. Macrina was indeed his biological sister and he portrays her in a very provocative way. But we will see that the provocative thing about Gregory is not that he wants to propose some "female spirituality" or that he wants to show that Macrina is a pseudo-man. He is much more ambitious than that. The primary reason why he wrote the *Vita* is to portray Macrina's life as a model of how to live between the beginning—that is, the creation of humankind in God's image—and the end, that is, the final resurrection, which leads to the ever increasing union with God. If one wants to understand the Christian anthropology that Gregory is trying to convey in his *Vita Macrinae*, and wants to consider his view of the consecration of women, there are at least seven important points that one must keep in mind.

1. Biography and Mutual Obedience in the Family

Macrina was born in 327 as the oldest of ten children in a Christian family in Cappadocia. Her grandmother is recognized as a saint in the East and West. Her brother Basil was promoted to bishop in 370. It was he who insisted that he ordain not only his brother Gregory of Nyssa and his friend Gregory of Nazianzus as bishops, but also his brother Peter as priest. If their brother Naucratius had not died at the age of twenty-five, Basil would most certainly have ordained him, too. Together with Gregory of Nazianzus, Basil of Caesarea and Gregory of Nyssa are known for their theological contributions as the three great Cappadocians. They were pioneers of the so-called Neo-Nicene theology and were largely responsible for the formulation of the Trinity Confession at the Council of Constantinople.[3] Perhaps the highest praise that Gregory of Nyssa could give to a member of such a prestigious family was that which he reserved for Macrina, whom he called "Macrina the Great."[4]

Virtue in Gregory of Nyssa (Oxford, 2015). See also C. Sunberg, *The Cappadocian Mothers* (Eugene, 2017).

3. See, e.g., A. Meredith, *The Cappadocians* (London, 1997) and J. Behr, *The Nicene Faith* (Crestwood, 2004).

4. For the biography (hereafter abbreviated DVM) I follow the English translation by *Macrina the Younger, Philosopher of God, The Life of St. Macrina* and the Greek

Although only men were ordained priests and bishops, Gregory's texts also refer to other power or, rather, "obedience" structures, that one would not expect at first. Gregory says, for example, that Naucratius placed himself in obedience under his mother, and he writes in his *Vita* that Macrina was responsible for Basil's conversion to ascetic life.[5] For Peter she was "father, mother and teacher of all good things." Conversely, Peter was her student and was a great help to her for her own spiritual life.[6]

2. The Eschatological Context of Gregory's Anthropology

Gregory's anthropology is based on a fusion of Gen 1:27 and Gal 3:28. Although he accepts gender categories, Gregory argues in his interpretation of Gen 1:27 that humanity was originally created in God's mind as God's image and only secondarily as man and woman with corporeal bodies and corresponding sex differences.[7] He also strongly holds to the teaching in Gal 3:28 that in Christ all are one and that, as a consequence of this, gender and class differences have no meaning.[8] Even though gender plays an important role in earthly relationships, Gregory considers it secondary in the larger context of origin and end. This is the necessary context in which to understand his portrayal of Macrina. On the one hand, he describes Macrina as "male" in her courage and in her mastery of passions.[9] However, she also performs every female role in

---

version by P. Maraval, *Grégoire de Nysse, Vie de Sainte Macrine* (Paris, 1971). DVM Silvas, 19.1, 128; Maraval, 16.10, 194–95.

5. Re: Naucratius: DVM Silvas, 10.5, S. 119; Maraval, chap. 8, 164–169; re: Basil: DVM A. Silvas, Kap. 8, 117; Maraval, chap. 6, 160–65.

6. DVM Silvas, 14.2, 122; Maraval, chap. 12, 182–83.

7. He develops these ideas in On the Creation of Humanity (*De hominis opificio*) (hereafter abbreviated with DHO); Greek Text in *Gregorii Nysseni Opera*, ed. W. Jaeger (Leiden, 1952). I follow the English translation by B. Jackson, *Hexaemeron* with *On the Making of Man* (Northampton, 2017).

8. See especially *On Virginity* (*De Virginitate*; here DV), Greek Text in *Gregorii Nysseni Opera*, ed. W. Jaeger (Leiden, 1952). Here I follow the translation of V. Woods Callahan in: *St. Gregory of Nyssa Ascetical Works*, The Fathers of the Church (Washington, DC, 1967).

9. After Naucratius's death she is described as *andreian*: courageous or manly. DVM P. Maraval, chap. 10, 172–75.

an exemplary manner.[10] By describing her in both these ways, Gregory tries to show what it looks like when a person grows not only beyond one's own gender but also beyond the limitation of sex as a whole. For him this is a return to the beginning as described in Gen 1:27, and as the fulfillment of Gal 3:28, in which all are one in Christ.

3. The Virgin Philosopher: Macrina and Thecla

In his *Vita* Gregory says that at Macrina's birth an angel came who called her "Thecla" three times.[11] He does not provide details that could illuminate how the listener should interpret this event, but we have two pictures of Thecla that help us.[12] The first comes from the *Acts of Paul and Thecla*, which tells the story of Paul's companion Thecla. The *Acts* describes how Thecla was so filled with the Holy Spirit that she miraculously escaped martyrdom twice. Her confidence in God was so great that she baptized herself; and, notably, she was not condemned for this act. The other work is *The Symposium*, a dialogue written by Methodius of Olympia, in which Thecla and nine other virgins philosophize about virginity. The text is clearly intended to mirror Plato's *Symposium*, a text in which Socrates and his companions philosophize about Eros. In Methodius's work, Thecla is regarded by her companions as a great teacher and philosopher. She begins her speech with a philosophical reflection on the basis of consecrated life and says: "The word virginity (parthenia) becomes the word 'near the divine' (partheia) if one leaves out only one letter."[13] Although such virginity certainly presupposes celibacy, the focus here is so entirely on higher beauty that it seems unimportant to the virgin philosophers to mention or regulate physical dimensions of virginity or even to regulate details of the necessary externalities. All speakers in the symposium are female, which is remarkable, because they are all presented as philosophers. Conversely, in the speech of the

10. Macrina is a virginal widow who waits for her fiancé, and who, at the same time, becomes a mother to her brother, Peter.

11. DVM Silvas, 3.2, 112; Maraval, chap. 2, 142–45.

12. See, for instance, L. Hayne, *Thecla and the Church Fathers* (Leiden, 1994) 209–18.

13. On this, H. Musurillo, *Methodius, the Symposium. A Treatise on Chastity, St. Methodius* (London, 1958) *Logos* 8, 105.

Virgin Marcella, Jesus is presented as a model of virginity. She says: "It is only appropriate that the one who is called arch-priest, arch-prophet and archangel should also be called arch-virgin."[14]

4. The Historical Context: Constantine, Councils and Ascetic Experiments

Macrina was born during the reign of Constantine and two years after the Council of Nicaea. At that time Christianity was becoming more and more accepted but was not yet fully established. During this time Christians were not only concerned with their relationship to the state but were also articulating nuances of theology and experimenting with ascetic ways of life. Many bishops felt that some of the new ideas and ways of life were disruptive or even destructive for the church. As Susanna Elm shows in her studies, on the one hand there were socially and ecclesiastically accepted "virgins of God" who were consecrated and who lived secluded lives of prayer either in a house with other virgins or, more often, in their family home. On the other hand, there were others who rejected marriage and typical gender roles and who saw no problem in the celibate, spiritual cohabitation of men and women.[15]

Eustathius of Sebaste was a particularly charismatic and prominent ascetic theologian in the fourth century who, in the end, decided on a direction that can be vaguely understood as "Arianist." We get an idea of the behavior of radical ascetic groups when we look at the so-called "Eustathinists." These were accused at the Council of Gangra for calling married people and others who did not want to completely despise their possessions as people "without hope of eternal life with God."[16] They were also accused of separating themselves from the church and for creating "their own assemblies and quasi-churches" in which they taught "foreign teachings," because they encouraged women to put on philosophical—that is, masculine—clothes and shaved their heads bare, and because they encouraged slaves to run away from their masters.

14. Methodius, *Logos* 1, 46.

15. S. Elm, *Virgins of God* (Oxford, 1994), esp. chaps. 1 and 4.

16. The dates of this council are not certain. If the complaints are, in fact, about Eustathius of Sebaste, for which there are good reasons to believe, then the date must be in the 360s or 370s. Basil gives the year 376.

That many people took this movement seriously and regarded it as dangerous for church unity after the Nicene Council can be seen by the fact that the Council of Gangra was not a small or local assembly. It was led by Eusebius, Metropolitan of Constantinople, and supported by twelve other bishops. The bishops who had gathered in Gangra were in a very precarious situation for they felt obliged, as Susanna Elm puts it, "to condemn Christians who did nothing but adhere to a literal interpretation of Holy Scripture."[17] One could even say that these people wanted to live lives as pure as the lilies of the fields and to demonstrate that in Christ there are no differences amongst persons. This, at its core, was the same doctrine on which the bishops based their authority.

The challenges facing the evolving church were immense. And it is important to remember that the church was not yet established at that time. Although Gregory of Nyssa was one of the leaders of the pro-Nicene party in Constantinople, he and his whole family were strongly influenced by the above-mentioned Eustathius of Sebaste, at least until Eustathius turned away from the pro-Nicene party, which caused Basil and Gregory to break off their relationship with him. And even after this separation, it would be too simple to maintain that they disagreed at all levels.[18]

5. Gregory's Understanding of Virginity

In the text *On Virginity*, which Gregory wrote around 371 at the request of his brother Basil, we hear many echoes of the philosophy that we have already considered in Methodius's *Symposium*. Even more: as Anna Silvas shows, the work was certainly marked by Gregory's experiences with Macrina and the ascetic community in Annisa.[19] The first part of the work clearly shows the greatness of the program and the connection between the ideal of virginity described by Methodius and the philosophi-

17. Elm, *Virgins of God*, 130.

18. Silvas analyzes this relationship in: *The Asketikon of St. Basil the Great*, especially chaps. 1, 4, and 5.

19. In his work on Basil, P. Rousseau questions the influence that Macrina had on Basil, since Basil himself never mentions his sister in his known works: *Basil of Caesarea* (Berkeley, 1994) 9–11. Silvas, however, shows that his works are very much influenced by the community in Annisa and, therefore, also by Macrina. Silvas, *Basil of Caesarea*, 43–49.

cal goal of beauty: "The holy appearance of virginity is precious to all who understand purity as the basis of beauty." The subsequent question he answers is what this purity actually looks like and what this "beauty" that leads to virginity consists of.

As an important contrast to texts written by Athanasius and John Chrysostom, Gregory's *On Virginity* is not primarily addressed to women. Even more: the primary model of virginity that Gregory emphasizes is not Mary, as we might expect. Instead, Gregory of Nyssa refers to the three Persons of the Trinity as a model of virgin life.[20] It is also extraordinary that the image of a woman who preserves her physical virginity for her true husband, Jesus Christ, is strikingly absent. Instead of a female example of virginity, he depicts King Solomon with his desire for a spiritual marriage with Lady Wisdom as a model of virginity. Even then Gregory tries to distance this image from gender conceptions. He says that such images are only tools and that the goal of motivating people to be united with wisdom applies to both women and men. For Paul writes in Gal 3:28, "There is neither male nor female," and Col 3:11, "Christ is all and in all."[21]

6. The Bride of Christ: Macrina and the Bride in the Song of Songs

In his *Vita*, Gregory gradually reveals Macrina as the bride of Christ. Like Thecla, she begins as a woman engaged. But after the death of her fiancé, she says that there is only one marriage and that it would be inappropriate to marry another because of the hope of resurrection.[22] The story develops in such a way that at the end of the text it becomes clear that the absent bridegroom is not the young man who died, but Christ himself.[23] If we look at the *Vita* in this light, and especially if we add the description of the Bride in Gregory's homilies on the Song of Songs, Macrina's spiritual significance is even clearer.

At first glance, the description of Macrina or the bride in the Song of Songs seems to be exclusively female. But in his homilies on the Song of Songs, Gregory explicitly says that, unlike in Proverbs or Ecclesiastes, in which the soul is portrayed as a man seeking Lady Wisdom,

20. Woods, DV, chap. 2, 10–12.

21. Woods, DV, chap. 20, 62–64.

22. DVM Silvas, chap. 6, 115; Maraval, chap. 5, 156–61.

23. DVM Silvas, chap. 24, 132; Maraval, chap. 22, 212–15.

when considering things on a higher spiritual level it makes more sense to describe the soul in feminine images, so that the human soul can be seen as the bride and Christ as the bridegroom. In the twelfth homily, he presents the bride as a closed and pure well from which the thirsty can drink. The picture is familiar to us, but Gregory changes it: it is no longer about the physical. Instead, Gregory recognizes "the discernment of the soul" in the "fountain." This, according to Gregory, "wells up in us with manifold thoughts, which then flow out like springs." Because the bride is pure and because she meets the bridegroom, she longs to be united with him, that is, with God, and to become like him. "For from the fountain the fountain is exactly modelled, from her life *the* life, from her water *the* water."[24] Gregory then mentions how this closed well shares wisdom with other virgins. He calls her a pomegranate tree and shows her as a person who can feed others. It is fertile and life-giving and the food she receives and passes on is God Himself.[25]

At its core, this is a description of the ideal theologian who knows and imitates God so well and who interprets Scripture and applies it practically in ways that are wholly reliable because the person lives in direct contact with God. This picture stands in stark contrast to the picture Gregory creates of his theological archenemy Eunomius, but not because of the use of feminine terms in his descriptions. Eunomius is described as arrogant and angry. Unlike the bride, he is not pure. He fights and fights until he finally spits out his statements about the nature of Christ. But in contrast to the fertility of the bride, Eunomius produces only "a poor abortion, born far too early."[26]

7. Parallels and Types

We have already seen that Gregory offers gender-based parallels and types; Macrina, Thecla, and the bride are connected with one another and can be used to understand and interpret one another. In his other

24. G. of Nyssa, Homily 9, in *Homilies on the Song of Songs*, ed. R. A. Norris (Atlanta, 2012) 309.

25. G. of Nyssa. Homily 9, 295.

26. See the first foreword: *Against Eunomius*: G. of Nyssa, *Contra Eunomium* (hereafter abbreviated CE), in: Nicene and Post Nicene Fathers, vol. 5 (Edinburgh, 1971).

texts Gregory compares Basil with Moses and Paul.[27] It is not difficult to put these models together: Moses and the bride can be seen together as Old Testament models, Thecla and Paul are old Testament models, and Macrina and Basil are his contemporaries; and both of these pairs are connected with each other in any case. However, the comparisons are not limited by gender. Although he does not mention Macrina in his encomium on Basil, Gregory says in his *Vita* that Macrina was responsible for the conversion of her brother Basil.[28] And although the bride is not mentioned in Moses' *Vita*, Gregory describes his education in bridal and maternal images.[29] At the beginning of the homilies on the Song of Songs, Moses is even explicitly shown in the role of the bride. Gregory writes: "Moses the bride kisses the bridegroom like the Virgin in the Song of Songs, who says 'let him kiss me with kisses of his mouth'."[30] Gregory's works are rich in such examples. Paul is striving not only to lead Christians to "masculinity," a quality also ascribed to Macrina: he is also honored as the "most fruitful in childbirth."[31] God is also described as a mother who breastfeeds her children, and Jesus is portrayed with breasts filled with wine.[32] These many examples should prevent us from making overly sharp separations between the genders and their roles in the works of Gregory of Nyssa. It has been shown that female images are not limited to women but also refer to Paul, Moses, and Jesus himself. His descriptions of Macrina do not serve primarily to offer a model of domestic, female Christian life; instead, she is presented as a teacher, philosopher, and theologian.

27. This is especially noticeable when one compares the *Vita Mose* and the *Encomium* with Basil. In the *Encomium* Gregory puts his brother in the role of Moses and makes the reader aware that his brother's death and feast days are to be seen in the context of the other winter feasts; in particular Christmas, St. Stephen, St. Peter, St. James, St. John, and St. Paul. Compare M. Williams, *Authorised Lives in Early Christian Biography* (Cambridge, 2013) chap. 2; G. of Nyssa, *The Life of Moses*, trans. A. Malherbe and E. Ferguson (New York, 1978).

28. DVM Silvas, chap. 8, 117; Maraval, chap. 6, 160–65.

29. See R. Norris, *Gregory of Nyssa on the Song of Songs* (Grand Rapids, 2013) 33–34.

30. Gregory explains that Moses desires God's kisses all the more because of the conversation that took place "face to face" with God, Norris, *Gregory of Nyssa*, 32–33.

31. *On Virginity*, ed. Jaeger, 19; 61.

32. Norris, *Gregory of Nyssa*, 34–35.

8. Macrina's Consecrated Life

The question remains whether Gregory's image of Macrina as a teacher and theologian opens doors so that we can see her in a liturgical and consecrated role. On a historical level, it is clear that Gregory would have strongly opposed such an idea. However, he does not reject freedom in Christ in principle. In his *Vita*, Gregory corrects interpretations of Gal 3:28 that go in this direction. On the one hand, he shows how Macrina assumes male roles in the management of the family estate; she does not withdraw, as one would expect from a "virgin of God."[33]At the same time, she acts in the accepted role of a widow and only after the death of her father. As a teacher she is also in a position of authority, but at the same time she remains ready to receive a blessing from her brothers who are ordained.[34]There is no thought that these roles should be switched.

Does this mean that Gregory has no openness for women in the priestly ministry? Perhaps. And yet when Gregory talks about the death of Emmelia, he describes the solemn blessing that Macrina and Peter receive from their mother. She ends her life like any liturgy, with a benediction. It is important that Gregory does not exclude the possibility that Emmelia may give and that Macrina may receive a formal blessing, in spite of the fact that both are women. He does not apologize when he puts words of Old Testament sanctification and blessing into Emmelia's mouth and when he names Macrina and Peter as recipients of this blessing.[35] It is also worth noting that shortly after this episode, Gregory describes how Basil, as bishop, ordained his brother Peter as priest in the "mystical rites."[36] It is clear that this ordination is a continuation of a process of consecration that had already begun and not the beginning of a new process. This consecration complements their philosophical life.

Gregory's description of Macrina's death is also worth considering: Although Macrina dies in her cell and not in the church, Gregory describes this as a sacred, quasi-liturgical space.[37] In her second conver-

33. DVM Silvas, chap. 7, 116; Maraval, chap. 5, 154–61.

34. DVM Silvas, chap. 19, 119–20, Maraval, chap. 17, 196–97.

35. DVM Silvas, chap. 15, 124; Maraval, chap. 13, 184–87. In this chapter the words εὐλογος and ἁγιας are used several times.

36. DVM Silvas, chap. 16, 125; Maraval, chap. 14, 188–91.

37. DVM Silvas, 19, 128; Maraval, 16, 194–97. Gregory goes to the "holy dwelling" ἐνττὸς τὴς ἱερᾶς ἐκεινεσ. DVM Silvas 25, 135; Maraval 23. Silvas points out that Macrina's bed was facing East.

sation, Macrina talks to Gregory about their family; "with the goal of gratitude" they exchange memories. This conversation is interrupted by the "voices of the psalm singers." They call on Gregory to continue this exchange in Vespers, where they pray the "thanksgiving of the lighting of the lamps."[38] The next day is Macrina's last. Gregory writes that she has moved her bed to the east—that is, the direction of prayer. Gregory places a formal prayer in Macrina's mouth, which is quite obviously to be understood as a high prayer or eucharistic prayer. It is similar to the eucharistic prayer of her brother Basil, but much more personal. In Basil, bread and wine are offered as sacrifices. But in this case, Macrina herself becomes the sacrifice and the gift.[39]

By this point, Macrina can already be recognized as the bride of Christ. Now the reader suspects that in this bride the whole church is to be seen as well. So Macrina is represented all at once as the church, the bride of Christ, and the elder sister of Gregory. After her death, Macrina's depiction is expanded. When the community mourns, it does so with the following words: "The lamp of our eyes has gone out! The light that led our souls has been taken away."[40] Now Macrina is no longer just a woman who prays the thanksgiving for the lighting of the lamps in the role of priest, but she is herself the lamp that shines for the community. Just as the bride can offer water because she is connected to the true well, Macrina can serve as a lamp because she is filled with the true light. Even more: by reading the *Vita*, Macrina's life and prayer find their place in the liturgy. In this way, Gregory gives Macrina an authority that is otherwise reserved only for priests and bishops. He does nothing more than this. But he also does nothing less.

38. DVM Silvas, chap. 23, 131; Maraval, chap. 22, 212–17.

39. DVM Silvas, chap. 26, 133–34; Maraval, chap. 24, 218–25. See especially Silvas, 133 Anm. 98.

40. DVM Silvas, chap. 28, 136–37; Maraval, chap. 26, 228–33.

"I Have Not Written You a Woman's Gossip, but the Word of God as a Member of the Christian Church."

Women in Ecclesiastical Offices—A Search for Traces in Church History

Andrea Strübind

1. Impulses from the Reformation

On the cover of the first pamphlet published by Argula von Grumbach in early November 1523[1] a unique scene is printed. A woman from the nobility, a laywoman, is standing in front of a group of men with an open Bible in her hand. One can tell from the way they are dressed that the men are scholars and academics. It is the council of the Faculty of Theology in Ingolstadt, led by a professor holding a gauntlet to the woman with her provocative stare. Argula von Grumbach[2] had sent an open letter, or rather a protest letter, to these scholars in which she defended the teaching of the Reformation and challenged the professors to a disputation. "I have no Latin," she writes, "but you could speak German with me, the tongue with which I was born and raised. I have not written you

1. On the printing history of this text, cf. A. von Grumbach, *Schriften*, ed. Peter Matheson (Gütersloh, 2010) 48–49.

2. On her biography cf. S. Halbach, *Argula von Grumbach als Verfasserin reformatorischer Flugschriften* (Berlin, 1992); P. Matheson, *Argula von Grumbach. A Woman's Voice in the Reformation* (Edinburgh, 1995); Matheson, *Argula von Grumbach. Eine Biographie* (Göttingen, 2014).

a woman's gossip, but the Word of God as a member of the Christian Church, against which the gates of hell shall not prevail."[3]

Argula's text found wide distribution and caused a sensation, so that fourteen editions appeared within two months.[4] For many years she corresponded with Martin Luther and other reformers. She stood up for the Reformation in the face of the Duke of Bavaria and other authorities, and she used her influence at the important Imperial Diets of the 1520s and 1530s as well as in her own networks. Her public activities led to serious conflicts with her husband, who was finally removed from his political office because he was unable to control his wife. From 1524 onward, she held her silence. Nonetheless, it was reported that she attracted attention even as an old woman by biblical readings that led people to convert to the new faith, as well as by clandestine sermons and funerals conducted without the participation of the responsible priest. That indicates that she was resistant to the very end.

She justified her public commitment by referring to Joel 3, according to which God would pour out his spirit, causing men and women to prophesy.[5] In her opinion the promise to the disciples in Matt 10:32, "Everyone who acknowledges me before others, I also will acknowledge before my Father in heaven," excluded neither men nor women.[6] She responds to the commandment regarding women's silence that Paul issued to his follower (1 Tim 2): " 'The women should keep silence, and should not speak in the church.' But now I cannot see any man who is up to it, who is either willing or able to speak, so I am compelled by the saying 'Everyone who acknowledges me.' . . ."[7]

In connection with the five hundredth anniversary of the Reformation, a considerable number of publications, exhibitions, and Internet pre-

3. Von Grumbach, *Schriften*, 75. "Jch kan kain Latein, aber ihr künde[n]t teutsch, jn dyser zung geborn vn[d] erzoge[n]. Jch hab euch nit weibs tedig geschribe[n], sund[er[dz wort gottess als ain gelyd der Christe[n]liche[n] kirche[n], vor welcher die pforte[n] der hell nit bestee[n] möge[n]."

4. Cf. von Grumbach, *Schriften*, 49.

5. Cf. von Grumbach, *Schriften*, 63.

6. Cf. von Grumbach, *Schriften*, 64.

7. Von Grumbach, *Schriften*, 67. "Die weiber sölle[n] schweigen vn[d] nit reden in der Kirchen. Nun ich aber in dyser artz kain man sehe, der reden will noch darff, dringt mich der spruch. Wer mich bekennt . . ."

sentations on women in the Reformation have appeared[8]. Every single female protagonist of that time was fascinating, especially since they had the courage to make public theological statements, to transcend the roles assigned to them, and thus to open up new horizons for women in the church. Nevertheless, the Reformation by no means pointed toward women's ordination, nor did it even stringently pave the way for it. Recent research has strongly argued that especially the Lutheran Reformation brought no emancipatory effect for women, but rather strengthened the patriarchal world order.[9] In addition, ecclesiastical offices that had developed in the medieval religious orders, such as that of the abbess, disappeared as a result of the flight from the monasteries induced by the Reformation and secularization. To be sure, the "priesthood of all believers" was one of the central teachings of the Reformation, as Luther wrote in his most important works of 1520 (among others "To the Christian Nobility" and "On the Freedom of a Christian") and also in his "Treatise on the New Testament, that is, on the Holy Mass": "All such, then, wherever they may be, are true priests, observe the mass aright and also obtain by it what they desire. For faith must do everything. It alone is the true priestly office and permits no one else to take its place. Therefore all Christians are priests; the men priests, the women priestesses, be they young or old, masters or servants, mistresses or maids, learned or unlearned. Here there is no difference, unless faith be unequal."[10]

In spite of this ecclesiological foundation, women were not admitted to an office for public preaching or to ordination as priests. In disputes with his opponents of the old faith, Luther did indeed defend the priesthood of all believers[11] to which all baptized Christians—men and women—

8. Cf. http://www.kirchliche-dienste.de/damfiles/default/haus_kirchlicher_dienste/arbeitsfelder/frauen/reformation/Literatur---Material---Medien--Frauen-und-Reformation-0-dbb65c2d1aea2cfdfd651ee3bdb23f63.pdf.

9. Cf. L. Roper, *The Holy Household* (Oxford, 1989).

10. M. Luther, "Treatise on the New Testament, that is, on the Holy Mass," 1520, translation at: http://www.godrules.net/library/luther/NEW1luther_a28.htm.

11. Cf. H.-M. Barth, *Einander Priester sein. Allgemeines Priestertum in ökumenischer Perspektive* (Göttingen, 1990); V. Leppin, Priestertum aller Gläubigen. Amt und Ehrenamt in der lutherischen Kirche, in: U. Heckel, J. Kampmann, V. Leppin, C. Schwöbel, eds., *Luther heute. Ausstrahlungen der Wittenberger Reformation* (Tübingen, 2017) 149–69.

were entitled, but on the basis of the subordination of women to men in Gen 3 as a consequence of the Fall, he nonetheless did not consider it appropriate for women to exercise the public ministry of preaching.[12] "This distinction is made in Nature and in God's creation also, where no woman (still less children and fools) can or ought to have rulership, as experience tells us, and Moses says, in Genesis 3:16, 'Thou shalt be in subjection to thy husband.' The Gospel does not abolish this natural law, but confirms it as the ordinance and creation of God."[13] Moreover, women were not suitable for such an office because of their weak voices.[14] This attitude prevailed in Lutheranism and was successively established in the other Reformation movements as well. Thus it is not possible to draw an unbroken line of tradition from the Reformation principle of the priesthood of all believers to the ordination of women. Rather, this topic is a product of modern times, specifically of the nineteenth and twentieth centuries, even in Protestantism.

The following sections represent an attempt to find traces in church history concerning the issue of women in ecclesial offices, concluding with the identification of potential for further development in ecumenism.

2. On Research into the History of Women

It was research on the history of women and gender, established in the 1970s, that contributed to serious changes in historiography in general and, consequently, in church historiography as well. The observation and analysis of gender relations in history is now part of the methodological inventory of historiography. The starting point for the research on the history of women in the churches of every confession and denomination was the feminist theology established in the 1970s.[15] In contrast to

12. Cf. K. G. Appold, Frauen im frühneuzeitlichen Luthertum, in: *Zeitschrift für Theologie und Kirche* 103 (2006) 253–79, 262–65; Leppin, *Priestertum*, 155.

13. "On the Councils and the Church" (1539), translation at: http://www.godrules.net/library/luther/NEW1luther_e14.htm; Weimar Edition 50, 633.

14. Cf. Appold, *Frauen*, 264.

15. Cf. U. Gause, *Kirchengeschichte und Genderforschung* (Tübingen, 2006) 2.

the history written and interpreted by men for centuries, which largely concentrated on great men and theologians as well as their theologies, feminist theology discovered women who had been successful and effective in church history and had helped to shape it.

This new research approach led the traditional, androcentric pursuit of church history to be complemented and compensated by a deliberate investigation into the women's history. Since then, a great many women from various eras have been discovered and their achievements made known. Historical sources on women have been edited, enabling further research. Thanks to this productive period, outstanding women from every historical epoch of the church and Christianity can be named who have transcended since ancient times the role assigned to them by patriarchal societies. It starts with the female disciples, apostles, leaders of house churches, and helpers in the early Christian communities,[16] goes on to the women martyred for their faith,[17] who were thus venerated in the same way as their male brothers, and includes the central role played by women in later heterodox movements such as Montanism or Gnosticism.[18]

One could also mention women in the Middle Ages who exerted great influence on the church as mystics and members of religious orders, such as Hildegard of Bingen,[19] or who, like Teresa of Ávila,[20] were even acknowledged by the pope as Doctors of the Church. The

16. Cf. S. Schreiber, Arbeit mit der Gemeinde (Röm 16,6.12). Zur versunkenen Möglichkeit der Gemeindeleitung durch Frauen, in: *New Testament Studies* 46 (2000) 204–26; L. Belleville,Ἰουνιαν . . . ἐπίσημοι ἐν τοῖς ἀποστόλοις. A Re-examination of Romans 16:7 in Light of Primary Source Materials, in: *New Testament Studies* 51 (2005) 231–49; C. Gerber, *Paulus und seine Kinder. Studien zur Beziehungsmetaphorik der paulinischen Briefe* (Berlin/New York, 2005).

17. Cf. E. Elm, Weibliches Martyrium—frauenspezifische Verfolgung—frauenspezifische Visionen?, in: *Pegasus-Onlinezeitschrift* VI/1 (2006) 15–26.

18. Cf. U. E. Eisen, *Amtsträgerinnen im frühen Christentum. Epigraphische und literarische Studien* (Göttingen, 1996).

19. Cf. T. Altenburg, *Soziale Ordnungsvorstellungen bei Hildegard von Bingen* (Stuttgart, 2007).

20. Cf. J. Burggraff, *Teresa von Avila. Humanität und Glaubensleben* (Paderborn, 1996).

rank of abbess[21] should be cited as another significant stage in the female leadership ministry of the church.

Important steps were taken by the new religious movements of the High and Late Middle Ages, such as the apostolic poverty movement, as well as by reform orders and communities such as the Cathars,[22] Waldensian sisters,[23] Beguines,[24] and Franciscan nuns.[25] Another important phase was the Reformation in all its facets—Lutheran, Reformed, Anabaptist, in which women often bore responsibility.[26] Making reference to the priesthood of all believers, women contributed to the dissemination and establishment of the Reformation, particularly in the early phase: as preachers, authors of pamphlets, co-reformers, and self-proclaimed church mothers, as is impressively demonstrated by the work and life of

21. Cf. T. Schröder-Stapper, *Fürstäbtissinnen. Frühneuzeitliche Stiftsherrschaften zwischen Verwandtschaft, Lokalgewalten und Reichsverband* (Cologne/Weimar/Vienna, 2015).

22. Cf. D. Müller, *Frauen gehen ihren eigenen Weg. Vom Leben und Sterben der Katharerinnen im 13. und 14. Jahrhundert* (Würzburg, 2004); U. Bejick, *Die Katharerinnen. Häresieverdächtige Frauen im mittelalterlichen Süd-Frankreich* (Freiburg, 1993).

23. Cf. J. Feuchter, Waldenserinnen im Mittelalter, in: G. Frank, A. de Lange, G. Schwinge. eds., *Die Waldenser. Spuren einer europäischen Glaubensbewegung* (Bretten, 1999) 51–69; P. Biller, The Preaching of the Waldensian Sisters, in: *Heresis. Revue d'hérésiologie médiévale* 30 (1999) 137–68.

24. See J. Voigt, *Beginen im Spätmittelalter. Frauenfrömmigkeit in Thüringen und im Reich* (Cologne, 2012); A. Conrad, *Welt-geistliche Frauen in der Frühen Neuzeit. Studien zum weiblichen Semireligiosentum* (Münster, 2013).

25. Cf. P. Zahner, ed., *Lebendiger Spiegel des Lichts. Klara von Assisi* (Münster, 2013); C. Jäggi, *Frauenklöster im Spätmittelalter. Die Kirchen der Klarissen und Dominikanerinnen im 13. und 14. Jahrhundert* (Petersberg, 2006).

26. Cf. A. Conrad, *"In Christo ist weder man noch weyb." Frauen in der Zeit der Reformation und der katholischen Reform* (Münster, 1999); U. Gause, Reformation und Genderforschung, in: M. Schattkowsky, ed., *Frauen und Reformation. Handlungsfelder, Rollenmuster, Engagement* (Leipzig, 2016) 21–37; C. A. Snyder, L. Huebert Hecht, eds., *Profiles of Anabaptist Women. Sixteenth-Century Reforming Pioneers* (Waterloo, 1997) 19–23 (on Anabaptists in Switzerland); M. Kobelt-Groch, *Aufsässige Töchter Gottes. Frauen im Bauernkrieg und in den Täuferbewegungen* (Frankfurt a.M./New York, 1993) 147–63; K. Reinholdt, *Ein Leib in Christo werden. Ehe und Sexualität im Täufertum der Frühen Neuzeit* (Göttingen, 2012).

Katharina Zell in Strasbourg.[27] One could also mention the prophetesses[28] as well as those female rulers who used their authority to introduce the Reformation in their territories, such as Countess Anna in East Frisia.[29]

Furthermore, one can refer to the relevant contributions of women in the various pietistic movements such as Pietism, Jansenism, and Revivalism[30] as well as to women's unconventional situations and assignments in overseas mission areas.[31] A further momentous facet in this overall

27. Cf. E. A. McKee, *Katharina Schütz-Zell. The Life and Thought of a Sixteenth-Century Reformer*, vol. 1 (Leiden/Boston/Cologne, 1999); T. Kaufmann, Pfarrfrau und Publizistin. Das Reformatorische "Amt" der Katharina Zell, in: *Zeitschrift für historische Forschung* 23 (1996) 169–218; A. Zimmerli-Witschi, *Frauen in der Reformationszeit* (Zürich, 1981) 73–90; H. Zschoch, Bileams Eselinnen. Frauen in der Publizistik der Reformationszeit, in: *Pastoraltheologie mit Göttinger Predigtmeditationen* 83 (1994) 477–97; R. H. Bainton, *Frauen der Reformation* (Gütersloh, 1995) 56–83; M. H. Jung, K. Zell geb. Schütz (1497/98–1562). Eine "Laientheologin" der Reformationszeit?, in: Jung, *Nonnen, Prophetinnen, Kirchenmütter. Kirchen—und frömmigkeitsgeschichtliche Studien zu Frauen der Reformationszeit* (Leipzig, 2002) 121–68; M. U. Chrisman, Women and the Reformation in Strasbourg 1490–1530, in: *Archiv für Reformationsgeschichte* 63 (1972) 143–68; A. Strübind, Katharina Zell. Eine Wegbereiterin für religiöse Toleranz, in: W. Ernst, U. Bohle, eds., *Geschlechterdiskurse zwischen Fiktion und Faktizität. Internationale Frauen—und Genderforschung in Niedersachen* (Hamburg, 2006) 171–201.

28. Cf. L. Y. Barrett, *Wreath of Glory. Ursula's Prophetic Visions in the Context of Reformation and Revolt in Southwestern Germany, 1524–1530* (Ann Arbor, 1992).

29. H. Ebbel Janssen, *Gräfin Anna von Ostfriesland—eine hochadelige Frau der späten Reformationszeit* (Münster, 1998).

30. R. Albrecht, Frauen, in: H. Lehmann, ed., *Geschichte des Pietismus*, vol. 4 (Göttingen, 2004) 522–55; U. Gleixner, E. Hebeisen, eds., *Gendering Tradition. Erinnerungskultur und Geschlecht im Pietismus* (Korb, 2007) 123–48; A. Sedgwick, *The Travails of Conscience. The Arnauld Family and the Ancien Régime* (Boston, 1998); R. Albrecht, "Daß wir andere zu Jesus rufen." Frauen in der Erweckungsbewegung Norddeutschlands, in: *Pietismus und Neuzeit* 30 (2004) 116–49; U. Gause, Frauen und Frömmigkeit im 19. Jahrhundert. Der Aufbruch in die Öffentlichkeit, in: *Pietismus und Neuzeit* 24 (1998) 309–27; V. Albrecht-Birkner, Gender Studies zu den Erweckungsbewegungen des 19. Jahrhunderts. Forschungsstand und -perspektiven, in: T. K. Kuhn, V. Albrecht-Birkner, eds., *Zwischen Aufklärung und Moderne. Erweckungsbewegungen als historiographische Herausforderung* (Berlin, 2017) 63–102.

31. Cf. B. Eulenhöfer-Mann, *Frauen mit Mission. Deutsche Missionarinnen in China (1891–1914)* (Leipzig, 2010); C. Keim, *Frauenmission und Frauenemanzipation. Eine*

picture is the women's diaconate, which originated in the reconstitution of the office of deaconess in the nineteenth century.[32]

Feminist church historians can refer to a wealth of new discoveries and interesting research results in women's history. Despite the patriarchal social systems that have left their mark on the last centuries, this research approach proved that women had borne and shaped the history of Christianity significantly, even if their life stories, theology, and piety had only been more clearly brought to light by research in the last fifty years.

However, there are also deficits in the feminist historical approach with its criticism of patriarchy. In a similar way to traditional church history, feminist research concentrated on making forgotten women "visible" and on elucidating their oppression. Women were seen to be first and foremost victims of history, underlining the unchanging bipolarity of the sexes.[33] The crux of women's history research, with all its merits, is that it highlighted exceptional women, who transcended or redefined their traditional roles, over against women who often functioned in the background as invisible and nameless supporters of the Christian churches. This should be critically reflected in the *memoria* of these women. Today numerous desiderata of understanding still remain as a reminder to continue discussing the gender perspective in the methodology of church history, especially since it has not yet been comprehensively received, as demonstrated by recent textbooks and anthologies.[34]

Extensive research results on this topic are available, but there are very few lines of continuity in church history regarding the pastoral and ordained ministry before the nineteenth century, apart from the diaconate in the early church.[35]

At the latest from the second century, the public activity of female church members was restricted or forbidden, not least due to a revalua-

---

Diskussion in der Basler Mission im Kontext der frühen ökumenischen Bewegung (1901–1928) (Münster, 2005).

32. Cf. S. Köser, *"Denn eine Diakonisse darf kein Alltagsmensch sein." Kollektive Identitäten Kaiserwerther Diakonissen 1836–1914* (Leipzig, 2006).

33. Cf. Gause, *Kirchengeschichte*, 71.

34. Cf. Gause, *Kirchengeschichte*, 80f.

35. Reference to the article by Theresia Hainthaler in this book.

tion of ritual purity.[36] In early Christianity, women were excluded from the ordained ministries, which became increasingly differentiated. For this reason, only a comparatively small number of them have been remembered over time. This deficit is essentially rooted in the fact that women, due to their exclusion from the ordained ministries and from preaching, were hardly able to occupy (leadership) positions commanding wide attention.

Against this backdrop of church history, it is appropriate to search for leitmotifs in churches, communities, and movements that have opened a door for the recognition of women in public preaching and ecclesiastical office. I will now go on to search for such traces.

3. Women in Preaching Ministry and Leadership Positions before the Nineteenth Century

From this point of view, it is particularly rewarding to examine pietistic movements that laid great emphasis on personal faith, the experience of spiritual "rebirth," sanctification, and the gifts of the Spirit. These movements include the separatist Puritans (Quakers), Pietists, Methodists, as well as the Revival and Pentecostal movements.

We may start with an example from Moravian Pietism. Anna Nitschmann (1715–1760),[37] later the second wife of Nikolaus, Count von Zinzendorf, came to Herrnhut as a religious refugee. As early as 1730, she was chosen by lot to be the Eldress for all the women in the community.[38] In the

36. Cf. H. Lutterbach, Starke Frauen in der Christentumsgeschichte, in: *Herder Korrespondenz* 70 (2016) Spezial 1, 26–30; E. Dassmann, Ämter und Dienste in den frühchristlichen Gemeinden (Bonn, 1994) 225–30; C. Markschies, *Das antike Christentum. Frömmigkeit, Lebensformen, Institutionen* (Munich, 2006) 208–9.

37. A. Nitschmann, *curriculum vitae* (1737), printed in: M. H. Jung, ed., *"Mein Herz brannte richtig in der Liebe Jesu." Autobiographien frommer Frauen aus Pietismus und Erweckungsbewegung. Eine Quellensammlung* (Aachen, 1999) 151–68; P. Zimmerling, Anna Nitschmann (1715–1760). Seelsorge unter Frauen, in: Zimmerling, ed., *Evangelische Seelsorgerinnen. Biografische Skizzen, Texte und Programme* (Göttingen, 2004) 103–23. Unfortunately, no scientific biography is available yet.

38. L. Martin, Anna Nitschmann (1715–1760). Priesterin, Generalältestin, Jüngerin der weltweiten Brüdergemeine, in: A. M. von Hauff, ed., *Frauen gestalten Diakonie*, vol. 1, *Von der biblischen Zeit bis zum Pietismus* (Stuttgart, 2007) 393–409, 396–97; cf. on this: P. M. Peucker, "Gegen ein Regiment von Schwestern." Die

unconventional system of the Herrnhut community, with its wide range of spiritual and organizational offices for men and women, the Reformation ideal of the priesthood of all believers was put into consistent practice. As Eldress, Anna Nitschmann held a senior position as spiritual counselor for women and girls, whereby she also became a member of leadership committees. A short time later she founded the "Choir of Single Sisters," an independent group or sisterhood within the Brethren community, which had a decisive effect on her personal history and that of the entire fellowship.[39]

On the overall level of the Moravian Church, the community of Herrnhut adopted the threefold hierarchical scheme of the early church: deacon, presbyter, and bishop.[40] Women were ordained as deaconess and presbyter, also called priestess. From 1746 women were already ordained into the office of priestess, but this was kept secret until 1758 due to social (anti-) convention. At the first official ceremony of ordination for women, Anna Nitschmann joined Zinzendorf at the benediction by the laying on of hands. From 1746 Anna Nitschmann bore the title of "Mother" of the Brethren community (*Gemeinmutter*) and actively participated in the ordination of other priestesses. She was also a cofounder of the Bethlehem settlement in Pennsylvania, traveled to the colonies as a lay preacher, and evangelized there.[41] This led to conflicts in some communities of other denominations that did not allow women to speak in public. Here the Quakers formed a particular exception, for she was received positively in their congregations and was able to preach there. For more than twenty years, Anna Nitschmann was one of the highest ranking administrators in her faith community.

4. Women as Preachers of the Revival Movement and the Dissenting Protestant Denominations

John Wesley (1703–1791), the founder of Methodism, had already allowed women to preach in England in the eighteenth century, although

Stellung der Frau in der Brüdergemeine nach Zinzendorfs Tod, in: *Unitas Fratrum* 45/46 (1999) 61–72; P. Zimmerling, Zinzendorfs Bild der Frau, in: *Unitas Fratrum* 45/46 (1999) 9–27.

39. Cf. Martin, Nitschmann, 397–400.

40. Cf. Martin, Nitschmann, 400. The author refers to source material that is supposed to prove that women also served as bishops within the Brethren congregations.

41. Cf. Martin, Nitschmann, 403.

he did not establish a special ministry for them.[42] For him, the criterion was a special vocation by God, which did not lead to an institutional ordination of women but rather justified and legitimized their missionary work. In the 1840s, about two hundred women were active as preachers in Methodist groups in England,[43] where the institution of itinerant female preachers also existed among the Quakers.[44] There is evidence of female preachers in the Baptist churches in North America in the early colonial period down to the eighteenth century, but after the foundation of the United States these churches were socially established and such egalitarian tendencies suppressed.[45]

In the revival movements of the nineteenth century, there was a decisive turn toward the institutionalization of the ordination of women.[46] Studies show that during the two great revivals in the USA more than one hundred women traveled through numerous states as itinerant evangelical preachers and evangelists and were successful missionaries. In addition, the first institutions were founded in which women could study theology, such as Oberlin College, which also admitted Black students.[47]

Some of them became well known, such as Harriet Livermore, who was allowed to preach before Congress in Washington in January 1827.[48] These protagonists were thoroughly conservative in their theology and also in their attitude to social gender roles, but they fought committedly

42. On the role of women in Methodism cf. C. A. Brekus, *Strangers and Pilgrims. Female Preaching in America 1740–1945* (London, 1998); P. Mack, *Heart Religion in the British Enlightenment. Gender and Emotion in Early Methodism* (Cambridge, 2008).

43. Cf. Brekus, *Strangers*, 133.

44. Cf. C. Baker, An Exploration of Quaker Women's Writing. Between 1650 and 1700, in: *Journal of International Women's Studies* 5 (2004) 8–20: http://vc.bridgew.edu/jiws/vol5/iss2/2; S. Wright, Quakerism and its Implications for Quaker Women. The Women Itinerant Ministers of York, 1780–1840, in: W. J. Sheils, D. Wood, eds., *Women in the Church* (Oxford, 1990) 403–14.

45. Cf. P. R. Durso, Zum Schweigen gebracht oder gehört. Die Stimmen baptistischer Frauen während der Kolonialzeit in Amerika, in: *Zeitschrift für Theologie und Gemeinde* 15 (2010) 197–220.

46. Cf. E. Geldbach, Die Stellung unterschiedlicher Kirchen zur Ordination von Frauen, in: *Zeitschrift für Theologie und Gemeinde* 4 (1999) 100–120, 104.

47. Cf. R. W. Hogeland, Coeducation of the Sexes at Oberlin College. A Study of Social Ideas in Mid-Nineteenth-Century America, in: *Journal of Social History* 6 (1972–1973) 160–76; Geldbach, *Stellung*, 104.

48. Cf. Brekus, *Strangers*, 1–3.

for women's right to preach and thus shaped, at least for a certain time, a new image of women in the churches and the critical public in the USA. Antoinette Brown Blackwell (1825–1921), who also studied at Oberlin College and was the first woman to graduate[49] as a full theologian, was ordained on September 15, 1853, in a congregational church in South Butler and appointed there as the first female pastor.[50] Luther Lee (1800–1889), a Methodist revival preacher and anti-slavery activist, took part at the ordination together with a Presbyterian.[51] In the following years Brown made a name for herself in particular as a lecturer in the anti-slavery movement and stood up for women's rights with other fellow campaigners.

Most of these revival preachers were not concerned with women's political, social, or economic equality, but with "spiritual equality" on a biblical basis, having a traditionally conservative religious socialization. Many of them also published important texts defending the female preaching ministry. It should be noted that most of them were not concerned with the ordination of women or the attainment of a certain ecclesiastical office—including administration of the sacraments—but with the proclamation of the word.

Another interesting example is the Salvation Army, in which Catherine Mumford Booth (1829–1890) and her husband created structures assigning equal value to women in service.[52] The admission of women to the preaching ministry and the first ordinations are also documented in

49. However, the degree was not formally awarded, and her name was not included in the list of graduates. Cf. M. Blume, *Antoinette Brown Blackwell. Die erste Evolutionsforscherin* (Filderstadt, 2013) 343.

50. Cf. E. Cazden, *Antoinette Brown Blackwell. A Biography* (New York, 1983); B. A. Zink-Sawyer, *From Preachers to Suffragists. Women's Rights and Religious Conviction in the Lives of Three Nineteenth-Century American Clergywomen* (London, 2003); Blume, *Antoinette Brown Blackwell.*

51. Cf. Geldbach, *Stellung*, 106–7; Blume, *Brown*, 434. Brown only remained a pastor for one year because of the tensions she experienced in her ministry.

52. Cf. E. Geldbach, C. Kenning, eds., *Gleichberechtigung in Uniform? Geschlechterverhältnisse in der Heilsarmee gestern und heute* (Münster, 2003); Geldbach and Kenning, Catherine Booth und die Heilsarmee, in: S. Fuhrmann, E. Geldbach, I. Pahl, eds., *Soziale Rollen von Frauen in Religonsgemeinschaften* (Münster, 2003) 141–54.

the Holiness movement and the early Pentecostal movement during the nineteenth century.[53]

For the Quakers, one should refer to Elizabeth Fry, whose biography and work have been repeatedly described.[54] Today she is still considered an icon of social reform, especially in her tireless efforts to improve detention conditions for women prisoners and as a driving force for diaconal and social projects on the European continent. During her lifetime she was already venerated as a new "saint" and achieved an amazing popularity.[55] On the other hand, researchers have so far paid little attention to her role as a preacher. In 1811 she became a preacher or Quaker Minister, an office which was open to both sexes in Quakerism.[56] What is striking, however, is that her way of teaching the Bible in prisons has made its mark in cultural memory. Her Bible study with the prisoners was promoted as a model of charitable commitment and selflessness. On the five journeys she made to the European continent between 1838 and 1843 she was active in the sense of prison reform, but also as a revival preacher and evangelist in the context of the Evangelical movement. She held religious conferences in the various countries and distributed Bibles and tracts as well as her own publications.

Erich Geldbach identifies the reference to the work of the Holy Spirit in view of the newly developed role of women as preachers and evangelists in the above-mentioned denominations as a starting point for the equality and emancipation of women in the church. "The Holy Spirit was the woman's emancipator."[57] However, with all respect for this dynamic development, it must be noted that at the turn of the century fundamentalism became widespread in the Evangelical movement, frequently leading to the end of egalitarian self-perceptions and practices.[58]

53. Cf. Geldbach, *Stellung*, 109f.

54. Cf. J. Kent, *Elizabeth Fry* (London, 1962); E. R. Pitman, *Elizabeth Fry* (New York, 1969); J. Rose, *Elizabeth Fry* (London, 1980); J. Hatton, *Betsy. The Dramatic Biography of Prison Reformer Elizabeth Fry* (Oxford/Grand Rapids, 2005); A. van Drenth, F. de Haan, *The Rise of Caring Power. Elizabeth Fry and Josephine Butler in Britain and the Netherlands* (Amsterdam, 1999).

55. Cf. Drenth and de Haan, *Caring Power*, 51.

56. Cf. Drenth and de Haan, *Caring Power*, 53.

57. Geldbach, *Stellung*, 109.

58. Cf. Geldbach, *Stellung*, 110.

5. Various Denominations and Their Path to Women's Ordination in the Nineteenth and Twentieth Centuries

5.1 Regional Protestant Churches in Germany

The long road leading to the pastorate of women within the Protestant regional churches has been extensively and bountifully researched in recent decades.[59] Step by step, research into the way women's ordination was introduced in the individual regional churches has also been carried out and specifically promoted in recent years.[60] Auguste Zeiß-Horbach has presented a study on the ordination of women in the Evangelical Lutheran Church in Bavaria that also presents the current state of the comprehensive research.[61] Under the bishop of that time, Hermann Dietzfelbinger, this regional church—together with Schaumburg-Lippe—was the one that opposed the ordination of women for the longest time. In my experience, current ecumenical discourses often do not seem to be aware of the fact that there is by no means a long tradition of equality

59. Cf. U. Baumann, *Protestantismus und Frauenemanzipation in Deutschland 1850 bis 1920* (Frankfurt a.M./New York, 1992); C. Drape-Müller, *Frauen auf der Kanzel? Die Diskussion um das Amt der Theologin von 1925 bis 1942* (Pfaffenweiler, 1994); A. Bieler, ed., *"Darum wagt es Schwestern . . ." Zur Geschichte evangelischer Theologinnen in Deutschland* (Neukirchen-Vluyn, 1992). Within the framework of this project a large number of biographies have been published concerning early female theologians within the Protestant regional churches: D. Herbrecht, *Emanzipation oder Anpassung. Argumentationswege der Theologinnen im Streit um die Frauenordination in der Bekennenden Kirche* (Neukirchen-Vluyn, 2000); H. Köhler, *Dem Himmel so nah—dem Pfarramt so fern. Erste evangelische Theologinnen im geistlichen Amt* (Neukirchen-Vluyn, 1996).

60. Cf. A. Funke, *"Kanzelstürmerinnen." Die Geschichte der Frauenordination in der Ev.-Luth. Landeskirche Sachsens von 1945 bis 1970* (Leipzig/Berlin, 2011; 2nd ed. 2016); R. Hering, Frauen auf der Kanzel? Die Auseinandersetzung um Frauenordination und Gleichberechtigung in der Hamburger Landeskirche, in: Hering and I. Mager, eds., *Hamburgische Kirchengeschichte in Aufsätzen*, vol. 5, *Kirchliche Zeitgeschichte (20. Jahrhundert)* (Hamburg, 2008) 105–53; H. Köhler, Angekommen! Frauen im Pfarramt der Evang.-luth. Landeskirche Hannovers, in: *Deutsches Pfarrerblatt* 114 (2014) 572–76; E. Kreutler, *Die ersten Theologinnen in Westphalen 1919–1974* (Bielefeld, 2007).

61. Cf. A. Zeiß-Horbach, *Evangelische Kirche und Frauenordination. Der Beitrag der Evangelisch-Lutherischen Kirche in Bayern zum deutschlandweiten Diskurs im 20. Jahrhundert* (Leipzig, 2017).

between men and women in the ordained pastoral ministry of the Protestant regional churches; the struggle to achieve this had to be conducted via several levels of lower-ranking ministries that, in part, existed for long periods.

The development began with the admission of women to the study of theology; later, women were allowed to become parish assistant or curate, then pastor in a "ministry of a special kind" or a particular women's ministry, clearly distinguished from that of the male clergy. Finally, equality between the pastors of both sexes was achieved, including the possibility of appointment as bishop.[62] During the German Empire, in the context of the civil women's movement, it was possible for the first time for women to be admitted to academic studies. From the beginning of the twentieth century, individual women with appropriate educational qualifications also managed to study theology as guest auditors and later as matriculated theologians.[63] However, they were not admitted to the church examinations and completed their studies with a licentiate.

In the period of the Weimar Republic, in which the public legal equality of women under public law was constitutionally guaranteed in Germany for the first time, things developed quickly. As a result, women could take examinations in one church after another. The profession of "pastoral assistant" or "pastoral helper" was established in some regional churches, and in the late 1920s church legislation followed the practice that had been created by women in many areas of church life. However, the Vicariate Law passed in May 1927 by the Evangelical Church of the Old-Prussian Union (ApU), the largest Protestant regional church, laid down a demonstrative demarcation and distinction between the status of the women appointed—who were not ordained, but only consecrated—and that of the male pastorate. Their activities were limited to certain areas (children, youth, the sick, prisoners), and they had to give up their position if they got married.[64]

62. Cf. Zeiß-Horbach, *Frauenordination*, 45.

63. Cf. D. Henze, Die Anfänge des Frauenstudiums in Deutschland, in: A. Bieler, ed., *"Darum wagt es Schwestern . . . ,"* 19–40; cf. Zeiß-Horbach, *Frauenordination*, 52ff.

64. C. Schlarb, Auf dem Weg zur Gleichstellung—Frauen im Geistlichen Amt im Bereich der EKD, in: *Pfälzisches Pfarrerblatt* 98 (2008) 392–96.

The work done by many female curates and theologians in the so-called emergency pastorates or vacant parishes during the National Socialist dictatorship and especially during the Second World War would deserve a presentation in its own right.[65] In January 1943, the president of the Brandenburg church, Kurt Scharf, ordained two women for the demanding service they undertook. For a certain time after the war, the ordination of women suffered a setback, since the increased rights and functions of the female curates that had come into force during the war were withdrawn again and the specific "women's ministry" was reemphasized. The pivotal decision was taken by the Law on Women Pastors passed in 1958 by the Evangelical Church of Anhalt, the Protestant Church of the Palatinate, and the Lutheran Church in Lübeck. This created a new legal situation by allowing female theologians to be ordained and giving them the fundamental right to preach and administer the sacraments.[66]

In this case, it is important to consider the asymmetry of the developments, especially since some member churches of the EKD already had large numbers of women pastors from the end of the 1950s, while the debates and the process of recognition (including church legislation) continued well into the 1970s in other regional churches.[67] The disparity of opinions in this matter that still existed in the mid-1970s can be illustrated by an article written by Hermann Sasse, a professor of theology in Erlangen, who stated that absolution given by ordained women was not valid in heaven. Sasse regarded women pastors as poor, pitiful "girls . . . who are misled by false doctrine."[68]

65. Cf. H. Erhart, Die Theologin im Kontext von Universität und Kirche zur Zeit der Weimarer Republik und des Nationalsozialismus. Ein Beitrag zur theologischen Diskussion, in: L. Siegele-Wenschkewitz, C. Nicolaisen, eds., *Theologische Fakultäten im Nationalsozialismus* (Göttingen,1993) 223–50; D. Herbrecht, I. Härter, H. Erhart, eds., *Der Streit um die Frauenordination in der Bekennenden Kirche. Quellentexte zu ihrer Geschichte im Zweiten Weltkrieg* (Neukirchen-Vluyn, 1997); D. Herbrecht, Der "Vikarinnenausschuß" der Bekennenden Kirche in der Altpreußischen Union, in: A. Bieler, ed., *"Darum wagt es Schwestern . . . ,"* 315–60.

66. Cf. Schlarb, *Weg*, 1.

67. Cf. Schlarb, *Weg*, 1.

68. H. Sasse, quoted in: Geldbach, *Stellung*, 102.

This asymmetry within the EKD and the confusing diversity of laws on women pastors can be attributed above all to the legal autonomy of the regional churches, which continued to determine church politics despite their association in the EKD. It is remarkable that all the laws appertaining to female theologians and the successive process of their recognition were connected with a gender-specific differentiation from the pastoral ministry of male clergy.[69] It was not until the mid-1970s that the equality of women in pastoral ministry was incorporated into and regulated by church law.[70]

Even today, the relationship to women's ordination is inconsistent, especially in Lutheran churches around the world. There is still opposition to women in the preaching ministry and even in nonordained leadership positions, for example in the Independent Evangelical-Lutheran Church (SELK) and the Lutheran Church–Missouri Synod as well as in numerous other churches belonging to the International Lutheran Council, but also in some churches of the Lutheran World Federation (LWF).[71]

5.2 Free Churches

In some free churches, women's ordination became possible from the 1970s onward and after a lengthy process. First to be mentioned is the Union of Evangelical Free Churches (BEFG), a merger of Baptist and Brethren congregations. At the early stages of its development in the 1830s, German Baptist churches adopted the egalitarian and anti-hierarchical tendencies of Baptist churches worldwide.[72] Congregationalist ecclesiology, which was based on the autonomy of the local congregation, initially led to the consistent rejection of institutionalized church offices. The priesthood of all believers, on the other hand, was supposed to unfold its full potential, and that included women in the early days. The training of mission workers for the expanding Baptist movement in Germany was advocated from the outset but limited exclusively to men ("brothers").[73]

69. Cf. Zeiß-Horbach, *Frauenordination*, 86.

70. Cf. Zeiß-Horbach, *Frauenordination*, 88–89.

71. See G. Appold, *Frauen*, 253.

72. Cf. E. Geldbach, Das Amt in den Anfängen des Baptismus, in: *Zeitschrift für Theologie und Gemeinde* 14 (2009) 249–60, 250f.

73. Cf. G. Balders, Kurze Geschichte der deutschen Baptisten, in: Balders, ed., *Ein Herr, ein Glaube, eine Taufe. 150 Jahre Baptistengemeinden in Deutschland*

The mission school also remained limited to men, as did the school for preachers founded in 1880, which later offered a qualifying study of theology. Right down to the 1960s, reservations based on the Bible obviously prevented any serious questioning as to whether women should be admitted to theological studies or to pastoral ministry.[74]

In view of student demands for reform and protests, the National Council, the highest synodal decision-making body of the Free Church, set up two working groups in May 1973 to discuss the "service of women" in the Union fellowship.[75] In its meeting the following year, the Council decided: "The Union does not intend to establish the ministry of a 'female pastor.' As a rule, the Theological Seminary does not provide any theological training for women. In justified individual cases, the Steering Committee may allow women to study theology (for various periods of time) at the Seminary if a) there is clarity about the professional goal; b) the intended service appears to require theological education; c) the applicants are prepared to bear the risk of not being employed within the Union fellowship."[76] In the following period five women were admitted to study at the Theological Seminary. A woman pastor from this first generation wrote in retrospect that they were accepted after a two-year assessment process in which they had to give an assurance that they did not intend to go into the ministry. Otherwise they would not have been admitted to study. Employment prospects for them were, in analogy to the development in the regional Protestant churches, only possible in the areas of children's and youth work, mission, or adult education in local congregations.

In 1979, the Union Council once again formed a commission to clarify the question of women's full-time service. The result was that the service of women had always been valued, desired, and expected on various levels of the Union and in many fields. When it came to the question of whether women should also be employed as pastors, the commission noted that all ministries in the congregation were dependent upon the calling and empowerment through Christ and upon the endowment with

---

1834–1984 (Wuppertal/Kassel, 1984) 17–168, 26.

74. Cf. Balders, Kurze Geschichte, 152.

75. Cf. Balders, Kurze Geschichte, 152.

76. Quoted from the minutes of the resolution, Balders, Kurze Geschichte der deutschen Baptisten.

spiritual gifts, which were granted to both men and women.[77] This charismatic equality, which in the opinion of the commission resulted from the testimonies in the New Testament, was to form the theological basis for the affirmation of women's pastoral ministry. "In spite of the fact that biblical statements are inconsistent, the majority of the Commission considers it possible in principle today to call women to full-time ministry as pastors in the fellowship of our Union."[78] Taking into consideration the different opinions and understandings in the Baptist congregations, it was recommended at the same time to refrain from using the term "pastor" and to designate the theologians appointed as "theological coworkers." In addition, the commission limited the activities of the theological coworkers to children's, youth, and women's work, internal and external mission, as well as to the area of religious instruction. In January 1981, the National Council endorsed the Commission's recommendations, thus giving the local congregations the opportunity to appoint trained theologians as theological coworkers in the areas outlined above.

Allow me to bring in a personal reminiscence at this point. In 1991, after completing my studies and doctorate, I was ordained as a "theological coworker," a kind of forerunner to pastoral minister in analogy to the parish assistants or curates in the regional Protestant churches. On the basis of this restriction, the man who ordained me, at that time Vice-President of the BEFG, refused to read out the text of my ordination certificate, since I was not to be called as a clergywoman but only for service to children, young people, and women. After this, there was a wearisome process of communication within the Free Church, culminating in a decision by the National Council in 1992 leaving it up to the congregations to ordain the women they had appointed as pastors. At this time there were fourteen theological coworkers who issued a joint declaration that they understood themselves to be pastors.[79] The local congregation was seen to be the decisive institution that could freely choose to call its coworkers "pastor."[80] This procedure corresponded to the congregationalist structure of this church union in which the indi-

77. Cf. Results of the Commission "Dienst der Frau" of April 22, 1982, in: C. Geisser, S. Post, eds., *Pastorin—ja oder nein? Documentation* (Elstal, 2005) 2.

78. "Dienst der Frau," 3.

79. Cf. "Dienst der Frau," 86.

80. Cf. "Dienst der Frau," 11.

vidual local congregations are autonomous. In 1993 I was finally ordained belatedly as a pastor. Today, women pastors make up about 12 to 15 percent of the BEFG's pastoral ministry, but in some congregations they are still not allowed or elected to serve as pastors because of their gender.

A few years later, a similar development process took place within the Union of Free Evangelical Churches (BFeG) in Germany that did not end until 2010 with the decision to ordain women pastors.[81] The road to the recognition of women as pastors in the Federation of Pentecostal Churches was similar, in that women also passed through an intermediate stage ("pastoral assistant") before achieving full recognition.[82] On women's ordination in the United Methodist Church, I refer to the section on the revival movement, which describes the acceptance of female preachers and evangelists since the early stages. Nevertheless, this free church also experienced a temporary setback prolonging the path to the recognition of women's ordination. The General Conference of Methodist Churches voted in 1956 for the full recognition of women in ordained ministries.[83] Women have also been entitled to be appointed bishop since 1980.

In the Mennonite congregations, the only denomination that can be traced back to Reformation Anabaptism in historical continuity, the first woman was ordained and inducted as pastor in the Netherlands in 1911.[84] In Germany, ordination to full-time ministry as a female preacher and pastor was not introduced until the 1970s and early 1980s.[85] In the case of the Seventh-day Adventists, the process of recognizing women's ordination is not yet complete in view of the worldwide structures of this

81. See W. Haubeck, W. Heinrichs, eds., *Pastorinnen. Aspekte zu einem aktuellen Thema* (Witten, 2008).

82. Cf. P. Schneider et al., eds., *Stellungnahmen zum Dienst der Frau* (Norderstedt, 2005) 131; K.-D. Passon, "Frauen in den Pfingstgemeinden," in: *Freikirchenforschung* 13 (2003) 71–84.

83. Cf. R. Wenner, Erfahrungen im bischöflichen Dienst der Evangelisch-Methodistischen Kirche, in: Ökumenische Rundschau 66 (2017) 560–66, 560.

84. Cf. B. Thiesse, Art. Amt, in: http://www.mennlex.de/doku.php?id=top:amt (30.06.2018).

85. Cf. Thiesse, Amt; B. Thiessen, C. Schmidt, Frauen in der VDM, in: *Auf dem Weg, 125 Jahre Vereinigung der Deutschen Mennonitengemeinden* (Krefeld, VDM, 2011) 37f.

free church, although women already work as pastors and hold leading positions in some regions.[86]

It should be noted that alongside these developments toward liberalization in the free churches there are still many opponents of women's ordination, an attitude consistently linked with the understanding of Scripture and with biblical hermeneutics.

5.3 Anglican Churches

The decisive date on the way to recognition of women's ordination was November 11, 1992, when the General Synod of the Church of England decided to admit women to the priesthood.[87] This ecumenically controversial decision was also preceded by more than twenty years of dialogue. In 1944 Florence Li Tim Oi was ordained a priest in Hong Kong,[88] but from 1945 onward, on the instructions of the Archbishop of Canterbury, she was no longer allowed to exercise her ministry. In 1971, the Anglican Consultative Council paved the way for women's ordination by granting each bishop permission to ordain women, provided he had the agreement of his own church province.[89] The majority of the church provinces subsequently implemented this decision, so that a large number of female priests were ordained; in some regions the episcopate is also open to them.

The Anglican Communion of Churches is an umbrella organization for independent regional churches, which is why it is in accordance with its structure that the decision is transferred to the authority of the church provinces. This resulted in a disparate overall picture, so that, for example, when the decision was taken in 1992, there was already one woman bishop in the Episcopal Church in the USA, while in Wales the situation looked completely different.[90] The ordination of women is still controversial in the Anglican Church, leading to asymmetry in the indi-

86. Cf. R. E. Fischer, *Freikirchliche pastorale Weiterbildung am Beispiel der Siebenten-Tags-Adventisten* (Berlin, 2015) 57–59.

87. Cf. Geldbach, *Stellung*, 111.

88. Cf. C. Methuen, Frauenordination aus anglikanischer Sicht, in: Ökumenische Rundschau 55 (2006) 26–30, 27; F. Li Tim Oi, *Raindrops of My Life. Memoirs of the Reverend Florence Li Tim Oi* (Toronto, 1996).

89. Cf. Methuen, *Frauenordination*, 27.

90. Cf. Geldbach, *Stellung*, 112.

vidual member churches and tensions within the church communion. The recognition of the ordination of women also led to ecumenical conflicts, particularly with the Roman Catholic Church, but also with the Orthodox churches. In contrast to the Lutheran, Reformed, and Free Church denominations of Protestantism, which all went their own ways in the recognition of women in the ministry from the middle of the twentieth century, it was not until the Anglican Communion began to ordain women as priests beginning in 1976 that it came to vehement protests in ecumenism and to emphatic counter-declarations on the part of the Vatican.[91]

5.4 Old Catholics

The discussion about the ordination of women in the Old Catholic Church in Germany has intensified since the 1970s.[92] After the introduction of the diaconate in 1981, it was a long road to the decision to introduce the unrestricted ordination of women to the apostolic ministry in the church in 1994. At the end of the 1990s, the first women priests were consecrated. It is necessary to point to the different processes in Switzerland, Austria, the Netherlands, and Germany. Here, too, the decisive steps were first taken at the level of individual local churches before the matter was regulated centrally.[93] The communication between Old Catholic churches worldwide was severely tested, and it came to serious conflicts. Nevertheless, despite the open dissent, the eucharistic fellowship among the Old Catholic local churches was maintained.

6. Summary

All the churches whose path to equal rights for women in church ministries has been depicted here went through lengthy phases of heated debates on this issue. It is striking that various churches first began to

91. Cf. A. Jensen, Ist Frauenordination ein ökumenisches Problem? Zu den jüngsten Entwicklungen in den anglikanischen, altkatholischen und orthodoxen Kirchen, in: *Internationale kirchliche Zeitschrift: Neue Folge der Revue internationale de théologie* 84 (1994) 210–28, 213.

92. Cf. A. Berlis, Frauenordination—ökumenische Konflikte und ihre Bewältigung—am Beispiel der Alt-Katholischen Kirche, in: Ökumenische Rundschau 55 (2006) 16–25, 16.

93. Cf. Berlis, Frauenordination, 18.

recognize women as pastors or priests at the local church level. Thus an exemplary procedure emerged in which women's ecclesiastical ministry first proved its merit within one church before it gradually found ultimate binding recognition within the whole church and codification under church law.

This course of decision-making, which always involved lay people due to the synodal constitution, is valid for the regional Protestant churches, the various free churches, and the Old Catholics, as well as for the Anglican Communion. A practice originated and exercised by women proved its worth within the various churches and was subsequently legitimized. This poses the question, as in other areas of doctrinal differences, as to how the member churches can enjoy a positive relationship to the church as a whole and how church practice can harmonize with dynamic doctrinal development in the course of dogmatic alterity.[94]

In the case of the developments within the churches that have been considered here, it was possible to detect a step-by-step progress beginning with the institution of specific interim "women's ministries" (for example, curate, deacon, theological assistant, pastoral assistant) intended to entrust church functions to women, who often had the same theological qualification as their male colleagues, without granting them complete equal rights. Although this path has ultimately proved successful, it is worth remembering the discrimination, rejection, and suffering of many women who were biographically disadvantaged by these intermediate stages and who had to live and defend their vocation in constant confrontation with degrading restrictions in the congregations. These women were constantly compelled to redefine their self-understanding as preachers, pastors, and leaders and to adapt it to the circumstances. Many broke down under this pressure and abandoned the ministry because of the permanent conflicts or moved to other churches in which the equal rights of women in pastoral offices had already progressed further.

Women often managed to find recognition for church ministries in those churches which took their preaching mandate of women seriously or which based equality on the spiritual gifts. The decisive role was played by a pneumatological accentuation of the theology of ministry.

94. A current example of such internal differentiation within the Roman Catholic Church is the dispute over the sharing of the Eucharist in interdenominational marriages and the *dubia* dispute between the dissenting bishops and the Vatican.

In view of new exegetical insights provided by feminist theology, the process of communication with regard to the ordination of women was reinforced and driven ahead in the churches that traditionally emphasized constant new teaching on the basis of Holy Scripture and the consequent permanent openness for reforms (*ecclesia semper reformanda*). Despite all systematic considerations, it should be placed on record that it was above all the women themselves who followed their vocation against all resistance in the different churches, who worked beneficially and thereby provoked a rethinking in questions of women's ordination.

7. To Conclude

It was in 1832 that a young, plainly dressed woman with strikingly large, expressive eyes asked the pastor of a parish in Ithaca, New York, to be allowed to preach a sermon in his church that evening, to which he agreed after some hesitation. But he insisted that she speak to the congregation after him, and not from the pulpit, but only from the steps in the sanctuary. After some discussion, the woman agreed to this compromise. In the evening the church was filled to capacity. After the greeting, some hymns, and the local pastor's sermon, it was her turn. Despite the angry looks of the pastor, she marched unswervingly up to the pulpit, the symbol of male authority in the church. There she held an impassioned sermon lasting ninety minutes. In retrospect, the clergyman she had duped said that they had never recovered from this performance.[95]

(Translation from German by Neville Williamson)

95. See Brekus, *Strangers*, 201.

III

Women's Diaconate

Ecumenical Perspectives

Women's Diaconate

Theresia Hainthaler

Introduction

In Kolwezi in the province of Katanga in the Congo, on February 17, 2017 (his name day), at the end of the Divine Liturgy, Patriarch Theodoros II of Alexandria consecrated a female catechist as mission deaconess as well as three nuns and two additional women catechists for ecclesiastical ministry. They are commissioned to support the mission of the church, in particular in the sacraments of baptism and marriage, and in catechesis.[1] The Holy Synod of the Orthodox Patriarchate of Alexandria decided at its meeting of November 17–19, 2016 to reintroduce the office of deaconess.[2] The decision has frequently been commented on.[3]

1. http://www.patriarchateofalexandria.com/index.php?module=news&action=details&id=1242 (20.02.2018): "At the end of the Divine Liturgy the Primate of the Alexandrian Throne . . . consecrated the Catechist elder Theano, one of the first members of the Missionary staff in Kolwezi, to 'Deaconess of the Missions' of the Holy Metropolis of Katanga and read the prayer for one entering the 'ecclesiastic ministry' for three Nuns and two Catechists, in order for them to assist the missionary effort of the Holy Metropolis, particularly in the Sacraments of Baptisms of adults and marriages, as well as in the Catechetical department of the local Church."

2. http://www.patriarchateofalexandria.com/index.php?module=news&action=details&id=1207 (20.02.2018), Second day of deliberations of the Holy Synod of the Patriarchate of Alexandria, 16.11.2016: "Regarding the issue of the institution of Deaconesses, it was decided to revive this and a tripartite committee of Hierarchs was appointed for a detailed consideration of the subject."

3. Cf., e.g., J. Dearie and C. Doody in: https://www.ncronline.org/news/theology/orthodox-move-women-deacons-called-revitalization-not-innovation (14.01.2018) and http://www.patheos.com/blogs/europeancommunion/2017/11/orthodoxy-validity-women-deacons/ (14.01.2018).

In an interview on February 18, 2017, this event was interpreted by the Orthodox theologian Evangelos Theodorou (1921–2018) from the University of Athens, who had probably done the most work on the question of women's diaconate; his doctoral thesis in 1954[4] had already been dedicated to this topic, and numerous further investigations and lectures followed. The women had been inducted into their office by the laying on of hands (*cheirothesia*), which is comparable to the ceremony for a subdeacon. Among other things, they had not been given an orarion (deacon's stole). He welcomed the consecration as a "fresh and important step" and as a "wise first step" but expressed his hope that women who were faithful and tested servants of God would be admitted into the diaconate sooner rather than later by *cheirotonia*[5]—in the same way as St. Phoebe (first century), St. Olympias (fourth century), St. Irene of Chrysovalanton (ninth century), and numerous other holy women.

Obviously, in Orthodoxy the validity of the decision of the Holy Synod has been called into question[6] (*inter alia* in an Orthodox monastery). For this reason, nine Orthodox liturgists—led by Theodorou but including

4. E. Theodorou, Die Weihe (Cheirotonia) oder Segnung (Cheirothesia) der Diakonissen, in: A. Jensen, G. Larentzakis, eds., *Diakonat und Diakonie in frühchristlicher und ostkirchlicher Tradition* (Graz, 2008) 36–128; this is the German translation of the Greek diss., Athens 1954, in: *Theologia* 25 (1954) 430–69, 576–601; 26 (1955) 57–76. The interest in deaconesses came from an encounter with German Protestant deaconesses, which resulted in a first article 1945/1946. Furthermore, Theodorou, *Heroines of Love. Deaconesses through the Ages* (Athens, 1949).

5. Interview in "Saint Catherine's Vision," February 24, 2017, in: http://www.saintcatherinesvision.com/assets/files/SCV%20Prof.%20Theodorou%20interview%20February%2024,%202017.pdf (20.02.2018). "This action undertaken by the Patriarchate of Alexandria, indeed is a wise first step. God-willing, may they sooner rather than later discern through cheirotonia (ordination) faithful and tested female servants of God to the diaconate; as were St. Phoebe (1st c), St. Olympias (4th c), St. Irene of Chrysovalanton (9th c) and numerous other holy women."

6. Professor emeritus Petros Vassiliadis (Department of Theology at the University of Thessaloniki and president of the Center of Ecumenical, Missiological and Environmental Studies "Metropolitan Panteleimon Papageorgiou" [CEMES]) reports that an Orthodox monastery objected to the decision of the Alexandrian patriarchate to revive the Order of deaconesses. There have been rumours that some "missionary agencies" (presumably associated with this monastic community) had threatened to stop supporting the African missions (cf. P. Vassiliadis, The Revival of the Order of Deaconess by the Patriarchate of Alexandria, in: https://publicorthodoxy.org/2017/11/17/support-alexandria-deaconess/ [20.2.2018]).

Paul Meyendorff and others[7]—signed and published a "Statement of Support for the Revival of the Order of Deaconess by the Patriarchate of Alexandria" on October 24, 2017.

Here it states:

- The order of deaconesses had gradually died out by the end of the fifteenth century but survived in the Oriental Orthodox churches and some monastic communities. The revival of the order was considered in the Russian Orthodox Church before 1917 and also in recent times. Greek bishops consecrated deaconesses in the twentieth century having established a school for deaconesses in Greece that eventually (1990) became a school for social workers.
- The order is not a new innovation but the revival of an office for publicly commissioned and authorized educators, evangelists, preachers, counselors, social workers, and so forth.
- Liturgical functions in the female diaconate seem originally to have been limited, but the rite of ordination is very similar to that of the male deacon, and the liturgical vestments are the same. It is for the bishops in the synod to decide whether to add additional liturgical functions in this day and age.
- It would be important to prepare and educate the faithful in the congregations accordingly. The quality and qualification of the candidates must be defined (the *canones* designate the minimum age, but not the education, marital status, clothing, remuneration, installation, or removal). Above all, the role and functions of the deaconess must be clearly regulated.
- The Inter-Orthodox Consultation in Rhodes already called for the revival of the female diaconate in 1988.

7. Emeritus Professor Evangelos Theodorou, Theological School of the University of Athens, Alkiviadis Calivas, Emeritus Professor of the Holy Cross Greek Orthodox School of Theology, Paul Meyendorff, Emeritus Professor of St Vladimir's Orthodox Theological Seminary, George Filias, Professor of the Theological School of the University of Athens, Panagiotis Skaltsis, Professor of the Theological School of the University of Thessaloniki, Stelyios S. Muksuris, Professor of the Byzantine Catholic Seminary, Nicholas Denysenko, Jochum Professor and Chair of Valparaiso University, Phillip Zymaris, Professor of the Holy Cross Greek Orthodox School of Theology, and John Klentos, Professor of Graduate Theological Union.

- No dogmatic questions or authoritative precedents are involved in the revival of the female diaconate. A local church may carry out such liturgical reform in its own territory.[8]

In addition, it should be mentioned that in the autumn of 2017 a deaconess was ordained in the Armenian Church of Iran.[9]

Research

There were already a surprising number of investigations and source collections available on this topic[10] in the 1990s; meanwhile, the number of publications has increased again. It is possible to find good compilations of the historical findings[11] and detailed discussions.[12] Thus, what

8. Cf. on this also: P. Vasilliadis, N. Papageorgíou, E. Kasselouri-Hatzivassiliadi, eds., *Deaconesses, the Ordination of Women and Orthodox Theology* (Cambridge, 2017). "The book is dedicated to the Patriarch of Alexandria, for his decision to revive the order of Deaconesses, and it was presented to him in the margin of this year's conference of Orthodox spirituality in Bose Monastery, Italy. The Patriarch expressed his thanks and requested the Orthodox theologians to continue to support his mission." At this conference in Saloniki Dr. Kyriaki Karidoyanes FitzGerald also held the laudation for Theodorou: http://www.saintcatherinesvision.org/assets/files/Theodorou%20Laudatum%2022-1-15.pdf (27.06.2018). She reports about allegations "that Orthodox men and women in favor of the ordination of deaconesses are the very same as 'post-Christian' liberal westerners."

9. Armenian Church of Iran has deaconess for first time in 100 years, 10.1.2018, in: https://news.am/eng/news/430380.html#.WlfAv50XPd4 (14.1.2018).: "Ani Kristi Manvelian has been serving at the Church for about 15 years, and she was ordained a deaconess in the fall of 2017, the Armenian Diocese of Tehran informed Armenian News-NEWS."

10. J. Pinius, Tractatus praeliminaris de ecclesiae diaconissis, in: *Acta Sanctorum Septembris I* (Antwerp, 1746) i–xxviii; A. Kalsbach, *Die altkirchliche Einrichtung der Diakonissen bis zu ihrem Erlöschen* (Freiburg i.Br., 1926); Sources: J. Mayer, *Monumenta de viduis diaconissis virginibusque tractantia* (Bonn, 1938) 55–63; H. Krimm, ed., *Quellen zur Geschichte der Diakonie*, vol. 1, *Altertum und Mittelalter* (Stuttgart, 1960). Unfortunately, it is not possible to give a detailed bibliography here.

11. R. Gryson, *Le ministère des femmes dans l'Église ancienne* (Gembloux, 1972); A. G. Martimort, *Les diaconesses. Essai historique* (Rome, 1982) (our study was conducted independently of Martimort). Cf. A. Jensen, *Gottes selbstbewusste Töchter. Frauenemanzipation im frühen Christentum?* (Freiburg i.Br., 2003) 141–64; A. Jensen, *Diakonat und Diakonie in frühchristlicher und ostkirchlicher Tradition* (Graz, 2008).

12. Cf. D. Reininger, *Diakonat der Frau in der einen Kirche. Diskussionen, Entscheidungen und pastoral-praktische Erfahrungen in der christlichen Ökumene und*

follows serves to recall what has been presented many times. These include a) the biblical testimony (whereby one must also consider the interpretation of the relevant passages by the church fathers), b) synodal legislation with its predecessors, the church orders, but also c) individual examples of deaconesses.

1. Biblical Testimony—The First and Second Centuries

For the female diaconate we have to consider the following passages in the New Testament.

1.1 Rom 16:1-2

The first person mentioned in the list of greetings at the end of the letter to the Romans is Phoebe, "our sister, being a *diakonos* of the church at Cenchreae." The church in Rome should "welcome her in the Lord as is fitting for the saints" and "help her in whatever she may require from you." Paul also explains that "she has been a benefactor of many (προστάτις, protectress) and of myself as well." Without going into detail on the exegetical discussion:[13] the *terminus technicus* of the deaconess is used and continues to be so;[14] even in the fifth/sixth centuries the office of the deaconess is called ἡ διάκονος. It is obvious that the ecclesiastical offices had not been developed at the time when the letter to the Romans was written. Here one only has to bear in mind that in Phil 1:1 Paul

---

ihr Beitrag zur römisch-katholischen Diskussion (Ostfildern, 1999) 56–126; a good and concise summary of the findings can be found in E. Theodorou, Frauenordination in der Orthodoxen Kirche? Anmerkungen zum Diakonat der Frau, in: D. W. Winkler, ed., *Diakonat der Frau* (Vienna/Berlin, 2010) 43–57. The book by Ph. Zagano, *Women Deacons? Essays with Answers* (Collegeville, 2016), provides a good overview of the state of discussion as well as English translations (from Italian) of important contributions. See also Ph. Zagano, B. Pottier, "What Do We Know about Women Deacons?," *Asian Horizons* 13,4 (December 2019) 647–58. Both belonged to the 2018–19 Pontifical Commission for the Study of the Diaconate of Women.

13. Indications on this in J. Ysebaert, The Deaconesses in the Western Church of Late Antiquity and Their Origin, in: G. J. M. Bartelink, A. R. Bastiaensen, A. Hilhorst, eds., *Eulogia. Mélanges offerts à Antoon A. R. Bastiaensen à l'occasion de son soixante-cinquième anniversaire* (Steenbrugge, 1991) 421–36.

14. The use of the same designation of office has also been pointed out by C. Marucci, History and Value of the Feminine Diaconate in the Ancient Church, in: Zagano, ed., *Women Deacons*, 30–56, here 55, on Rom 16:1, 30-31.

addresses his letter "to all the saints in Christ Jesus who are in Philippi, with the bishops (or overseers) and deacons." The "bishops" in the plural in Philippi are not the bishops as we understand them today. It should, however, be noted with regard to the later development of the ministries that the deacons are mentioned together with the bishops, so that they stand in a certain relationship to each other. Their activity or function is not described in detail.

Later deaconesses were apostrophized as "second Phoebe" (inscription from the fourth to the seventh centuries, Palestine[15]).

1.2 1 Tim 3:11

Within the framework of a qualification profile for deacons (1 Tim 3:8-13), which comes immediately after that for bishops (so that a relationship between *episkopoi* and *diakonoi* is also evident here), verse 11 (parallel to verse 8 with the requirements for deacons) abruptly states: "Women likewise must be serious, not slanderers, but temperate, faithful in all things." Who is meant by these "women"? It has been suggested that it was about 1) women in the church in general, or 2) wives of deacons, or 3) a separate group of women doing service to women, or 4) female deacons functioning together with deacons. Jennifer Stiefel[16] gives a detailed exegetical analysis, and after weighing up all the arguments in each direction she concludes that the structure of the entire deacon's code reveals that these are women who function as deacons together with men. It may be that 1 Tim 3:8-10 uses inclusive language that is then extended to female deacons in 3:11 and to male deacons in 3:12. It is possible that androcentric language conceals the reality of a diaconal ministry of men and women. Women exercise a service that cannot be forbidden and has

15. U. Eisen, *Amtsträgerinnen im frühen Christentum. Epigraphische und literarische Studien* (Göttingen, 1996), particularly 154–92, here 154–55.

16. J. H. Stiefel, Women Deacons in 1 Timothy. A Linguistic and Literary Look at "Women likewise . . . " (1 Tim 3:11), in: *New Testament Studies* 41 (1995) 442–57. Cf. C. Wessely, *Gekommen, um zu dienen. Der Diakonat aus fundamental-theologisch-ekklesiologischer Sicht* (Regensburg, 2004) 323–30 (excursus on 1 Tim 3:11), considers it "more probable that the author of the pastoral epistles has found women working as deacons or in a relatively similar ministry, but no longer wants to see them . . . in an official position. . . . they are . . . reduced to a minor role that corresponds . . . neither to their function nor to their history" (329–30). Cf. also Stiefel, Women Deacons in 1 Timothy, n. 42.

to be mentioned, but not with the title of deacon. The ambivalent situation of the women described can be detected in a variety of signals.

The evidence for a diaconal office for women is not entirely compelling, but it is strong. Contradictory interpretations arise because the syntactic signals are ambiguous. Nonetheless, the syntax of 3:11 and the entire section support the interpretation that the women served as partners of men in a diaconal ministry. The statement was not intended to do so, but it testifies to the ministry of women at that time.

John Chrysostom clearly understood that the women in 3:11 had the rank of deacon, and he considered that the stipulation of monogamy for deacons in 3:12 applied equally to deaconesses, for this was necessary, useful, and appropriate in the church.[17] Theodore of Mopsuestia remarks in connection with 1 Tim 3:11 that it is not about deacons' wives, but about women who are themselves deacons.[18] Theodoret of Cyrus interprets the passage in a similar way. In his opinion, Phoebe in Rom 16:1f. is also a deaconess.[19]

1.3 Further Evidence in the New Testament

It should be mentioned that 1 Tim in 5:3-16 deals with the order of widows with the clear intention of restricting something that already existed.[20] The minimum age of sixty years was later also applied to deaconesses.[21]

The appointment of the Seven in Acts 6:1-6 is first and foremost proof of the ministry of the Seven, which apparently expires. As from Irenaeus of Lyon's *Adversus haereses* (written at the time of Bishop Eleutherius of Rome, ca. 174–189), it is documented that Acts 6 was understood as the introduction of deacons.[22] Canon 15 from the Synod of Neocaesarea

17. Gryson, *Le ministère des femmes*, 135. John Chrys., Hom. 1 Tim 11,1 (PG 62, 553CD).

18. Gryson, *Le ministère des femmes*, 143. Theodore of Mops., Comm. 1 Tim 3,11, ed. H. B. Swete, *Theodori episcopi Mopsuesteni In epistolas B. Pauli commentarii*, vol. 2, I (Cambridge, 1822) 128,9–129,12.

19. Gryson, *Le ministère des femmes*, 145.

20. J. M. Bassler, The Widow's Tale. A Fresh Look at 1 Tim 5:3–16, in: *Journal of Biblical Literature and Exegesis* 103 (1984) 23–41, 36. Cf. also B. B. Thurston, *The Widows* (Minneapolis, 1989) 40–55.

21. Cf. Gryson, *Le ministère des femmes*, 143 with n. 3; Theodore of Mops. comments on it.

22. Irenaeus of Lyon, Adversus haereses I 26:3: "The Nicolaitans have Nicholas as their teacher, one of the seven appointed by the apostles as the first deacons (Acts

(314–319) speaks of the requirement of seven deacons in one city in accordance with Acts.[23]

Thus there is a repeated connection in the New Testament between *episkopoi* and *diakonoi* (Phil 1:1; 1 Tim 3) without any exact description of their functions. The term *diakonos* is used for both men and women (as in the pagan environment) (Rom 16:1). It is likely that the function of the *diakonos* mentioned in 1 Tim 3 was performed by both women and men. This is to be distinguished from the order of widows mentioned in 1 Tim 5, which is apparently fully established, but which the author of 1 Tim wishes to reduce by setting stringent requirements, such as registration, the fulfillment of numerous conditions, and possibly pledges (vows?).

1.4 Pliny the Younger (2nd century)

From about 111, Pliny was governor in Bithynia (today Izmit in Turkey) and therefore responsible for accusations made by the population against Christians living there. In an exchange of letters with Emperor Trajan, which he later included in his ten-volume collection of letters (*Epistulae*), he obtained legal confirmation for his proceedings with them. In epistula X/96 he described his interrogation methods, the Christian customs he had come to know, and his impression of their faith. He mentions among the Christians *ancillae quae ministrae dicebantur.*

2. Montanism

In a report on the Montanist movement, in which prophecy was strongly pronounced,[24] Epiphanius of Salamis tells of a vision of Christ

6:5f). They have no moral inhibitions. . . . (Rev 2:14f., 6)" (N. Brox, FC 8/1, 1993, 317). Adversus haereses III 12,10: "Stephen further, who was first elected deacon by the apostles, and who first followed the traces of suffering of the Lord by all men, being first killed because of the confession of Christ. . . " (E. Klebba, BKV2, 1912, 257). Adv. haer. IV 15: "And Stephen, who was first chosen as a deacon by the apostles and first killed because of his testimony for Christ, thus spoke about Moses according to Luke (Acts 7:38-43)" (E. Klebba, BKV2, 1912, 364).

23. P.-P. Joannou, *Discipline générale antique* (IIe-IXe s.), 1,2, *Les canons des synodes particuliers* (Fonti IX 1.2) (Grottaferrata, 1962) 82; K. J. Hefele, *Conciliengeschichte*, vol. 1 (2nd ed. Freiburg i.Br., 1873) 251. Cf. [Concilium] Trullanum 692, can. 16, in: Joannou, Fonti IX 1.2, 144–148; FC 82 (2006).

24. On this, Eusebius of Caesarea, *Historia ecclesiastica* (CPG 3495), V 14.16.17.18. For easier identification the CPG number is given here and in the following.

in the form of a woman Wisdom (49:1) and then mentions "their ordination of women as clergy" and that they (the Montanists) (49:2) "have woman bishops, presbyters and the rest; they say that none of this makes any difference because 'In Christ Jesus there is neither male nor female' (Gal 3:28)."[25] In a dialogue between a Montanist and an Orthodox Christian there is mention of the fact that women are not allowed to speak in church or rule over men (1 Tim 2:12), but also that women are prohibited from "writing books in their name. For this means that they pray and prophesy bare-headed and thus dishonour the head (cf. 1 Cor 11:5), i.e. the man. Could Mary the Mother of God not have written books in her own name? But she did not do so, in order not to dishonour the head by ruling over the men."[26] In this dialogue the "Orthodox" person confirms this statement in response to an enquiry by the "Montanist."[27]

3. Church Orders

This literary genre includes: 1. *Didache* (around 100) (Syria), 2. *Traditio apostolica* (early third century, ca. 215) (Rome), 3. (Syriac) *Didascalia Apostolorum* (ca. 230) (Northern Syria), 4. the *Apostolic Church-Order* (end of the third century or beginning of the fourth century) (perhaps Egypt, possibly Syria), 5. the *Apostolic Constitutions* (CA), (ca. 380 in Antioch), an adaptation and compilation of the three earliest church orders;[28] a collection of eighty-five Apostolic Canons

25. Epiphanius, *Panarion* (CPG 3745), 49:1.2, from: P. de Labriolle, *Les sources de l'histoire du montanisme* (Fribourg/Paris, 1913) 139–41.; English: F. Williams, *The Panarion of Epiphanius of Salamis Books II and III*. De Fide (Leiden/Boston, 2013) 22–23.

26. Ps.-Didymus Al., *Dialexis Montanistae et orthodoxi* (CPG 2572), in: G. Ficker, Widerlegung eines Montanisten, in: *Zeitschrift für Kirchengeschichte* 26 (1905) 447–63, also in: de Labriolle, *Les sources de l'histoire*, 93–108, 105f.

27. "Montanist: So praying or prophesying with a bare head is equivalent to writing books?—Orthodox: Exactly." Cf. (Ps.-)Didym. Al., *De trinitate* (CPG 2570), in: de Labriolle, *Les sources de l'histoire*, 159–60. On these statements, which tend toward the comical, see also R. Nürnberg, "Non decet neque necessarium est, ut mulieres doceant." Überlegungen zum altkirchlichen Lehrverbot für Frauen, in: *Jahrbuch für Antike und Christentum* 31 (1988) 57–73.

28. The collection consists of texts from three main documents, the *Didascalia* (CA I-VI), *Didache* (VII,1-32), and *Traditio apostolica* (VIII, 3-45). Within this

(from Nicaea, Antioch [around 330], Laodicaea [343–381], Ankyra [314], Neocaesarea [around 319]) added as the last chapter;[29] the CA are considered the culmination of the Ancient Church Orders. The Pseudo-Ignatian Epistles and the Arian Commentary on Job come from the same author. However, the *Apostolic Constitutions* gained a high degree of authority and apostolic rank in the Orthodox churches through the Council in Trullo (691), but probably also before that in the non-Chalcedonian churches of the East (Western Syrians, Eastern Syrians, Armenians, Copts, Ethiopians), partially or in their own church orders.

One must pay attention to the literary genre when reading the texts. There is a debate about the intended purpose of drafting church orders. Do they represent a protocol of the life of the congregations, wanting to regulate it more or less comprehensively institutionally, or are they tendentious texts, wanting to take up and regulate new questions (problems, grievances) in the life of the congregations without consideration of much of their practice?[30] According to Schöllgen, it is "improbable" that they "simply reflect the normal practice of the congregations in order to establish it in the sense of ecclesiastical law." It cannot be proven that these are "official congregational documents." That the regulations they contain were actually enforced should not be "taken for granted without proof."[31] I believe that one ought to look into their validity on a regional or supraregional level (cf. the *Syriac Didascalia* or the Egyptian Church Order); this is a question I would suggest.

The *Syriac Didascalia* states that a woman may not baptize, because Christ was not baptized by Mary, but by John. A deacon may baptize on the authority of the bishop; but a deaconess (*mshamshanīta*) may not baptize. She is allowed to give instruction to the women baptized.

---

framework it contains euchological, conciliar, and other traditions, also from other texts, especially the Bible and the Pseudo-Clementine writings. Numerous interpolations of varying importance originate from the editor. The collection is from a single compiler, including the 85 canons. There are certainly contradictions due to the diversity of sources, which the editor did not harmonize.

29. It is uncertain whether the editor compiled them himself or whether a collection was already available.

30. G. Schöllgen, Der Abfassungszweck der frühchristlichen Kirchenordnungen. Anmerkungen zu den Thesen Bruno Steimers, in: *Jahrbuch für Antike und Christentum* 40 (1997) 55–77, 57.

31. Schöllgen, Der Abfassungszweck, 77.

The editor Marcel Metzger[32] sums up the findings on the deaconess in the *Apostolic Constitutions* (CA) as follows. Her place in the clerical lists varies. In the ordination ritual she follows immediately on the deacon (VIII 19), as well as in the passage inspired by the *Didascalia*, which compares the deacon with Christ and the deaconess with the Holy Spirit (II 26). Other lists do not explicitly mention the deaconesses but seem to include them when referring to the diaconate or the deacons (VIII 10. 12. 13. 46). Elsewhere, deaconesses are only mentioned after male offices (II 26; VIII 28. 31) but take the first place among women before the widows (VIII 13), who are subordinate to them (III 8). There is also hesitation regarding terminology. The compiler sometimes writes ἡ διάκονος and sometimes ἡ διακόνισσα. But that does not depend on the sources of the compilation, because ἡ διάκονος is not only found in passages from the *Didascalia* (II 58; III 8), but also in VIII 13.

According to the CA, the ministry of the deaconess is first required at the baptism of women (III 16; VIII 28). Other functions in the liturgical assembly concern the guarding of the entrance doors for women (II 57; VIII 11; 28); the ordination ceremony (VIII 20) only names this function, which also includes the reception of strangers (II 58). In addition to liturgical functions, deaconesses participate in the charitable ministry of the church, under the bishops and deacons (III 16. 19); and they serve as mediators between women and the male clergy (II 26).

The *Apostolic Constitutions* (VIII 20) also contain the prayer for the consecration of a deaconess, which is attributed to the Apostle Bartholomew.

> Concerning a Deaconess, I Bartholomew make this constitution: Bishop, thou shalt lay thy hands upon her in the presence of the Presbytery, and of the Deacons and Deaconesses; and shalt say:
>
> O Eternal God, the Father of our Lord Jesus Christ, the Creator of man and of woman, who replenished with the Spirit Miriam (Ex 15:20), and Deborah (Jgs 4:4), and Anna (Lk 2:36), and Huldah (2 Kgs 22:14); who did not disdain that Your only begotten Son should be born of a woman; who also in the tabernacle of the testimony, and in the temple, ordained women to be keepers of Your holy gates—do Thou now also look down upon this Your servant (δουλήν), who is to be ordained to the office of

32. M. Metzger, ed., *Les constitutions apostoliques* III–VI, in: *Sources Chrétiennes* 329 (Paris, 1986) 55–56.

> a deaconess (εἰς διακονίαν), and grant her Your Holy Spirit, and cleanse her from all filthiness of flesh and spirit (2 Cor 7:1) that she may worthily discharge the work which is committed to her to Your glory, and the praise of Your Christ, with whom glory and adoration be to You and the Holy Spirit forever. Amen.

The Byzantine consecration of a deaconess[33] can also be compared to this consecration. After the anaphora and the opening of the doors, the candidate for consecration is led to the bishop. He calls out: "Divine Grace, which always heals what is infirm and makes up for what is lacking, promotes this servant N. to be a Deaconess." This is followed by the laying on of hands, the sign of the cross, and the prayer of the bishop, as well as the litany of intercessions. Then the bishop speaks a prayer and places the orarion (stole) around her neck—under the maphorion (headcloth)—with both ends of the orarion at the front. The liturgy continues. At communion, she also receives the cup, which she replaces on the altar herself. Subdeacons (readers and cantors) may not wear an orarion (Laodicaea, can. 22 and 23). The Latin rite of consecration for deaconesses dates from the twelfth century (with roots in the Carolingian period).[34]

4. The Synodal Legislation

4.1 Ecumenical Synods

Nicaea (325), can. 18 reduces the rights of deacons vis-à-vis presbyters. As for the deaconesses, can. 19 is relevant but only concerns the deaconesses of a heretical group, the Paulianists, which made the interpretation controversial.

At the Council of Chalcedon (451), which counts as the Fourth Ecumenical Council, can. 15 stated: "No woman under forty years of age is to be ordained a deacon (διάκονος), and then only after close scrutiny. If after receiving ordination (χειροτονία) and spending some time in the ministry (λειτουργία) she despises God's grace and gets married, such

33. A.-A. Thiermeyer, Der Diakonat der Frau. Liturgiegeschichtliche Kontexte und Folgerungen, in: *Theologische Quartalschrift* 173 (1993) 226–36, 232f.

34. Thiermeyer, Der Diakonat der Frau, 234f.

a person is to be anathematized along with her spouse."[35] —This canon was repeated word for word at the Synod of Worms (868), apparently because it was considered necessary and the order of deaconesses had not yet died out.

4.2 Particular Synods in East and West

Local synods in the East made no decisions on deaconesses, as far as I can see. In the West, on the other hand, the Synod of Orange (Concilium Arausicanum, 441) stated in can. 25 that deaconesses (*diaconae*) should not be ordained under any circumstances; if they had already been ordained, they were to bend their heads at the blessing granted to the people.

The Synod of Epaon (Concilium Epaonense 517) decreed in can. 21: "We abrogate the consecration of widows whom they call 'deaconesses' completely from our region." This clearly implies that this institution existed. That can also be established from the regulation of the Synod of Orléans (Concilium Aurelianense 533), where can. 17 states: "Women who have so far received the *benedictio diaconatus* against the prohibitions of the canons, if it can be proved that they have returned to matrimony, should be banned from communion. But if they have given up this living together after they have acknowledged their error in front of the bishop, let them return to the grace of communion after fulfilling a penance."

Nevertheless, St. Radegund, the wife of King Clothar, was probably consecrated as *diacona* around this time (555) by Bishop Medard of Noyon (see below).

5. Imperial Legislation

In addition, one should pay attention to the legislation of the emperors Theodosius and Justinian. In Codex Theodosianus (CTh) 16.2.27 of June 21, 390, Theodosius prescribes the minimum age of sixty years for deaconesses. CTh 5.3.1 lists the deaconess after bishop, priest, and deacon, and before the subdeacon.[36]

35. N. P. Tanner, ed., *Decrees of the Ecumenical Councils I* (London/Washington, DC, 1990) 94.

36. CTh 16, 2, 27, in: SC 497 (Paris, 2005) 170–75; CTh 5, 3, 1, in: SC 531 (Paris, 2009) 80–81. Gryson, *Le ministère des femmes*, 119–22.

In Justinian's legislation,[37] deaconesses are clearly counted among the clergy. Novella 3 of March 16, 535 states that at the Hagia Sophia (and at other large churches) there should not be more than 60 presbyters, 100 deacons, 40 deaconesses, 90 subdeacons, 110 readers, and 25 singers, a total of 425 clerics (the deaconesses are included), in addition to 100 doorkeepers.[38] It even literally refers to "male and female deacons." The deaconesses are ordained (χειροτονία), but not absolutely (as with other clerics), that is, they belong to a particular church or monastery. The minimum age is reduced to fifty years in Nov. 6.6 and finally to forty years in Nov. 123.13. A future deaconess must be a virgin or the widow of only one man (*univira*) (Nov. 6.6). She must remain completely chaste; transgressions will be severely punished. They get their living from the church. Their jurisdiction lies in the hands of the bishop, before any civil judge.

The functions of deaconesses are not described in more detail, except that they are said to have a ministry at the celebration of holy baptism and—without further details—that they are present at other sacred functions customarily done by them in connection with the venerable mysteries (Nov. 6.6).

Gryson notes, correctly, that in the Armenian Church and in the Nestorian Church the role of the deaconess is limited to her baptismal assistance.[39]

6. Examples of Female Deacons in the First Six Centuries

A number of deaconesses are known to us by name, many of them particularly in Constantinople in the second half of the fourth century or at the beginning of the fifth century, as well as in Antioch and Cappadocia.[40]

37. Gryson, *Le ministère des femmes*, 122–27.

38. *Corpus Iuris Civilis*, vol. III, *Novellae*, ed. R. Schoell, W. Kroll (Berlin, 1912) ed. stereotypa IV, 21 (Nov. III 1).

39. This is also confirmed in the article by J. Dum-Tragut, Diakoninnen in der Armenisch-Apostolischen Kirche, in: Winkler, *Diakonat der Frau*, 71–88. According to this, the earliest evidence of a women's diaconate dates from the eleventh century; their functions are preaching and proclaiming the gospel to women, as well as "bathing" children and women (baptism!).

40. Cf. Gryson, *Le ministère des femmes*, 146–50; Jensen, *Gottes selbstbewusste Töchter*, 148–57.

6.1 Constantinople

When John Chrysostom († September 14, 407) became Archbishop of Constantinople in the year 397, Olympias († July 25, 408) was already serving there as deaconess, having been consecrated by his predecessor, Nektarios (381–397), probably after 391, at the age of about twenty-five.[41] She is probably the most famous deaconess.[42]

John himself consecrated Elisanthia, Martyria, Palladia, the sisters or relatives of Olympias, to deaconesses (ἡ διάκονος).

Vita Olymp. 7 reports: John Chrysostom "consecrated to deacons (χειροτονεῖ διακόνους) of the Holy Church also her [Olympias's] three relatives Elisanthia, Martyria and Palladia to absolve the four ministries (τὰς τέσσαρας διακονίας) uninterrupted."[43]—What are the four ministries? They have been translated as diaconal services, but it cannot be a question of round-the-clock charitable or ecclesiastical service, even if it were nursing.[44] Is it possible to imagine here continuous prayer,[45] such as was customary at that time in the monastery of the Acoemetae (sleepless monks), founded by Alexander the Acoemete?[46]

The three had joined Olympias (Vita Olymp. 6). Later Elisanthia was to become the second successor of Olympias as ἡγουμένη; the first was Marina. Elisanthia preserved the rule and changed nothing.

Pentadia[47] should also be mentioned, to whom Chrysostom wrote three letters from exile (Ep. 94, 104, 185) that have survived. Originally Pentadia had been married to the general Timasius, who was condemned

41. C. Baur, *Der heilige Johannes Chrysostomus und seine Zeit*, Vols. 1–2 (Munich, 1929–1930) II 87.

42. Sozomenus, *Historia ecclesiastica* 8, 9, 1; 8, 24, 8; 8, 27, 8; Socrates, *Historia ecclesiastica* VI 16.

43. A.-M. Malingrey, *Jean Chrysostome, Lettres à Olympias. Augmentée de la Vie anonyme d'Olympias* (SC 13bis) (Paris, 1968) 420f.

44. Also L. Neureiter, Networking von Christinnen in der Spätantike. Diakoninnen, Witwen, diakonisch tätige, einflussreiche und wohlhabende Frauen in der Umgebung des Johannes Chrysostomus, in: Jensen, Larentzakis, eds., *Diakonat*, 171–89, 181.

45. So Malingrey, *Jean Chrysostome, Lettres à Olympias*, 421, n. 5.

46. See R. Riedinger, Art. Akoimeten, in: TRE, vol. 2, 148–53; A. Grillmeier with T. Hainthaler, *Christ in Christian Tradition*, vol. 2/2 (London/Louisville, KY, 1995), 12–13 (and index).

47. Malingrey, *Jean Chrysostome, Lettres à Olympias*, 234–35. Cf. John Chrys., *Epistulae* (CPG 4405): PG 52.

by the chamberlain and court eunuch Eutropius for high treason and, according to Sozomenus, died in the penal colony of the Oasis Magna in Egypt, in the desert.[48] She was a deaconess at the Hagia Sophia and one of those to whom John bade farewell at his deportation, together with Olympias and Prokla, exhorting her to continue her ministry in the church.[49] Chrysostom also wrote three letters to the deaconess Prokla/Amprukla at the Hagia Sophia (Ep. 96, 103, 191).

Mention should also be made of Silvina (lat. Salvina), daughter of Gildo in Numidia, married to a certain Nebridius. Jerome wrote to her, asking her to remain a widow. She was ordained deaconess by Chrysostom.[50]

The fact that the deaconess belonged to an order in the church is proved by the example of Nicarete, who, according to Sozomenus (HE 8, 23,4-7), did not strive for the status of deaconess *(ἀξίωμα διακόνου)* and did not want to "be in charge of church virgins." John Chrysostom also speaks of τὸ ἀξίωμα τῆς διακονίας (PG 62, 553CD).

Sabiniana (ἡ κυρία μου . . . ἡ διάκονος) was, according to Palladius, Chrysostom's aunt, presumably a sister of his father[51] who came from Antioch to visit him in exile in Kukusus.[52]

Sozomenus (HE 9,2) also tells of a deaconess Eusebia at the end of the fourth century who belonged to the heretical Macedonian sect and lived outside Constantinople.

6.2 Antioch

Apart from Sabiniana, Chrysostom's aunt mentioned above, Theodoret of Cyrus speaks of Pouplia or Publia (Πουπλία) in Antioch,[53] who led

48. Baur, *Der heilige Johannes Chrysostomus*, II 42.

49. Palladius, *Dialogue sur la vie de Jean Chrysostome*, introduced and trans. A.-M. Malingrey, SC 341, 206–7.

50. Baur, *Der heilige Johannes Chrysostomus*, II 90. Jerome, Ep. 79 ad Salvinam (400 oder 401), in: J. Labourt, *Saint Jérôme, Lettres* IV (Paris, 1954) 93–104. Jerome knew the father of Nebridius, Salvina's husband.

51. Baur, *Der heilige Johannes Chrysostomus*, II 1, 2 n. 6. Palladius, *Historia Lausiaca*, 41.

52. Baur, *Der heilige Johannes Chrysostomus*, II, 298f.; 324. John Chrysostom, Epistula 6 an Olymp. 1d, in: Malingrey, *Jean Chrysostome, Lettres à Olympias*, 130–31.

53. Theodoret of Cyrus, *Historia ecclesiastica* III 19, in: BKV, 192f.

"a chorus of virgins who had sworn lifelong virginity and joined them unceasingly in praising God the Creator and Redeemer." The psalms they sang mocking the weakness of idols were a provocation to Emperor Julian (the Apostate), who then had Publia beaten. The text does not speak of a deaconess or a diaconal ministry,[54] but the table of contents at the beginning of the third book lists a chapter "about Publia the deaconess (ἡ διάκονος) and her frankness regarding God"[55] and thus provides the reference to her diaconal ministry.

Shortly beforehand, Theodoret tells in his church history (HE III 14) of an unnamed deaconess who brought the son of a pagan priest to convert to Christianity at the time of Emperor Julian (360–363) (and was baptized by Cyril of Jerusalem).

Theodoret writes letters to three deaconesses. Axia and Casiana receive letters of condolence,[56] but the main addressee is Celerina.[57] In his letter (around November 448), which he apparently writes to ἡ διάκονος without knowing of the condemnation of Eutyches—she probably lives in Constantinople—it becomes clear that she obviously knows about the christological problems. Theodoret asks Celerina to dedicate herself to the teachings of the Gospel and the peace of the churches; this presumably means instruction, but it could also be meant in the sense of church politics. Celerina is well versed in the questions and is also aware of Theodoret's christological position, so that he does not have to explain very much to her.[58]

54. SC 530, n. 2, p. 155, informs more generally about deaconesses, but nevertheless states that the *kephalaion* 19 speaks of a deaconess, although the text depicts her as a choir leader.

55. In the edition by L. Parmentier, *Die griechischen christlichen Schriftsteller der ersten drei Jahrhunderte*, vol. 19 (Leipzig, 1911) 176,4 (*kephalaion*). According to Parmentier, Einleitung (ci), *Historia ecclesiastica* was written before 450. The Latin translation of Theodoret's *Historia ecclesiastica* III 19 is in Cassiodor's *Historia Tripartita* VI 36. The titulus, which summarizes III 18 and 19, is: *De Artemio martyre et Publia abbatissa* (CSEL 71, ed. R. Hanslik, [Vienna, 1952], 304, 50). In other words, the deaconess (ἡ διάκονος) in the *kephalaion* (Theodoret) became the abbatissa in Cassiodor.

56. SC 40, 118; SC 98, 62–64.

57. Theodoret, ep. 101: ed. Y. Azéma, SC 111 (1965) 18–20.

58. Theodoret of Cyrus writes to Celerina: "It is however needless for me to inform your piety of my sentiments, for you have exact knowledge of what I preach, and how I instruct the ignorant. I beseech you therefore, since the workers of lies have

The deaconess Anastasia was presumably also in the region of Antioch. Severus of Antioch (who, as a non-Chalcedonian, was deposed as archbishop) wrote her at least four letters,[59] which are dated around the middle of the year 522. One of the letters exists in Syriac (partly in Coptic, Arabic, and Greek) and deals with exegetical questions that Anastasia had posed to him. Severus praises her for treading the path of righteousness, that is, of asceticism and monastic life, and meditating on the inspired Scriptures. In a long letter he gives comprehensive answers to her questions, referring to the church fathers. That means that he assumes that the addressee has advanced theological education.[60] In addition, Severus wrote to at least three other deaconesses who were at the same time archimandritesses—which was not the case for Anastasia—namely, Jannia (489–512), Valeriana (513–518), and Eugenia (513–538).[61]

In a letter from the time of exile (519–538), Severus writes: "In the case of a female deaconess, especially in monasteries, ordination is received not so much for the sake of the requirements of the mysteries, but for the sake of honour only (for the deaconesses in the cities are in the habit of ministering to the divine laver of regeneration in the case of females who are baptized)."[62] Here, the practice in the cities appears to differ from that in rural communities.

---

poured their insults upon all the godly bishops of the East at once, and overwhelmed the churches with a storm, that your piety will show all possible zeal on behalf of the doctrines of the gospel and the peace of the churches."

59. Ep. 69 (PO 14, 75–103), 70 (PO 14: A collection of letters of Severus of Antioch from numerous Syriac manuscripts, ed. E. W. Brooks [Paris, 1920], 104–7) 71 (PO 14, 107–17) and ep. 72 (PO 14, 117–118). Cf. CPG 7070 (2) and (12).

60. R. Albrecht, *Das Leben der heiligen Makrina auf dem Hintergrund der Thekla-Traditionen. Studien zu den Ursprüngen des weiblichen Mönchtums im 4. Jahrhundert in Kleinasien* (Göttingen, 1986) 145–49 and 366–68 (Diakonissen im Kloster), here 367, n. 168, already saw in this letter of Severus to Anastasia illuminating evidence for the theological education of deaconesses.

61. Ep. 110 (to Eugenia): PO 14, 273–74; ep. III, 10.15 (to Valieriana): W. Brooks, ed., *The Sixth Book of the Select Letters of Severus, Patriarch of Antioch*, vol. 2 (London, 1904) (hereafter: Brooks, *Select Letters* II) 364–68; ep. IV, 118.121 (to Jannia): Brooks, *Select Letters* II, 368–71.

62. Ep. I.62: Brooks, *Select Letters* II, 193–94.

The story of St. Pelagia, who came from Antioch, brings us into the region of Syro-Palestine in the fifth century.[63] On behalf of the prostitute Pelagia, who converts and asks to be baptized, the bishop sends for the deaconess Romana, who becomes her godmother and takes her into her household. The deaconess also gets in touch with the bishop when Pelagia donates all her belongings to him. After one week, Pelagia leaves Romana's house secretly at night to go on a pilgrimage to Jerusalem in men's clothes in order to live as a recluse on the Mount of Olives.—This is the only story I know that tells of a deaconess by name who plays a role in a baptism.

6.3 Cappadocia

In 372, Basil of Caesarea wrote a letter (ep. 105) to deaconesses who are the daughters of Comes Terentius.[64]

The mother of the monastic father Euthymius [*377], Dionysia, was consecrated *diaconos* around 379 (διάκονος ἐχειροτόνησεν).[65]

In connection with the death of Macrina, the sister of Basil of Caesarea and Gregory of Nyssa, around 380, Gregory mentions the deaconess Lampadion in his *Vita Macrinae*.[66] She led the choir of virgins in the convent of Macrina on the Iris in Cappadocia (προτεταγμένη τοῦ χόρου τῆς παρθενίας) with the rank of diaconia (ἐν τῷ διακονίας βαθμῷ)[67] and she knew of the decrees Macrina had made for her death.

At the shrine of St. Thecla outside the city of Seleucia in Isauria, the deaconess Marthana was in charge of monasteries, as the pilgrim Egeria tells in her report.[68] This pilgrimage took place from 381 to 384.

63. S. P. Brock/A. Ashbrook Harvey, *Holy Women of the Syrian Orient* (Berkeley, 1987) 41–62; esp. 52–58; cf. Albrecht, *Makrina*, 148f.

64. Gryson, *Le ministère des femmes*, 148.

65. Cyril Scyth., *Vita Euthym.* 2–3: E. Schwartz, ed., *Kyrillos von Skythopolis (Texte und Untersuchungen zur Geschichte der altchristlichen Literatur)* 49, 2 (Leipzig 1939), 10,22–11,1; cf. 8,20; 10,6. French: A.-J. Festugière, *Les moines d'Orient*, vol. 3 (Paris, 1961) 59–61.

66. Gregory of Nyssa, *De vita Macrin.* 29.2 (διακονία), 32.2 (ἡ διάκονος): Maraval, ed., SC 178 (1971); BKV, 360–63.

67. Albrecht, *Makrina*, 51; 145: The abbess of the convent is Macrina, while the deaconess Lampadion has a prominent function in the choir of the virgins.

68. Egeria, *Peregrin.* 22.3, in: H. Donner, *Pilgerfahrt ins Heilige Land. Die ältesten Berichte christlicher Palästinapilger (4.–7. Jh.)* (Stuttgart, 1979) 134f.

6.4 Gaul

In his will, Bishop Remigius of Reims († 533) speaks of his daughter Helaria the deaconess (*diacona*).[69]

We are particularly well informed about the life of Radegund[70] (ca. 520–587),[71] who was probably born in 520 in Erfurt and was taken as a prisoner of war from Thuringia to Neustria in 531 by King Clothar I before she was twelve years old. Her father, Bertachar, was king of a part of Thuringia and was killed by his brother Baderic. Radegund was raised at the court of this uncle Baderic. Clothar brought her to the royal city of Athies in Vermandois, where she received a first-class education (with a view to her possible later marriage to Clothar). When she was about twenty, Clothar sent for her to come to Vitry to marry him. After her brother was killed at Clothar's instigation, she left the court to be ordained by Medard of Noyon to *diacona,* as Venantius Fortunatus reports:[72]

"[S]he came to the blessed Medardus of Noyon (Noviomagus) and implored him to consecrate her . . . to the Lord. But remembering the words of the apostle, if a woman be bound to her husband, she should not seek to be free (1 Cor 7:27), he did not fulfil the queen's request, telling her not to don the nun's habit. Moreover, the nobility attacked the blessed man, dragging him roughly through the basilica away from the altar, so that he would not be able to give the veil to someone bound to the king, not that the bishop (*sacerdos*) might dare to deprive the prince of his queen, not the publicana, but his officially wedded wife; when the saint recognised this, she went into the sacristy, put on a nun's habit, returned to the altar, and addressed these words to the most blessed Medard: If you hesitate to consecrate me, fearing one man more than God, the shepherd will de-

69. Remigius, *Testamentum*, ed. H. M. Rochais, CCL 117 (Turnhout, 1957) 477, 95–98.

70. Venantius Fortunatus, *Vita Radegundis* (CPL 1042), in: *Monumenta Germaniae historica. Scriptores*, vol. 2, *Scriptorvm rervm Merovingicarvm* (1937) 364–77.

71. Cf. R. Aigrain, *Sainte Radegonde* (vers 520–587) (Paris, 1918); H. Leclercq, Art. Radegonde, in: *Dictionnaire d'archéologie chrétienne et de liturgie* 14 (1948) 2044–2055; J. Lanczkowski, Radegunde von Thüringen, in: *Erbe und Auftrag* 67 (1991) 85–109; J. Hofmann, Verständigung im Zeichen des Kreuzes. Königin Radegundis und Kaiserin Sophia als christliche Brückenbauerinnen zwischen dem Frankenreich und Byzanz, in: E. Möde, S. E. Müller, B. M. Zapff, eds., *Jesus hominis salvator. Christlicher Glaube in moderner Gesellschaft. Festschrift für Bischof Dr. Walter Mixa* (Regensburg, 2006) 13–35.

72. Venantius Fortunatus, *Vita Radegundis*, 12, in: PL 88, 502.

mand from you the soul of the sheep. Deeply shaken by the force of this invocation, he laid his hands upon her and consecrated her as diacona."[73]

She then made a pilgrimage to the tomb of St Martin and dedicated herself to the poor and sick in a way reminiscent of Elisabeth of Thuringia, who lived much later. Radegund lived extremely ascetically and entered the monastery of Poitiers. She appointed her adopted daughter as abbess and adhered to Caesarius's "Rule for Virgins," thus gaining exemption for the monastery and creating a bridge between Martinian monasticism and that of Lérins. From Constantinople she requested and received a relic of the True Cross—the first one north of the Alps—for which Venantius Fortunatus composed hymns in 569 which are still sung today in Holy Week (Vexilla Regis and Pange, lingua, gloriosi). Radegunde died on 13 August 587, was buried in the Church of St. Mary outside the Walls, later to be renamed Sainte Radegonde.

Apart from this, the presence of deaconesses both in the East and in the West (6th century) is also attested by inscriptions.[74]

7. Summary

In the sources (frequently from the second half of the fourth century), names of well-known deaconesses are mentioned who are called ἡ διάκονος. Their ministry appears to be taken for granted in Antioch, Constantinople, and Cappadocia; it belongs to the church and is not seen to be a problem. It is probably assumed that people knew what was meant by the title "deaconess."

It is noticeable that, with only one exception (Romana), the deaconesses who are specifically named are not mentioned in the context of baptismal assistance. This function, which is mentioned in church orders, should probably not be overestimated; one should recall the warning to be careful in using these texts in historical research.[75]

73. On *diacona* cf. J. Forget, Art. Diaconesses, in: DThC, vol. 4 (1920) 685–703; H. Leclercq, Art. Diaconesse, in: DThC, vol. 4 (1920) 725–33; P. Philippi, Art. Diakonie I, in: TRE, vol. 8 (1981) 626–27.

74. Gryson, *Le ministère des femmes*, 149–50. Cf. Eisen, *Amtsträgerinnen im frühen Christentum*, 188–92.

75. Schöllgen, *Der Abfassungszweck*, 77: "Therefore, church historical research should be much more cautious in dealing with them than is generally the case."

They were often women living ascetically and also heavily involved in charitable care for others, particularly for the poor and the sick. Some of them were educated women interested in theology, or women who exerted—or were able to exert—influence (Olympias, Celerina). There were women from the highest social class, rich women who placed their wealth at the disposal of the bishop or who erected buildings. This is especially true of Olympias, who was extremely active in charitable works and used her huge fortune to this purpose, even leaving her fortune at the disposal of the Archbishop of Constantinople.

Elisanthia, Martyria, and Palladia are known to have been consecrated (χειροτονεῖ διακόνους) for the four kinds of ministry (διακονία). There are some indications that they held liturgical church services.

One should certainly beware of reinterpreting such activities as a kind of job description for the deaconess. It is not within the scope of the respective narrative to describe the profile of a deaconess. The consecration of a deaconess is not the same as the consecration of a virgin, for by no means every virgin in a convent or outside was consecrated as a *diacona.* There are said to have been 250 nuns in the convent of St. Olympias, but only four deaconesses are mentioned. Not every rich and religious widow became a *diacona.*

It was, clearly, rather the *leadership responsibility* that was connected with the deaconesses' ministry. The "leadership of the choir of virgins" is a function that is mentioned several times.

The deaconess was also not inevitably the head of the monastery or convent. There are cases in which this is true, but in the letters of Severus, for example, the fact that a deaconess was abbess of the convent is specifically mentioned. In Macrina's case, the deaconess was not in charge of the convent, and there were also a number of deaconesses in the convent of Olympias, including the later abbess.

The deaconesses in Constantinople belonged to the clergy.

This diversity of activities would also provide leeway for redefining the tasks of a deaconess, should this diaconal ministry be revived.[76]

76. The Orthodox Metropolitan and long-time Oxford Professor Kallistos Ware clearly summarized the current state of this issue in April 2017: https://www.youtube.com/watch?v=Mh_NIFmnFyI&list=WL&index (27.06.2018).

The rather restrictive interpretation presented by Aimé Georges Martimort needs to be revised in some cases.[77] The reality of deaconesses in the time of the early church up to the seventh century was very varied, depending on the time and the region.

(Translation from German by Neville Williamson)

77. Regarding the Coptic evidence, U. Zanetti, Y eut-il des diaconesses en Égypte?, in: *Vetera Christianorum* 27 (1990) 369–73, has submitted a correction to Martimort.

The Discussion on the Diaconate of Women in the Catholic Church

Peter Hünermann

Introduction

In discussions about the possibility of admitting women to the diaconate, it is repeatedly argued that the diaconate is part of the one sacrament of holy orders (*ordo*), and that consequently only men can be admitted. The episcopate, the presbyterate, and the diaconate are all stages of the *one ordo* and historically only men can be considered for sacramental ministry—as has been clearly attested since the Middle Ages—for theological reasons. Women could therefore only be entrusted with a non-sacramental ministry. All that was necessary for this ministry was an ecclesiastical commission and a benediction. In this argumentation, systematic and historical justifications are closely intertwined. Both justifications are flawed. In order to ensure a transparent critical analysis, both justifications are examined separately below.

1. Diaconate as Part of the One Order—A Formal Logical Analysis

1.1 Part and Whole as a Purely Quantitative Determination

Diaconate as part of the one sacramental order can be understood in different ways logically. The part of a whole can be understood purely quantitatively. To take a simple example: think of a piece of cheese, cut out of an Emmenthal cheese wheel. The unity of part and whole is here determined *purely quantitatively*. In both cases it's cheese, the same cheese!

What does that mean in relation to the reference to diaconate and the one order?

If the sacramental order is defined purely as *potestas*, that is, as spiritual power or authority, then the diaconate belongs to the *sacramentum ordinis* as a purely quantitative part. This part can be "widened" or "enlarged," so to speak, to the presbyterate or episcopate. The only difference between the three ministries is then the extent of their power. This kind of hierarchy functions as a pure command hierarchy, for example in the military field. In modern armies, this hierarchy is severely limited by the qualitative differences in the various branches of the armed forces and the highly specialized functions assigned to officers and NCOs. Whoever claims, like the present-day cardinals, bishops, clerics, or laymen with a traditionalist attitude, that any person consecrated as deacon must also be entitled to ordination as presbyter or bishop favors such a one-dimensional hierarchy of pure power.

At this point, a historical reminiscence: the plans for church structure that were prepared for the Second Vatican Council by the theological commission under Cardinal Ottaviani are based on such a *potestas* concept in their understanding of ministry. This remarkable official understanding comes to light particularly in the first chapter of this draft ecclesiology with the title "The Nature of the Church Militant." The Fathers of the Second Vatican Council rejected this conception.[1]

It is not possible to invoke the Council of Trent for this concept. There it was said that one had to pass through different stages of the ministries, because at that time the church order only knew a consecrated diaconate, a transitional stage on the way to the presbyterate; apart from that, the so-called minor orders and the subdiaconate were also preserved as purely transitional stages without further practical meaning. In Trent the focus lay on issues of ministry contested by Luther. The question of an order for the *ministeria* as such was not a conciliar issue.[2] This also means, however, that the logical way in which the different ministries are related

1. Cf. P. Hünermann, Theologischer Kommentar zur dogmatischen Konstitution über die Kirche *Lumen Gentium*, in: *Herder theologischer Kommentat zum Zweiten Vatikanischen Konzil*, vol. 1, *Die Dokumente des Zweiten Vatikanischen Konzils. Konstitutionen, Dekrete, Erklärungen*, ed. P. Hünermann (Freiburg i. Br., 2009) 291–316; in particular 295–99, 314–17, and 320–24.

2. Cf. DH 1771–1778; in particular 1776; 1772.

to one another is not the topic of the Tridentine anathemas. In addition, one must recall that for many centuries in the first millennium deacons who served as the right hand of the bishop in the church administration were often consecrated directly to bishops.

1.2 Part and Whole as Qualitative Determination

But how should one understand the systematic and logical unity of these different *ministeria* that evolved in the early church—bishop, presbyter, deacon—if it cannot be a purely quantitative determination?

First of all, a *preliminary consideration:* the *ministeria* in the church are publicly recognized services to a community. Services for society, for a public community, are essentially determined on the grounds of their duties on behalf of the community in which they form *complementary* units. There are many different types of relationship between such units. One might take as an example the basic services of the judiciary, of legislature and administration, which form a unity—despite all the differences between judges, the elected representatives of the people who legislate in the parliaments, and the political executive (government and administration). These different kinds of service are all concerned with the necessary enabling and realizing of the rule of law in society. They all serve the public order. This means that the individual services are qualitatively differentiated according to their different duties, thus forming a coherent unit that is naturally organized by rules of responsibility, precedence, and subordination or superordination.

What should be said of ecclesial ministries and their unity? Naturally, ecclesial ministries are not the same as services to the general public. The disciples sent out by Jesus Christ are those who bear witness to him as the risen Lord, that is, to proclaim the kingdom of God.[3] The power given to the risen Christ is power in the Holy Spirit through which he himself becomes present in the faith of the believers—that is, he awakens faith in people and thus takes his dwelling in them, together with the Father. He makes them members of his body and holds them in fellowship with himself. He is the one who works in the apostles' proclamation. He is the one who calls people to be his disciples.

3. Cf. Matt 28:16-20.

Discipleship includes getting to know him, practicing repentance, keeping his commandments. This is all sealed in baptism, rebirth in Jesus Christ, participation in the paschal mystery through the Spirit. This comprehensive commission to the disciples, aimed at the salvation of the whole human and the whole of humanity, demonstrates all its complexity very quickly as the young churches take shape.

This also involves order within the fellowship, which is also guaranteed by the apostles' discipleship in Christ: "Whoever listens to you listens to me."[4] This mission of the apostles in the public service of the church very quickly branched out into different ministries, leading to the formation of a common ministerial order after two or three generations: episcopate, presbyterate, and diaconate. The concrete tasks also varied according to the different local churches and epochs.

The Second Vatican Council rediscovered the diaconate as an independent ministry, thereby indicating a certain qualitative differentiation from the other ministries by referring to deacons "who receive the imposition of hands 'not unto the priesthood, but unto the ministry' " (cf. LG 29). This is followed by a characterization that is, at first glance, astonishing in its generality: "For, strengthened by sacramental grace they are dedicated to the People of God, in conjunction with the bishop and his body of priests, in the service of the liturgy, of the Gospel and of works of charity. It pertains to the office of a deacon, in so far as it may be assigned to him by the competent authority, to administer Baptism solemnly, to be custodian and distributor of the Eucharist, in the name of the Church, to assist at and to bless marriages, to bring Viaticum to the dying, to read the sacred scripture to the faithful, to instruct and exhort the people, to preside over the worship and the prayer of the faithful, to administer sacramentals, and to officiate at funeral and burial services. Dedicated to works of charity and functions of administration, deacons should recall the admonition of St Polycarp: 'Let them be merciful, and zealous, and let them walk according to the truth of the Lord, who became the servant of all' " (LG 29). This characterization was clearly formulated at the beginning of a new development that still requires common reflection and concretion.

Benedict XVI took an important step toward such a concretion in the second part of his encyclical *Deus Caritas Est*, which developed the

4. Luke 10:16.

doctrinal theology. At the beginning of the second part of the encyclical (the first part of which deals with God's love and the relationship of God's love to the individual), speaking of the church as a whole, Benedict says:

> Love of neighbour, grounded in the love of God, is first and foremost a responsibility for each individual member of the faithful, but it is also a responsibility for the entire ecclesial community at every level: from the local community to the particular Church and to the Church universal in its entirety. As a community, the Church must practise love. Love thus needs to be organized if it is to be an ordered service to the community. The awareness of this responsibility has had a constitutive relevance in the Church from the beginning: "All who believed were together and had all things in common; and they sold their possessions and goods and distributed them to all, as any had need" (Acts 2:44-5). . . . As the Church grew, this radical form of material communion could not in fact be preserved. But its essential core remained: within the community of believers there can never be room for a poverty that denies anyone what is needed for a dignified life. . . . (DCE 20)[5]

And further on: "As the years went by and the Church spread further afield, the exercise of charity became established as one of her essential activities, along with the administration of the sacraments and the proclamation of the word: love for widows and orphans, prisoners, and the sick and needy of every kind, is as essential to her as the ministry of the sacraments and preaching of the Gospel. The Church cannot neglect the service of charity any more than she can neglect the Sacraments and the Word" (DCE 22) (DH 5103). He goes on to explain that the church's threefold task—proclaiming the word of God, celebrating the sacraments, and exercising the ministry of charity—are duties that "presuppose each other and are inseparable. For the Church, charity is not a kind of welfare activity which could equally well be left to others, but is a part of her nature, an indispensable expression of her very being" (DCE 25). In this encyclical Benedict expresses in general language what he laid down in ecclesiastical law in a *motu proprio* and in the altered text of the World Catechism, in which he expressly uses the words of the Second Vatican Council, that the deacon receives the imposition of

5. Benedict XVI, Encyclical Letter *Deus Caritas Est*, December 25, 2005, http://www.vatican.va/content/benedict-xvi/en/encyclicals/documents/hf_ben-xvi_enc_20051225_deus-caritas-est.html.

hands "unto the ministry." Whoever is ordained to the diaconate represents Christ, who made himself the "deacon" or servant of all, serving the whole person, but in particular the marginalized, the poor, the outcast: the sick, the widows, and orphans. The theological justification for this is provided by *Deus Caritas Est*. Thus Benedict XVI has substantially clarified the qualitative characterization given in *Lumen Gentium* for this office of deacon, without, however, explicitly mentioning the deacon at this point in the encyclical.

Thus the Second Vatican Council and following developments have provided a clear definition of the present form of the ministry. Each individual, like the church as a whole, participates in the mission of Jesus Christ. The ministries of the church are together supposed to bear public responsibility in order to make sure that the church, in its individual groupings, can and does join in carrying out these functions as the body of Christ. The unity of the Order, the unity of ministries, is thus rooted in Jesus Christ and in his commission to the apostles, and at the same time it represents the fullness of the church as a community of believers who together form the body of Christ in history. Seen systematically and logically, the position of the diaconate as part of the one order is a qualitative relationship, not a purely quantitative one.

Neither the deaconesses of the Eastern Churches in the first millennium and today (in Syria, Armenia, Greece, Africa, and so forth) nor the women today in the Latin Church can be denied access to the sacramental diaconate by arguing that the diaconate is part of the one order, in the sense of a purely quantitative relationship. The ecclesiastical hierarchy is not a pure command hierarchy.

2. Historical Justification for the Impossibility of Admitting Women to the Sacramental Diaconate Today—A Critical Analysis

In order to find the errors in this line of argumentation, somewhat more than just formal-logical analysis is required.

2.1 How the Historical Argumentation Originated

At the turn of the nineteenth to the twentieth century, and slightly more strongly during the Weimar Republic and the Nazi years, a discussion arose concerning the diaconate of women in the Catholic Church, its history, and whether it should be revived. The founder generations of Catholic women's organizations were the ones asking such questions. Among the outstanding theological thinkers were Adolf Kalsbach, Michael Faulhaber, later Archbishop of Munich, Edith Stein, Josefine Meyer, and others.[6]

The discussion was considerably intensified after the Second World War: as early as 1951 there was a public initiative in Germany, prompted by the Department for Pastoral Care in the diocese of Rottenburg-Stuttgart and by the KDFB, then in 1954 a corresponding initiative in Switzerland, and in 1959 in France. After the Vatican Council (1962–1965) decided to revive the independent diaconate for celibate and married men, demands for the admission of women to the sacramental diaconate came from many sides. At the Third World Congress for the Lay Apostolate in Rome in 1967 there was an insistent call for clarification of women's place in the sacramental order. There are broad-based initiatives in the Netherlands, Germany, Canada, the USA, Switzerland, Austria, France, and Belgium.[7] This topic was widely discussed at the postconciliar German synod of Würzburg (1971–1975), and Rome was called upon to examine the question of the possibility of consecrating women to the diaconate.[8] A reply never came.

In 1976, at the instigation of Paul VI, the Congregation for the Doctrine of the Faith published its declaration *Inter Insigniores* on the question of the admission of women to the priesthood.[9] This response to the admission of women by the Anglican churches of Canada and England in 1975 refers formally to admission to the priesthood. However, as a

6. Cf. F. Kukula, I. Schüller, Der Streit um den Diakonat der Frau—zur Geschichte vor und nach dem II. Vatikanum, in: P. Hünermann, A. Biesinger, M. Heimbach-Steins, A. Jensen, eds., *Ein Amt für Frauen in der Kirche—ein frauengerechtes Amt?* (Ostfildern, 1997) 304–66.

7. Cf. Kukula and Schüller, Der Streit um den Diakonat der Frau, 304–66.

8. Cf. *Gemeinsame Synode der Bistümer in der Bundesrepublik Deutschland. Beschlüsse der Vollversammlung, Offizielle Gesamtausgabe* I (Freiburg/Basel/Vienna, 1976) 595f.; 616f.

9. Congregation for the Doctrine of the Faith, Declaration on the Question of the Admission of Women to the Priesthood *Inter Insigniores*, October 15, 1976, English text at http://www.vatican.va/roman_curia/congregations/cfaith/documents/rc_con_cfaith_doc_19761015_inter-insigniores_en.html.

consequence, part of the argumentation is broadly applied to the diaconate as well.

The background is Paul VI's recourse to tradition in relation to the Middle Ages. This argumentation is the basis of the texts from Rome. The same justification is also found in theological explanations from liturgical scholars, systematic theologians, and experts on canon law, who also rule out the diaconate for women on the same grounds.[10]

In *Inter Insigniores,* Paul VI first refers to "the Church's constant tradition" and states: "The Catholic Church has never felt that priestly or episcopal ordination can be validly conferred on women" (II 1). Paul VI explicitly refers in this context to the *Didascalia Apostolorum* and the *Constitutiones Apostolicae*. These acknowledge deaconesses, but they have no knowledge of the ordination of women to presbyters or bishops.

With reference to the Middle Ages and the modern era he writes: "The same conviction animates medieval theology, even if the Scholastic doctors, in their desire to clarify by reason the data of faith, often present arguments on this point that modern thought would have difficulty in admitting, or would even rightly reject. Since that period and up till our own time, it can be said that the question has not been raised again for the practice has enjoyed peaceful and universal acceptance" (II 1).

"Jesus Christ did not call any women to become part of the Twelve" (II 2), although he would never have prevented women as such from being near him.

In this way, his behavior was different from that of his Jewish fellow citizens. Moreover, referring to the practice of the apostles, who elected a man to complement their college of twelve, the pope questions whether this does not prohibit the church from departing from this attitude today (II 2).

The question can only be decided by a theological reflection clarifying "the proper nature of the sacrament of Order, with its specific reference to the mystery of Christ" (II 5). Of medieval theology and in particular Thomas Aquinas, the pope points out, "The whole sacramental economy is in fact based upon natural signs, on symbols imprinted on the human psychology: 'Sacramental signs,' says Saint Thomas, 'represent what

10. Cf. H. Jorissen, Theologische Bedenken gegen die Diakonatsweihe von Frauen, in: P. Hünermann et al., eds., *Diakonat. Ein Amt für Frauen in der Kirche—frauengerechtes Amt?* (Ostfildern, 1997) 86–97.

they signify by natural resemblance.' The same natural resemblance is required *for persons as for things*: when Christ's role in the Eucharist is to be expressed sacramentally, there would not be this 'natural resemblance' which must exist between Christ and his minister if the role of Christ were not taken by a man: in such a case it would be difficult to see in the minister the image of Christ. For Christ himself was and remains a man" (II 5). He then expressly rejects the reference to Gal 3:28 that, according to Paul, in Christ Jesus "there is no longer any distinction between men and women." He writes, "this passage does not concern ministries: it only affirms the universal calling to divine filiation, which is the same for all" (II 6). The principle of this Pauline statement, which is intended to highlight the difference from the salvation history of the Old Testament, is not discussed.

Indeed, Thomas Aquinas—along with numerous other medieval theologians—rejected the admission of women to Holy Orders completely. Thereby, on closer analysis, Thomas's opinion proves to be exactly opposite to the justification brought in by Paul VI. Thomas's argument favoring the exclusion of women from the sacramental office is not based on "theological" but on "cultural" factors: "*De necessitate sacramenti*" the woman is excluded from the reception of the *sacramentum ordinis*, "since it is not possible in the female sex (*in sexu femineo*) to signify eminence of degree, for a woman is in *status subiectionis*, the state of subjection."[11] Thomas adopts the designation of the sacrament of order from Peter Lombard, who assumes from the outset that there are *ordines* (plural). "But there are seven degrees (ranks) or ordines (spiritual offices). The degrees are ostiary . . ."[12] and so forth. Clerics are to be entrusted with these offices. One enters the clergy by receiving the tonsure or corona (crown), the sign of being appointed (*mancipatio*) for the administration of the church. Peter Lombard explicitly sees 1 Peter 2:9, "You are a chosen race, a royal priesthood," as a reference to the clergy.

As a result of Thomas adopting this concept of the order, medieval and modern theology represent the topos that women are not entitled to

11. Th. Aquinas, STh, Suppl. q. 39, a. All medieval theologians quoted by Paul VI—alongside Thomas—such as Bonaventure, Richard of Middleton, John Duns Scotus, or Durandus argue in the same way as Thomas.

12. Peter Lombard, *Sententiae in IV libris distinctae*, ed. Collegii S. Bonaventurae ad Claras Aquas (Rome, 1971), lib. IV, dist. 24, cap. 1.

attain a *gradus regendi* in the church because of their *status subiectionis*. They cannot even receive the tonsure as a condition of the seven *ordines*. The Council of Trent makes use of this theology—which seems strange to us—in its own decree on the Order:

> And whereas the ministry of so holy a priesthood is a divine thing; to the end that it might be exercised in a more worthy manner, and with greater veneration, it was suitable that, in the most well-ordered settlement of the church, there should be several and diverse orders of ministers, to minister to the priesthood, by virtue of their office; orders so distributed as that those already marked with the clerical tonsure should ascend through the lesser to the greater orders.[13]

2.2 *On the Theological Evaluation of This Historical Justification for the Exclusion of Women from Receiving Holy Orders*

Let us summarize the result of this clarification of the history of theology and dogma:

(1) The conception of the *sacramentum ordinis* in the second millennium—from the tonsure to the *sacerdotium* and the determination of the *status subiectionis* of women—is understandable in a feudal society characterized by the unity of empire and church. With the tonsure and the corresponding special ecclesiastical rights for the clergy, the church created a fundamental structure for its officials that was publicly recognized: its own group of "nobility." They were "ennobled" by showing the gifts of the Spirit,[14] said Peter Lombard in his *Sentences*. At the same time, this form of office is elevated to a "pre-political," God-given level by rooting the *status subiectionis* in human nature, namely, in the *status* of the *sexus femineus*. In this way, this understanding of office achieved the

13. Philip Schaff, *The Creeds of Christendom*, vol. 1 (New York, 1877) 187.

14. This legal position also applies to members of the monastic orders and subordinately to women in religious orders. It does not apply to Beguines, however, but only to *regulated women's religious orders*, which are assigned legally to the male orders in a certain sense. In this way, for example, for Carthusians, the consecration to deacon can be connected with the consecration to virgin, being permitted to read the Gospel, etc. Cf. H. Becker, A. Franz, Die Frau mit der Stola. Zum Ordo Consecrationis Virginum proprius Monialium Ordinis Cartusiensis of 1978, in: *Theologische Quartalschrift* 192 (2012) 320–28.

rank of divine law, taking priority over the historical, privileged authority of the "nobles" in feudal society.

(2) This premodern understanding of office was basically abolished by the Second Vatican Council, but the alteration of the concept was not redefined institutionally and canonically in the various documents. To name just two examples: In *Sacrosanctum Concilium* the *sacerdos* is no longer the one "*qui perficit sacramentum*" (who accomplishes the sacrament). The faithful are not called to participate in "his" eucharistic sacrifice. The pastor is, rather, the one who celebrates the eucharist together with the whole congregation. He holds the presiding office, on the basis of divine and ecclesiastical legitimation and authority.

In *Lumen Gentium* the public, sacramental ministry is not understood as "*gradus dignitatis regendi*" but as entrustment with the appointment as "shepherd," with "pastoral ministry" in the succession of the apostles. This gives the ecclesiastical office a particular profile, a particular authority over positions in civil law. Here there is no need for *status subiectionis*.

(3) In this context, the statement of John Paul II in *Mulieris Dignitatem* of 1988 on Gen 3:16 is especially significant: "Therefore when we read in the biblical description the words addressed to the woman: 'Your desire shall be for your husband, and he shall rule over you' (Gen 3:16), we discover a break and a constant threat precisely in regard to this 'unity of the two' which corresponds to the dignity of the image and likeness of God in both of them. But this threat is more serious for the woman. . . . This 'domination' indicates the disturbance and loss of the stability of that fundamental equality which the man and the woman possess in the 'unity of the two' " (MD 10).[15] The characterization of the woman through the *status subiectionis* is thus condemned as an expression of sin.

Let us summarize the result of this critical analysis of the historical reasons for the exclusion of women from Holy Orders from the Middle Ages to modern times: This "proof by tradition" has no formal theological, that is, normatively binding justification, but is only a material tradition that derives its unquestioned plausibility from cultural, social, and biological beliefs which were taken as a matter of course in the

15. Pope John Paul II, Apostolic Letter *Mulieris Dignitatem*, August 15, 1988, http://www.vatican.va/content/john-paul-ii/en/apost_letters/1988/documents/hf_jp-ii_apl_19880815_mulieris-dignitatem.html.

Middle Ages and the modern era. On the basis of new insights, what was then taken for granted has now been put into perspective, both by contemporary civil society and by the magisterium of the church, as historical attitudes conditioned by the times. It is therefore a serious theological mistake to designate this tradition as one that is binding for faith.

3. Conclusion

Humanity's concrete yearning for salvation, with its spiritual and bodily neediness, may act as *one* specific motivation for the sacrament of holy orders, the mandate and empowerment of the church to carry out pastoral ministry. For this reason, pastoral ministry essentially branches out into a qualitative plurality of specific services (*ministeria*). The unity of these ministries is founded in Jesus Christ himself, who continues his mission in the power of the Spirit in and through these ministries.

Since the understanding of ministry that formerly prevailed in the Latin Church was abolished by the Second Vatican Council and the postconciliar magisterium of the church, there can be no justification for the exclusion of women from the diaconate.

This also massively contradicts the de facto diaconal work performed by women in and for the church as well as the necessity not only to conceive and promote diaconal work in relation to the individual, but also to see this service as "the practice of love by the Church as 'a community of love' " (*Deus Caritas Est*, Part II). "Love of neighbour, grounded in the love of God, is first and foremost a responsibility . . . for the entire ecclesial community at every level: from the local community to the particular Church and to the Church universal in its entirety. . . . Love thus needs to be organized if it is to be an ordered service to the community" (DCE 20). Pope Benedict XVI emphasizes: "The Church's deepest nature is expressed in her three-fold responsibility: of proclaiming the word of God (*kerygma-martyria*), celebrating the sacraments (*leitourgia*), and exercising the ministry of charity (*diakonia*). These duties presuppose each other and are inseparable" (DCE 25a). I am surprised that Pope Benedict does not say a single word about deacons and/or deaconesses in this context.

(Translation from German by Neville Williamson)

Deaconesses in the Orthodox Church

Reflections and Perspectives

Thomai Chouvarda

The question about women's position in the Orthodox Church in general, as well as the issues related to women's ordination or the upgrading of women's various roles, are essentially brought into the Orthodox theological discussion through the multilateral and bilateral inter-Christian theological dialogues. In this context special attention was paid to the ancient institution of deaconesses. In our study we will try to outline the recent developments in this regard and to expose briefly this special interest in the revival of the institution of deaconesses.

The Orthodox Church reacted to the reflections and theological discussions of the 1960s that were influenced by the feminist movement by holding a meeting of thirty representatives of the church at the Orthodox Centre of the Ecumenical Patriarchate in Chambesy, Switzerland in 1974. This meeting sought full participation of men and women in the life of eucharistic community. Participants were only men. Two years later (1976), the First International Orthodox Women's Conference was held in the Monastery of Agapia in Romania, discussing the subject "The Role of Women in Society,"[1] in which Orthodox women from different countries were gathered for the first time. The meeting addressed issues such as women's position in the family, monastic life, the various ministries in the church, catechism, charity, and theological education.

1. Organized by the WCC's Department of Education and Renewal, with the subject "The Role of Women in Society."

In the context of the inter-Christian dialogue, however, the discussion on the ordination of women, improving their position and broadening their diverse roles in the revival of the ancient institution of deaconesses, dominated all the theological meetings of the time. After the historic meeting of Sheffield in 1980, with the extensive list of questions it raised and discussed,[2] the Orthodox Church was activated even more and was called upon to give its answers. Certainly, the obvious orthodox and theologically documented response is the sacrificial, self-offering ministry of men and women according to the example of Christ, the diversity of charisms and ministries, parity and equality in salvation.[3] The interest in the position of women in the church continued with the inter-Orthodox Assembly in Boston in June 1985, at which, the question of the revival of the institution of deaconesses was raised along with other vital issues.[4]

While these debates were taking place, the Ecumenical Patriarchate convened the Orthodox Congress in Rhodes in 1988, on the "Position of Women in the Orthodox Church and the Issue of Women's Ordination." One-third of the delegates were women. This conference was devoted to such issues as the mystery of the priesthood, the place of the Mother of God in the Orthodox Church, the fuller participation of women in the life of the church, and the possibility of restoring the institution of deaconesses. This inter-Orthodox meeting was an important event for Orthodox theology,[5] since its findings revealed new, fertile theological

2. C. F. Parvey, ed., *Ordination of Women in Ecumenical Perspective. Workbook for the Church's Future*, Faith and Order 105 (Geneva, 1980) 60–64.

3. 1 Cor 12:4-11: "Διαιρέσεις δὲ χαρισμάτων εἰσί, τὸ δὲ αὐτὸ Πνεῦμα· καὶ διαιρέσεις διακονιῶν εἰσι, καὶ ὁ αὐτὸς Κύριος· καὶ διαιρέσεις ἐνεργημάτων εἰσίν, ὁ δὲ αὐτός ἐστι Θεός, ὁ ἐνεργῶν τὰ πάντα ἐν πᾶσιν. ἑκάστῳ δὲ δίδοται ἡ φανέρωσις τοῦ Πνεύματος πρὸς τὸ συμφέρον . . . πάντα δὲ ταῦτα ἐνεργεῖ τὸ ἓν καὶ τὸ αὐτὸ Πνεῦμα, διαιροῦν ἰδίᾳ ἑκάστῳ καθὼς βούλεται."

4. For a detailed presentation of the subject cf. G. Limouris, Woman in Dialogue within Orthodoxy and the Ecumenical Movement in the 20th century. A historical survey, in: *Kanon* XVI (2001) 1–24.

5. "It is needless to say that this Inter-Orthodox assembly was a milestone in the history of the Orthodox Church and theology, because it was the first time that the subjects of an Inter-Orthodox Conference gave material for contemplation and speculation, while many of the Christian Churches and Denominations have officially reached their decisions on the issue of women's ordination in the ecumenical movement and assemblies of the last decades." Limouris, Woman in Dialogue, 11.

reflection on the upgrading of the position of women in the church and, in particular, on the revival of the institution of deaconesses. On the latter question the meeting especially emphasized that "[t]he apostolic order of deaconesses should be revived. It was never altogether abandoned in the Orthodox Church though it tended to fall into disuse."[6]

At the same time, the WCC Ecumenical Decade of Churches in Solidarity with Women (1988–1998) led to the convening of several inter-Orthodox meetings, such as the Second International Conference on Women's Issues (WCC) in Chania, Crete in 1990 on the topic "Church and Culture." Following the Rhodes decisions, the conference emphatically underlined the absence of female witness as well as the need for the revival of the institution of deaconesses. In the words of the final report: "The female ministry, in particular, would offer to the Church an opportunity for the faithful to experience much more widely a feminine form of ministry for which both men and women feel the need."[7]

In the following inter-Orthodox meeting in Levadia, Greece in 1994 on the topic "Orthodox Women in a United Europe," the participants discussed the immediate revival of the institution. It was additionally pointed out that the Rhodes decisions and recommendations on reviving the order of deaconesses had found no great response or implementation.

Two years later, in 1996, the same issue was discussed at another inter-Orthodox meeting,[8] this time in association with the theme of mission and evangelism. The meeting posed the question, "Why do our churches avoid with qualms and reservations the materialization of the proposal for the revival of the institution of Deaconesses, when this issue is so important and necessary?"[9]

The same concerns were discussed during the next two conferences, in Damascus in 1996 and in Istanbul in 1997 on the same subject: "Discerning the 'Signs of the Times' (Mt. 16:3). Women in the Life of the

6. G. Limouris, ed., *The Place of the Woman in the Orthodox Church and the Question of the Ordination of Women*, Interorthodox Symposium, Rhodes, Greece, October 30–November 7, 1988, Ecumenical Patriarchate (Katerini, 1992) 31.

7. Limouris, Woman in Dialogue (see n. 4), 14.

8. Held in Addis Ababa, Ethiopia, from January 19 to 27, 1996, organized by the WCC during the preparations for the World Conference on Evangelism and Mission.

9. Limouris, Woman in Dialogue (see n. 4), 15.

Orthodox Church."[10] At the first conference, women mainly from Asia, Africa, and the Middle East again raised the question of the revival of the institution of deaconesses, with the expectation "that our church leaders discern prayerfully and courageously the presence of the Holy Spirit in those many places where the ministry of ordained deaconesses, as well as other forms of ministry, are needed."[11] In Istanbul, where the participating women represented churches from Europe, Asia, the Middle East, America, and Oceania, the dominant theme was again the revival of the institution, this time ascertaining that the ancient institution, its history and contribution is not sufficiently known. Therefore, the need for further and fuller information and understanding was highlighted, whereas the final report states, "Many of us believe that the introduction of deaconesses in the life of the Church will aid the atmosphere of love and learning in the life of the Church."[12]

The interest in issues concerning the status of women and the institution of deaconesses continued. The next inter-Orthodox encounter, held in 1998 in the USA,[13] discussed the question of deaconesses in relation to the liturgical renewal and unity in the church. The importance of the role of deaconesses in the life of the church was emphasized in the conclusions of the Pan-African Orthodox Women's Meeting in Nairobi, Kenya: "We wish to unite our voices with those who support the woman deacon, because she is of great importance, since the majority of our communities is comprised of women and young people."[14]

Finally, it is worth mentioning the initiative of the Center for Ecumenical, Missionary and Environmental Studies in Thessaloniki, which, more than twenty years after the Rhodes Congress, organized an inter-

10. The conferences were held at the invitation of the WCC and blessed by four Patriarchs, s. Kyriaki Karidoyanes-FitzGerald, ed., *Orthodox Women Speak. Discerning the "Signs of Times"* (Geneva, 1999) 1.

11. Karidoyanes-FitzGerald, *Orthodox Women Speak*, 10.

12. Karidoyanes-FitzGerald, *Orthodox Women Speak*, 31.

13. The Consultation entitled "Orthodox Liturgical Renewal and Visible Unity" was held in New Skete Monastery, Cambridge, New York from May 26 to June 1, 1998 by the WCC.

14. Orthodox Conference of Women in the Life of the Church, Makarios III Seminary, Nairobi, Kenya, June 1–4, 1998, Orthodox Archbishopric of Kenya and Irinoupolis; see Limouris, Woman in Dialogue (see n. 4), 18.

national conference on "Deaconesses, the Ordination of Women and Orthodox Theology." Its intention was to provide the Orthodox Church and the global Christian community with authentic theological arguments on the subject.[15]

The Congress of Rhodes, as a milestone in this matter, as well as the subsequent inter-Orthodox meetings and the developments that occurred at them, paved the way for a series of in-depth theological studies, dissertations, or monographs that illuminate the subject from various aspects.[16] It is, of course, well known that since the 1950s, the studies of Professor E. Theodorou constitute a point of reference for the issue of deaconesses.[17] The interest in reviving the institution of deaconesses is also expressed through other actions and initiatives, such as the publishing of theological magazines (*MaryMartha*, *St. Nina's Quarterly*) or websites (Saint Catherine's Vision) that inform about the position of women in the Orthodox Church or promote the revival of the order of deaconesses.

This brief historical review demonstrates the continuous interest in strengthening the roles of women with concrete recommendations and indeed by the immediate revival of the ancient institution of deaconesses, particularly after the conference of Rhodes, which encouraged the churches to proceed to it. A second finding is that it concerns the entire Orthodox world, even if the faithful from the various local churches

15. P. Vassiliadis, N. Papageorgiou, E. Kasselouri-Hatzivassiliadi, eds., *Deaconesses, the Ordination of Women and Orthodox Theology* (Newcastle upon Tyne, 2017) 4.

16. Numerous are the publications on the topic. See, e.g., K. Yokarinis, Η ιερωσύνη των γυναικών στο πλαίσιο της οικουμενικής κίνησης (The Priesthood of Women in the Ecumenical Movement) (Katerini, 1995); K. FitzGerald, *Women Deacons in the Orthodox Church. Called to Holiness and Ministry* (Brookline, MA, 1998); T. Chouvarda, Η παρουσία της γυναίκας στη βιβλική και πατερική παράδοση των πρώτων αιώνων. Η περίπτωση των χηρών (The Presence of the Woman in the Biblical and Patristic Tradition of the First Centuries. The Case of Widows), PhD diss., Thessaloniki, 2004; D. Koukoura, Η θέση της γυναίκας στην Ορθόδοξη Εκκλησία (The Place of Women in the Orthodox Church), (Thessaloniki, 2005).

17. E. Theodorou, Ηρωίδες της χριστιανικής αγάπης. Αι διακόνισσαι δια των αιώνων (Heroines of Love. Deaconesses through the Ages) (Athens, 1949) and Η "χειροτονία" ή "χειροθεσία" των διακονισσών (The "Ordination" or "Appointment" of Deaconesses), PhD diss., Athens, 1954.

dealing with the subject have different assumptions on the role of a deaconess. The need for all the faithful to be properly informed about both the institution itself and the developments carried out in these meetings has also been emphatically pointed out. The immediate necessity of the revival of the institution of deaconesses is also stressed, as it is correlated with missionary, liturgical, pastoral, catechetical, and other contemporary demands of the church. Consequently, the actual task of theology is to be in dialogue with the problems that arise, in every age, and to offer its conclusions to the service of the church, in order to use them whenever she needs them.

Certainly the issue of the position of women is inevitably related to the issue of ordination, but this constitutes a subject in its own right. As has been pointed out, the solution to this problem that concerns the Christian world and has divided the various Christian confessions cannot be found only on the basis of arguments from sociology and tradition or arguments ex silentio. What is needed is mainly theological arguments, based on the spiritual self-consciousness of the church and the living experience and practice of the church's life. According to a prominent professor of dogmatics, it is a fact that "[f]rom the beginning to date, a long tradition has ruled out the priesthood of women. It is worth noting, however, that this exclusion has been imperceptible and tacit, without having been adopted as a dogma. On the occasion of this reflection, a very interesting and fruitful dialogue can be born, capable of overcoming all prejudice and changing forever the society itself, changing first of all the human person for the better."[18]

While, as it is commonly said, the question of women's ordination came "from outside," the issue of the ministry of deaconesses comprises an authentic, lengthy tradition of the ancient church, whose revival comes "from within," from the bosom and needs of the church. For this reason, regarding the revival of the institution, we ought to recall, point out, and examine the following historical, liturgical, canonical, and hagiographical testimonies, along with the modern pastoral needs and requirements:

18. N. Matsoukas, Η ιερωσύνη των γυναικών ως θεολογικό και οικουμενικό πρόβλημα (The Ordination of Women as a Theological and Ecumenical Problem), in: P. Vassiliadis, ed., Ορθόδοξη Θεολογία και Οικουμενικός Διάλογος (Athens, 2005) 123–27, 124.

- The history of deaconesses is a long one. Its origins are found in New Testament era and extend to the late Byzantine period. The institution fell into disuse but has never been abolished by any synodal decision of the church.[19]
- The implementation of the institution varies by places and times. It is differently experienced in East and West, while at times in concrete local churches it is flourishing and in others it becomes inactive.
- It is necessary that the real meaning and conception of diakonia (διακονία) be reexamined and emphasis given to its spiritual authority and not to the potential power to be derived from it.[20] It is a fact that in many cases authority and supremacy tendencies are creeping in that are sometimes a step for claiming attitudes and practices that go beyond the actual understanding and contribution of the diaconal ministry. The latter, moreover, concerns all the baptized believers, the "royal priesthood," who wish to respond to Christ's vocation and that is being realized through Jesus' injunction "Whosoever will come after me, let him deny himself, and take up his cross, and follow me."[21]
- Regarding the revival of the institution, its "reception"[22] by the believers is of particular importance, since information about the female diaconate is incomplete and the modern needs of the local churches

19. Although in the fourteenth century we encounter a recommendation by Patriarch Athanasios I for the inertia of the institution, possibly due to the conditions of the time, see the "ἔνταλμα" (subscription) of the Patriarch Athanasios I (1303–1309) in: V. Laurent, *Les regestes des actes du Patriarcat de Constantinople*, vol. I., *Les actes des Patriarches*, fasc. IV, *Les regestes de 1208 à 1309*, Institut Francais d'Études Byzantines (Paris, 1971), N. 1747, 526: "Ils proscriront les monastères doubles et feront cesser la coutume des diaconesses."

20. Βλ. J. Chrissavgis, Men and Women "in the Service of Christ": Reflections on the Diaconate in the Orthodox Church, in: P. Vassiliadis, N. Papageorgiou, E. Kasselouri-Hatzivassiliadi, eds., *Deaconesses* (see n. 15) 53–58, passim and G. Limouris, ed., *The Place of the Woman* (see n. 6), 29; cf. J. N. Collins, *Diakonia. Re-interpreting the Ancient Sources* (New York/Oxford, 1990) 193–263.

21. Mark 8:34.

22. D. Koukoura, Problems in the Rejuvenation of the Ministry of Deaconesses, in: P. Vassiliadis, N. Papageorgiou, E. Kasselouri-Hatzivassiliadi, eds., *Deaconesses* (see n. 15) 403–11, 410.

are different. Some churches are not even aware of the developments achieved, while others are anxiously awaiting the implementation of the Rhodes findings. It is imperative that the faithful be informed regarding the history and importance of this institution for the building up of the church, as well as the progress made in inter-Christian meetings and theological research.

- An equally significant parameter is that the revival of the institution should take into account the new conditions of reevangelization.[23]
- The fields of work and contribution of deaconesses extend to a wide range of ecclesiastical life, i.e. liturgical, pastoral, catechetical, educational, missionary and social work inside and outside the temple. At this point, it is worthwhile to mention the fields of this offer briefly.

One of the most important, well-known, and extensive areas of the ministry of deaconesses was philanthropical activities. These included visiting all those in need, the sick,[24] the mourning, needy women,[25] and imprisoned Christians, and generally caring for women's hospitali-

23. "The re-evangelization of God's people in modern, secularized societies and the evangelization of those who have still not come to know Christ remain an unceasing obligation for the Church," Message of the Holy and Great Council of the Orthodox Church, https://www.holycouncil.org/-/message?_101_INSTANCE_VA0WE2pZ4Y0I_languageId=en_US (retrieved on 20-12-2017).

24. *Didascalia Apostolorum* 16 in: A. Vööbus, *The* Didascalia Apostolorum *in Syriac*, Part 2 (CSCO 408) (Louvain, 1979) 155f. Epiphanius of Salamis, *Adversus Haereses*, PG 42, 744–45 and 824f.

25. *Constitutiones Apostolorum* III, 19 in: Metzger, *Les Constitutions Apostoliques* II (SC 329) (Paris, 1986) 160:"Εστωσαν δὲ καὶ οἱ διάκονοι ἐν πᾶσιν ἄμωμοι ὡς καὶ ὁ ἐπίσκοπος, μόνον δὲ εὐσκυλτότεροι, ἀνάλογοι πρὸς τὸ πλῆθος τῆς Ἐκκλησίας, ἵνα καὶ τοῖς ἀδυνάτοις ὑπηρετεῖσθαι δύνωνται ὡς ἐργάται ἀνεπαίσχυντοι· καὶ ἡ μὲν γυνὴ τὰς γυναῖκας σπουδάζουσα θεραπεύειν, ἀμφότεροι δὲ τὰ πρὸς ἀγγελίαν, ἐκδημίαν, ὑπηρεσίαν, δουλείαν, ὡς καὶ περὶ τοῦ Κυρίου Ἡσαΐας ἔλεγεν φάσκων, http://stephanus.tlg.uci.edu/help/BetaManual/online/Q6.html. "Δικαιῶσαι δίκαιον εὖ δουλεύοντα πολλοῖς."Εκαστος οὖν τὸν ἴδιον γνωριζέτω τόπον καὶ ἐκτελείτω αὐτὸν σπουδαίως, ὁμοφρόνως, ὁμοψύχως, γινώσκοντες τὸν τῆς διακονίας μισθόν. Ἔστωσαν δὲ καὶ ἀνεπαίσχυντοι εἰς τὸ ὑπηρετεῖσθαι τοῖς δεομένοις, ὡς καὶ ὁ Κύριος ἡμῶν Ἰησοῦς ὁ Χριστὸς οὐκ ἦλθεν διακονηθῆναι, ἀλλὰ διακονῆσαι καὶ δοῦναι τὴν ψυχὴν αὐτοῦ λύτρον ἀντὶ πολλῶν."

ty.[26] The deaconesses developed significant catechetical and missionary work for non-Christian women, instructing them in the Christian faith.[27] Among the main ministries of the deaconesses was the general supervision of the spiritual formation of Christian women, which was carried out not only in the church but also privately. They were also responsible for the virgins and widows,[28] while they could undertake the duties of an abbess. During church worship, some deaconesses worked as "doorkeepers,"[29] and were responsible for the order and decency of the women present, watching and encouraging women's participation in worship, for example, in chanting. The deaconesses undoubtedly entered the sanctuary, not only at the time of the Divine Liturgy but also in other circumstances.[30]

Deaconesses provided an important service in the celebration of the sacrament of baptism by helping the presbyters "ἐν τῷ βαπτίζεσθαι τάς γυναίκας διά τό εὐπρεπές."[31] Since infant baptism did not exist in the ancient church, the deaconesses participated in the baptism of adult women, anointing their bodies with holy oil and myrrh.[32] The distribution of the Holy Eucharist to sick women who could not attend worship

26. *Constitutiones Apostolorum* II, 58, in: Metzger, *Les Constitutions Apostoliques* I (SC 320) (Paris, 1986) 322: "Εἰ δὲ πτωχὸς ἢ ἀγενὴς ἢ ξένος ἐπέλθοι πρεσβύτης ἢ νέος τὴν ἡλικίαν καὶ τόπος οὐχ ὑπάρχει, καὶ τούτοις τόπον ποιήσει ἐξ ὅλης τῆς καρδίας αὐτοῦ ὁ διάκονος, ἵνα μὴ πρὸς ἄνθρωπον αὐτοῦ γένηται ἡ προσωπόληψις, ἀλλὰ πρὸς Θεὸν ἡ διακονία εὐάρεστος. Τὸ δ' αὐτὸ ποιείτω καὶ ἡ διάκονος ταῖς ἐπερχομέναις γυναιξὶν πτωχαῖς ἤτοι πλουσίαις."

27. Palladius, *Historia Lausiaca* CXLIV, *De Olympiade*: "Πολλάς δέ τῶν ἀπίστων κατηχήσασα γυναῖκας," PG 34, 1249.

28. *Constitutiones Apostolorum* III, 7, in: Metzger, *Les Constitutions Apostoliques* (see n. 25) 140.

29. Ps.-Ignatius, *Ad Antiochenos* XII, PG 5, 908: "Ἀσπάζομαι τάς φρουρούς τῶν ἁγίων πυλῶν, τάς ἐν Χριστῷ διακόνους. Ἀσπάζομαι τάς Χριστολήπτους παρθένας."

30. Saint Macrina, "ἐντός γενομένη τοῦ Θυσιαστηρίου, παννύχιον προσπίπτει τῷ Θεῷ τῶν ἰάσεων," Gregory of Nyssa, *Vita S. Macrinae* 31, in: P. Maraval, *Gregoire de Nysse, Vie de Sainte Macrine* (SC 178) (Paris, 1971) 244. The occasional prohibitions had no absolute character.

31. *Constitutiones Apostolorum* VIII, 28, in: Metzger, *Les Constitutions Apostoliques* III (SC 336) (Paris, 1987) 230.

32. *Constitutiones Apostolorum* III, 16, in: Metzger, *Les Constitutions Apostoliques* (see n. 25), 155–56.

was part of their liturgical activities. They also took an active part in the shrouding, decoration, and burial of Christian women.[33]

All the aforementioned ministries of the deaconesses were carried out in close cooperation with the bishop, whom they represented in the ranks of the women.[34] Sometimes they were also entrusted with particularly sensitive pastoral affairs, such as the "ἐπίσκεψις πάθους."[35] Finally, theological research on the sources has clearly proved that since the fourth century the ordination rite for deaconesses is almost the same as that for deacons.[36]

The purpose of this multifaceted ministry of women was primarily the building up of the Body of Christ. The essential presupposition for this building up, however, is the unity of the Body through the diversity of its members' gifts. The pastoral care of the church focuses on the community of men and women, namely, all its members, and the exploitation of their charisms according to their receptiveness.[37] The church bestows gifts and activates institutions to use them for the maximum benefit of its members in the perspective of salvation. Regarding the position of women, we should point out a two-sided reality, which was also acknowledged at the Congress in Rhodes: in the church as the mystical Body of Christ,

33. Gregory of Nyssa, *Vita S. Macrinae*, 29–32, in: Maraval, *Gregoire de Nysse* (see n. 30) 236–46.

34. *Constitutiones Apostolorum* III, 19, in: Metzger, *Les Constitutions Apostoliques* (see n. 25) 162–64: "Χρὴ οὖν ὑμᾶς τοὺς διακόνους ἐπισκέπτεσθαι πάντας τοὺς δεομένους ἐπισκέψεως, καὶ περὶ τῶν θλιβομένων ἀναγγέλλετε τῷ ἐπισκόπῳ ὑμῶν· ψυχὴ γὰρ αὐτοῦ καὶ αἴσθησις εἶναι ὀφείλετε, εὔσκυλτοι καὶ εὐήκοοι εἰς πάντα ὄντες αὐτῷ ὡς ἐπισκόπῳ ὑμῶν καὶ πατρὶ καὶ διδασκάλῳ."

35. Epiphanius of Salamis, *Adversus Haereses* III, II, LXXIX, PG 42, 744–45.

36. E. Theodorou, Η "χειροτονία" ή "χειροθεσία" των διακονισσών [The "Ordination" or "Appointment" of Deaconesses], 64–65.

37. Eph 4:11-16: "καὶ αὐτὸς ἔδωκε τοὺς μὲν ἀποστόλους, τοὺς δὲ προφήτας, τοὺς δὲ εὐαγγελιστάς, τοὺς δὲ ποιμένας καὶ διδασκάλους, πρὸς τὸν καταρτισμὸν τῶν ἁγίων εἰς ἔργον διακονίας, εἰς οἰκοδομὴν τοῦ σώματος τοῦ Χριστοῦ, μέχρι καταντήσωμεν οἱ πάντες εἰς τὴν ἑνότητα τῆς πίστεως καὶ τῆς ἐπιγνώσεως τοῦ υἱοῦ τοῦ Θεοῦ, εἰς ἄνδρα τέλειον, εἰς μέτρον ἡλικίας τοῦ πληρώματος τοῦ Χριστοῦ . . . ἀληθεύοντες δὲ ἐν ἀγάπῃ αὐξήσωμεν εἰς αὐτὸν τὰ πάντα, ὅς ἐστιν ἡ κεφαλή, ὁ Χριστός, ἐξ οὗ πᾶν τὸ σῶμα συναρμολογούμενον καὶ συμβιβαζόμενον διὰ πάσης ἁφῆς τῆς ἐπιχορηγίας κατ' ἐνέργειαν ἐν μέτρῳ ἑνὸς ἑκάστου μέρους τὴν αὔξησιν τοῦ σώματος ποιεῖται εἰς οἰκοδομὴν ἑαυτοῦ ἐν ἀγάπῃ."

all the baptized members are equal to the variety of gifts, while in the church as an institutional expression in the world, inequalities among its members exist.[38] Women's history in the church has been marked by revolutions or discrimination and degradation due to specific social, political, and cultural conditions in each era.[39] However, social and other constraints may temporarily lead to ecclesiastical restrictions but not to theological exclusions. This explains many of the alleged contradictions and paradoxes encountered in Orthodox Church life.[40]

In previous times, in the patriarchal structured societies that excluded women from public activities, the church offered women that liberating step in order to minister according to their virtues and gifts. In the prevailing public-domestic view of life,[41] when men participated in public life and women were occupied only with domestic activities, the church encouraged women in responsible positions in the public sphere of life. This is even more true today when women's fuller participation in public life is not only obvious but sometimes acceptable as superior to that of men.[42]

38. "It is necessary to confess in honesty and with humility, that, owing to human weakness and sinfulness, the Christian communities have not always and in all places been able to suppress effectively ideas, manners and customs, historical developments and social conditions which have resulted in practical discrimination against women." Limouris, ed., *The Place of the Woman* (see n. 6), 29.

39. For example, the time of iconoclasm, which caused many upheavals in ecclesiastical life and inevitably in the status of women, or later in the Eastern Church, the period of Ottoman rule, during which the female presence was largely marginalized because of political conditions.

40. E. Behr-Sigel's statement is characteristic: "We see there juxtaposed and intermingling the liberating message of the gospel and outmoded taboos, a theological doctrine of humankind both spiritual and personal, and misogynic stereotypes inherited from patriarchal societies." E. Behr-Sigel, K. Ware, Bishop of Diokleia, *The Ordination of Women in the Orthodox Church* (Geneva, 2000) 1.

41. E. Stegemann, W. Stegemann, *Urchristliche Sozialgeschichte. Die Anfänge im Judentum und die Christusgemeinden in der mediterranen Welt* (Stuttgart u.a., 1995) 310, 317.

42. "The Orthodox Church accepts the fuller participation of women in everyday tasks—tasks for which the women often excel and have superior qualities to those of men." Message of His All Holiness the Ecumenical Patriarch Dimitrios I.; Limouris, ed., *The Place of the Woman* (see n. 6), 18.

According to the historical evidence the institution became inactive because the ministry of deaconesses and other active orders of women, such as widows and virgins, were absorbed by the work of nuns. The contribution of the female diakonia, which was neither limited nor entirely auxiliary but rather broad and demanding, extended to a wide range of ecclesiastical functions[43] that demonstrate the dominant presence of women as gifted members with significant responsibilities. Nowadays, many of the ministries of the Byzantine deaconesses are still being performed by women, lay members of the church, with a blessing by the local bishop, while simultaneously new fields of action arise dictated by the contemporary needs of the society. For this reason, the ministry of deaconesses should be redefined in relation to the past. It should be reexamined which part of that still exists or the new fields of action that can be performed today through the revival of the deaconess ministry.[44] For example, the Patriarchate of Alexandria attempted to strengthen the role of women by reviving the institution of deaconesses in harmony with the liturgical tradition of the church. The Patriarch emphasized that the initiative of reviving the institution is connected with the pastoral and missionary needs of the church on the African continent. The institution of deaconesses was also reactivated in 2004 by a decision of the Holy Synod of the Church of Greece.

After the Symposium in Rhodes (1988), which encouraged the churches to strengthen and broaden the roles of women, we realize that some churches show particular concern for the revival of the women's diaconate up to the present, others show no interest, while others have already proceeded to make use of the gifts and roles of women.[45] The conclusions

43. "Καὶ γὰρ εἰς πολλὰς χρείας γυναικὸς χρῄζομεν διακόνου," *Constitutiones Apostolorum* III, 16 in: Metzger, *Les Constitutions Apostoliques* (see n. 25), 156.

44. Besides, in the conclusions of Rhodes it is stated: "Furthermore, would it not be possible and desirable to allow women to enter into the 'lower orders' through a blessing of the Church (Cheirothesia): sub-deacon, reader, cantor, teacher without excluding new orders that the Church might consider to be necessary? This matter deserves further study since there is no definite tradition of this sort." G. Limouris, ed., *The Place of the Woman* (see n. 6), 32.

45. The first case refers to the orthodox parishes in the Western societies, the second relates to the Eastern Slavic-speaking churches, while in Orthodox mission countries such as in the Patriarchate of Alexandria, where adult women are being instructed into the faith and baptized, the pastoral need for the ministry of deaconess is more than obvious.

of Rhodes are applied according to the needs and, where appropriate, to local churches. Changes are not rapid, since the Orthodox Church around the world does not live under the same sociocultural conditions everywhere.

The church in all the aspects of its historical presence always lived according to certain theological and ecclesiological principles, such as those of *oikonomia*, discernment, need, unity and, above all, love.[46] As it is aptly stated, "What the Orthodox Church should do is to be prepared not with damaging theological arguments but with the perfect social organization of its life, with men and women being fully equal, to bring out rich fruits of charismatic life and to cultivate education and culture."[47] In other words, all the "royal priesthood," clergy and laity, men and women, who are called to various vocations by Jesus Christ, must be aware of their responsibilities and bear witness, since "the activity of discipleship is manifested by each both in the liturgical assembly and in the liturgy of daily life in the world,"[48] especially in the modern world, where there is a great need for substantial reevangelization.

For this reason the church has always been activating institutions and making use of people's gifts, according to their distinctiveness and receptiveness, always striving for unity, as a nonnegotiable ecclesiological request, in the community of its devoted members, for the equality in the salvation of men and women on their way to the Eschaton.

46. 1 Cor 12 and 13.

47. N. Matsoukas, Η ιερωσύνη των γυναικών (see n. 18), 127.

48. Limouris ed., *The Place of the Woman* (see n. 6), 33.

IV

The Debate on the Admission of Women to Ministry

From the Perspective of Systematic Theology and Canon Law

The Debate on the Admission of Women to Ecclesial Ministry

Cultural Patterns of Justification and Theological Perspectives

Isolde Karle

Introduction

In the Protestant Church the right to the ordination of women has slowly and laboriously asserted itself in the course of the last century. It was not until the beginning of the twentieth century that women were generally admitted to university studies, and beginning with the academic year 1919–20 Protestant female theologians were able to complete their studies with a faculty examination. It then took several decades before they were allowed to become pastors, and this was fiercely contested. The arguments put forward against women's ordination were primarily cultural and social: It would be contrary to the custom and nature of women to admit them to the pastorate. The woman was supposed to be first and foremost a mother, giving birth and bringing up the children, in accordance with her place in creation. Women were supposed to be incapable of thinking intellectually, organizing, and administrating. Therefore, even at times when there were far too few pastors, a "ministry *sui generis*" was invented, assigning mostly pedagogical and pastoral-diaconal tasks to female theologians but continuing to exclude them from the ministry of proclamation of the Word and administration of the sacraments.

In 1930, Annemarie Rübens and Ina Gschlössl from the Vereinigung evangelischer Theologinnen (Association of Protestant Women Theologians) had already commented on this development in no uncertain terms. It was not theological reflection, a recourse to the cause of the Gospel and its proclamation in this world, that excluded women from the fully valid pastorate. "Let it be said quite clearly, it results from . . . a certain conviction that women are inferior, that is to say, unsuited to proper ecclesiastical office, and there are sometimes attempts to justify this attitude biblically. Further reasons behind this attitude are the notion of rivalry and the legend of the superiority of the male sex, which has long since been settled in other areas of life."[1] There was actually no more to be added, but it was not until the 1970s that most Protestant regional churches allowed the ordination of women. In Schaumburg-Lippe this did not happen until the 1990s. And it was not predominantly theological reasons that paved the way for the ordination of women, but "catching up with women's individualization"[2] in the 1960s and 1970s, which increased the pressure on the Protestant church and led to a rethinking.

Meanwhile, it is taken for granted in the EKD that women can be ordained. They are accepted without question by the congregations (even by Evangelicals, as a rule). More than 50 percent of the people studying theology at present are women. The high proportion of female theology students corresponds fairly closely to the general trend that sees more women graduating from high school than men. Just over a third of the pastors in the member churches of the EKD are female. Thus the Protestant pastorate is in the process of becoming emancipated from the male-dominated occupational profile that only applies when there is more than 30 percent female participation in one profession. Beyond that, it has become more or less normal to elect women as deans and bishops too, even though the number of female bishops is relatively small at the moment. But on a global and ecumenical level there is still much to be done in the churches, including the Lutheran churches. For example, the Lutheran Church in Latvia decided in 2016 to revoke the ordination of women. This required a constitutional amendment with a three-quarters

1. I. Gschlössl/A. Rübens, Ein notwendiges Wort in Sachen der Theologinnen, in: *Die christliche Welt* 44 (1930) 216–20, 218.

2. On this expression cf. the groundbreaking essay by E. Beck-Gernsheim, Vom "Dasein für andere" zum Anspruch auf ein Stück "eigenes Leben." Individualisierungsprozesse im weiblichen Lebenszusammenhang, in: *Soziale Welt* 34 (1983) 307–40. See also I. Karle, *Der Pfarrberuf als Profession. Eine Berufstheorie im Kontext der modernen Gesellscahft* (3rd ed., Gütersloh, 2011) 283.

majority, which was actually achieved in the synod. An authoritarian system could not afford a liberal theology, was the shameful explanation of Archbishop Vanags.[3]

Why does the question of women still provoke such intense reaction when it comes to access to offices in the church? What deep-seated fears continue to play a role here? What are the theological and cultural lines of argument justifying further exclusion? I want to explore these questions in this article, starting with the creation stories, which usually serve as a basis for the arguments against the equality of women; after that, I will add a few thoughts on the way the modern professionalization of the pastorate affects the gender question.[4]

1. Lines of Argument Derived from the Bible and Culture

When ecclesiastical statements refer to the creation narratives, one can often detect attempts to elicit from these texts an ontological theory and anthropology of the sexes that is independent of history, as it were. Such an interpretation is not only unhistorical, but it also misses the point of the creation narratives.[5] The stories of creation do not present teaching about the nature of the sexes but are, rather, classical etiologies trying to explain present experiences with the help of a past event. I will briefly outline the most important interpretations.

1.1 The Story of Paradise (Gen 2–3)

Let us first turn to the narrative in Gen 2–3, the so-called Story of Paradise. It has had a particularly stigmatizing effect on women—the woman is supposedly created as a subordinate helper for the man. Recent exegetical research has now drawn attention to the fact that, although the narrative originated in an androcentric context, on closer look it is surprisingly critical of the patriarchy. This begins with the first human,

3. https://www.evangelisch.de/inhalte/135040/01-06-2016/lutherische-kirche-lettland-will-frauenordination-abschaffen (08.02.2018).

4. Cf. for more on this question: I. Karle, Pfarrerinnen im Pfarrberuf: Gender und Professionalität, in: *Grüß Gott, Frau Pfarrerin: 40 Jahre Theologinnenordnung – Aufbrüche zur Chancengleichheit* (Gütersloh, 2009) 101–24.

5. Cf. I. Praetorius, *Anthropologie und Frauenbild in der deutschsprachigen Protestantischen Ethik seit 1949* (2nd ed., Gütersloh, 1994) 85.

Adam, who is usually naturally thought to be a man. However, in the story Adam is not initially conceived as the first man, but as the first human being, as yet sexually undifferentiated. "Adam" is a sexually undifferentiated earth-being, created from the ground, *adamah*. If you like, "Adam" is a hermaphrodite or androgynous and only becomes *isch* and *ischah*, man and woman, through the division.[6] The point of the narrative is not the introduction of the woman into human history as an inferior helper, but the problem of human loneliness. This problem can only be solved by an opposite number on an equal footing. That is why Adam is also disappointed when the animals are brought to him first of all. People need other people in order to be human, someone to speak to them, to challenge and support them. The formula of kinship therefore emphasizes *the unlikely similarity* of the first two humans, not their difference ("This at last is bone of my bones and flesh of my flesh!").

In addition, the account of the joy that they share in sexuality still does not make any reference to reproduction and the risks and burdens of birth. Surprisingly, the formula in Gen 2:24 states that *a man* leaves his father and mother and binds himself to his wife (clings to her), not vice versa, although this matrilinearity was not foreseen in ancient Israel. The Catholic Old Testament scholar Erich Zenger therefore also sees Gen 2 as a *utopian draft contrasting with the oppressive patriarchal everyday reality*.[7] Gen 2 is a fictitious "alternative to the universally established patriarchal order."[8] Gen 3, the so-called Fall of Man, on the other hand, describes the regrettable existing state of affairs, making it clear that the punishment of Gen 3:16 ("Your husband shall rule over you") is not to be read as confirmation of patriarchy, but as God's own regret at patriarchal everyday life: it was not supposed to be like this. God's intention at the creation was different. The masculine hegemony described in Gen 3:16 is the result of sin and therefore is embedded in neither natural law

6. Cf. F. Crüsemann, Eva—die erste Frau und ihre "Schuld." Ein Beitrag zu einer kanonisch-sozialgeschichtlichen Lektüre der Urgeschichte, in: *Bibel und Kirche* 53 (1998) 2–10, 3.

7. Cf. E. Zenger, Die Schöpfungsgeschichte der Genesis im Kontext des Alten Orient, in: *Welt und Umwelt der Bibel. Archäologie und Geschichte* 1 (1996) 20–33, 32.

8. H. Spieckermann, Ambivalenzen. Ermöglichte und verwirklichte Schöpfung in Gen 2f., in: A. Graupner et al., eds., *Verbindungslinien. FS W. H. Schmidt* (Neukirchen-Vluyn, 2000) 363–76, 368.

nor God's order of creation. It indicates the perversion of God's good intentions. The vast majority of Old Testament scholars agree that the story of Paradise was not supposed to legitimize an asymmetric gender relationship or to present it as God's will.

1.2 The Creation Story in Genesis 1

We find the second creation narrative in Genesis 1 with the crucial verse with the greatest historical impact, verse 27: "God created humankind in his image, / in the image of God he created them; / male and female he created them." This text had a much more fundamental effect. To this day, it has been used to assert and justify a fundamental difference between the nature of women and the nature of men, in the sense of the modern bourgeois gender role model of opposing gender-differentiated virtues, abilities, character traits, attitudes, ways of thinking, and patterns of perception. On the one hand, this is unhistorical because, as already mentioned, this model only developed in the modern era. On the other hand, the modern, complementary gender role model superficially suggests that man and woman are on eye level with each other—each of them, being completely different, needs the other as a complementary counterpart in order to form a whole—but is in fact accompanied by clearly asymmetrical notions of status. For the role of the "virtuous housewife" and mother was and is assigned to women, whereas men must venture out into hostile life and are thus the ones who hold social power.

A polarizing differentiation between women and men always goes hand in hand with discriminating consequences and always produces an imbalance in which one side benefits significantly more than the other from power and social participation. This also applies to the interpretation of Gen 1:27, as we find it in the Letter on the Collaboration of Men and Women in the Church and in the World issued by the Congregation for the Doctrine of the Faith.[9] Here, too, this passage is used to establish the fundamental complementarity of man and woman at all levels and to perpetuate it for eternity: "Their equal dignity as persons is realized as physical, psychological and ontological complementarity" (8). Man

9. Congregation for the Doctrine of the Faith (CDF), Letter to the Bishops of the Catholic Church on the Collaboration of Men and Women in the Church and in the World (Rome, 2004) http://www.va/roman_curia/congregations/cfaith/documents/rc_con_cfaith_doc_20040731_collaboration_en.html.

and woman are considered to be completely and fundamentally bipolar. The explanations show that this intrinsic complementarity goes hand in hand with very different opportunities for inclusion: thus it lies in the nature of the woman to exercise restraint. It excluded their participation in social power and leadership. At the same time, the text praises the woman for her love of what is concrete, which is the opposite of abstractions and thus of reason and rationality.[10] As much as the woman is praised for her emotions, intuition, and care, so little is she apparently capable of cognitive, rational, and abstract thinking. The mythologization and idealization of femininity cannot conceal the simultaneous stigmatization of "the woman."

The decisive factor for our context is first of all this: the patterns of interpretation used by the Vatican are not taken directly from Holy Scripture but are typically modern patterns of explanation and gender clichés that first emerged in the eighteenth and nineteenth centuries. It was not until the private and public spheres were separated in the modern era that the sexes were polarized and dichotomized, assigning the women completely to the family and men to their work and public engagement. In Luther's day, such a strict division of labor would have been inconceivable. Therefore, despite his patriarchal view of the world, Luther could well imagine women working as teachers and could speak of his wife Katharina von Bora as "My Lord Katie." However, the gender metaphysics developed by the bourgeoisie, especially in Romanticism, was only consistently practiced in the nineteenth and even well into the twentieth century in the upper middle classes. The bourgeois "mother myth"[11] ensured that the role of mother was expanded in a way never seen before. The working class and the rural population did not attribute particular roles to the genders, for they could not afford to do so. It was not until the "golden age of marriage" in the 1950s that the model became more or less established throughout society, leading to a renewed reduction in women's gainful employment, which had begun to become established in the 1920s.[12]

10. Cf. CDF, On the Collaboration of Men and Women, 13.

11. I. Karle, *"Da ist nicht mehr Mann noch Frau . . . " Theologie jenseits der Geschlechterdifferenz* (Gütersloh, 2006), particularly chap. 4, 121–60.

12. Cf. H. Tyrell, Ehe und Familie—Institutionalisierung und Deinstitutionalisierung, in: K. Lüscher, F. Schultheis, M. Wehrspaun, eds., *Die "postmoderne" Familie. Familiale Strategien und Familienpolitik in einer Übergangszeit* (Konstanz, 1988) 145–56, 153.

Meanwhile, it is obvious that the bourgeois gender role model is exactly what it says—*a model, a social construction*. There is nothing about it that is timeless or transhistorical. This is true from both a synchronic and a diachronic perspective. In Western societies, too, the complementarity model is becoming more and more recognizable as a model: women have become increasingly individualized and their ways of life pluralized due to "women catching up on individualisation" (Beck-Gernsheim) in recent decades. Women participate in education and sometimes even overtake men or boys at school and university. This gives them completely new opportunities to participate in society and help shape it. They can get married and have children, but they do not have to. And if they do have children, they are no longer banished to privacy, but can continue to go to work. It is therefore no longer possible to speak of "the woman" or "the man"; there is, rather, a great individual diversity of women and men.[13] The fact that women are very well capable of thinking abstractly and exercising political power competently and responsibly over a long period of time is demonstrated not least by Federal Chancellor Angela Merkel. Forbes magazine voted her the world's most powerful woman for the seventh time in a row in 2017.[14]

But how is Gen 1:27 now to be interpreted, if we do not read modern gender metaphysics into this text? What is innovative and surprising about Gen 1:27 is the likeness to God, to which only the Pharaoh was entitled in ancient oriental royal ideology, but which is indiscriminately attributed to all human beings in this creation narrative. Gen 1:27 thus propagates a *democratizing and egalitarian tendency*. Not only the king, but all people are called to be the image of God and to shape the world according to God's will.[15] It is not the bisexualism of the human being that is in the foreground here, but rather the fact that in view of the humans' theomorphism no distinction can or may be made between males and females. The point of the text is precisely that there is no difference in status between man and woman, but that all are included. It is the

13. In November 2017, the Federal Constitutional Court took this diversity into consideration and called for the introduction of a third gender category in official registers: http://www.zeit.de/gesellschaft/zeitgeschehen/2017-11/bundesverfassungs gericht-fuer-drittes-geschlecht-im-geburtenregister (08.02.2018).

14. https://www.forbes.com/profile/angela-merkel/ (08.02.2018).

15. Cf. A. Schüle, Made in the "Image of God," The Concepts of Divine Images in Gen 1–3, in: *Zeitschrift für die Alttestamentliche Wissenschaft* 117 (2005) 1–20, 8.

inclusiveness of God-likeness that is emphasized here, not the bipolarity of the sexes.

1.3 New Creation in Christ

From the beginning, Christianity was not just a religious conviction but also a certain way of life, a practice expressed in new social forms. With his message of the kingdom of God and his deliberate inclusion of those usually excluded, Jesus himself demonstrated how social and cultural boundaries can be transcended. The sick, the sinners and prostitutes, the "lost," the weary and heavy laden, people from other ethnic groups—they should all be accepted and no longer excluded. Paul takes up this message and develops it further. In Gal 3:28 this boundary-crossing perspective of the Christian faith is expressed in a pronounced way: "There is no longer Jew or Greek, there is no longer slave or free, there is no longer male and female; for all of you are one in Christ Jesus." In a remarkably radical fashion, the early Christian baptismal formula declares that customary social differences are no longer relevant. That in Christ the distinction between Jew and Greek no longer applies is a sign of the universal breadth of Christianity: in Christ, ethnic differences are no longer decisive. Neither does social rank determine the value of a person. Even the distinction between man and woman loses its discriminatory character. This is the beginning of a new coexistence of men and women.

It is interesting to notice that modern exegesis had no problem with the first two pairings that Paul names. But the notion that the new creation in Christ had also profoundly relativized the gender difference was almost inconceivable in the modern era, so that it was only in the last few decades that exegetes acknowledged that it was indeed meant seriously. Gal 3:28 is not simply a utopia, but a "report of what was actually happening in the Pauline churches."[16] Here there was a living community which "was no longer structured according to discriminatory demarcations and distinctions as in the customary forms of social life"[17] but transcended them. The New Testament exegete Hans Dieter Betz formulates clearly "that in the Christian church the gender differences between men and women

16. J. Roloff, *Die Kirche im Neuen Testament* (Göttingen, 1993) 91.

17. Roloff, *Die Kirche*, 91.

have become meaningless."[18] The barriers between men and women are broken down as an expression of the new creation in Christ; differences of gender are profoundly relativized and transformed.

Paul therefore cooperated quite naturally with women in leadership positions—with Junia, the apostle, with Phoebe, the leader and "deacon" of the congregation of Cenchreae, with Prisca, the preacher in Rome, Corinth, and Ephesus. Women were decisive in supporting and shaping the early Christian movement. Relativizing gender borders did not, and does not, mean that human beings are pressed into uniformity, as is repeatedly claimed; quite the opposite is true: it enables the liberating development of experiences beyond culturally imposed constraints, it is about a plurality of identities, charisms, and talents that cannot be forced into a corset of gender stereotypes. There is no justification for preventing women from further developing such abilities and talents in the name of Jesus Christ, whether as volunteers or in a paid capacity.

2. Women in the Pastoral Profession: Gender Perspectives

This extensive reference to biblical traditions seemed necessary to me, because the recourse to supposedly timeless biblical truths still determines the arguments against women's ordination, and not least because the Congregation for the Doctrine of the Faith in its reading of the creation stories concludes that women cannot enter the priesthood. The woman was created by nature to be there for the other person and could therefore not be "self" in the same way as the man. Her real purpose was to be seen in the area of the family or in activities similar to those of a family ("actions which elicit life, and contribute to the growth and protection of the other").[19]

Gender research shows us that these ideas are contingent and historically relative, that they are neither biblical nor covered by the highly plural experiences of women in the present. Despite all emancipation and despite all progress with regard to equality between women and men, we are nevertheless still strongly determined by the modern bourgeois,

18. H. D. Betz, *Der Galaterbrief. Ein Kommentar zum Brief des Apostels Paulus an die Gemeinde in Galatien* (Munich, 1988) 344.

19. CDF, On the Collaboration of Men and Women, 13.

dichotomous patterns of perception, accompanied by feminization and masculinization of our bodies, so that we perceive men and women differently even when they are doing the same thing, such as undertaking the same tasks as pastors.

Despite admitting women to ordination, it was often questioned in the Protestant Church whether female pastors were not quite different from their male colleagues. Difference feminism in particular has been trying to suggest that women pastors are better people: more intuitive, more emotional, less interested in power, socially more competent, less authoritarian, and so on. Such attributions do not just read like a modernized form of the gender arrangement of recent centuries, but they also appear to be suspect. Apart from that, it is always problematic to attribute special abilities to a certain group of people because such an attribution is always stereotypical and does not take the individual person with his or her charisms into account, and, on the other hand, it always implies devaluations and exclusions. Erving Goffman already pointed out this mechanism in the 1970s and emphasized that the glorification of women's abilities was part of their discrimination. According to Goffman, the enhancement of femininity serves as compensation for everyday sexism.[20] "Although women are considered to be below men, they are credibly idealised and mythologised by such values as maternity, innocence, gentleness, sexual attractiveness, and so on."[21] Goffman therefore warns against any kind of idealization of females that could turn out to be a dubious blessing.

Professions encourage a relativization of gender. The most important point is whether a person is able to perform a task competently, not whether he or she is male or female. This is why the guiding social orientation in our modern society is individual performance, independent of gender and origin. Gender attribution indeed exists as a background expectation in every interaction, but it is by no means always in the forefront. For example, when suffering a bereavement, people are primarily interested in pastoral care that is sensitive, supportive, and competent, not in whether the pastor is a man or a woman.

20. E. Goffman, Das Arrangement der Geschlechter, in: H. A. Knoblauch, ed., *Interaktion und Geschlecht* (Frankfurt a.M., 1994) 105–58, 109.

21. Goffman, Das Arrangement der Geschlechter.

In professions such as the "male profession" of the Protestant pastor, both sexes increasingly make use of the behavioral repertoire of the other sex, thus diminishing the polarization of gender opposition. A female pastor in a cassock is no longer wearing a male symbol, as used to be the case, but signals that she is an academic and a preacher in her own right. Similarly, the sermon from the pulpit, administration of the sacraments, or reference to the biblical-Christian tradition can no longer be identified as substantially male activities. Thus, in Protestantism, when it comes to the conception and practice of the ministry or the dogmatic orientation, one can no longer differentiate within the pastorate along the lines of gender distinction. Since the number of female pastors in the Protestant church has increased significantly, the male pastor can no longer be regarded as the prototype of a cleric. When women take over men's activities, and men those of women, it no longer makes sense to define activities, occupations, qualities, competences, or abilities according to gender differentiation.

And yet, gender difference can still play an important role in certain contexts. In pastoral care, for example, some women specifically seek advice from female pastors, especially when they have problems with men in their marriage, in the family, or at work. On the other hand, it is also true that men usually find it easier to admit their weaknesses to a male pastor rather than to a woman, to acknowledge their brokenness and give way to feelings and tears. Therefore, it is still sensible to differentiate between the work of women and of men for certain groups of people and in certain circumstances. Overall, however, the individuality of the clerical person and his or her professional and pastoral competence are likely to be of much greater importance with regard to successful interaction with people seeking spiritual help and accompaniment. At any rate, this is confirmed by the church membership studies of the EKD, which indicate a very high acceptance of women pastors among the population.

The pioneer female theologians understood and fulfilled their ministry in very different ways. Some attached particular importance to their "otherness," others crossed the gender borders boldly and self-confidently. Their courageous behavior and their identification with their profession have changed the face of the church. They have contributed significantly to the fact that the pastorate is oriented toward criteria of professionalism and no longer toward those of gender. Many of them lived to a great old age. According to their biographers, this resulted not least from the fact that they loved their work above all else, in spite of all the difficulties. They should be to us an incentive and a role model.[22]

(Translation from German by Neville Williamson)

22. Cf. Hannelore Erhart et al., eds., *Dem Himmel so nah—dem Pfarramt so fern. Erste evangelische Theologinnen im geistlichen Amt* (Neukirchen-Vluyn, 1996) 5; I. Karle, *Der Pfarrberuf als Profession. Eine Berufstheorie im Kontext der modernen Gesellschaft* (3rd ed., Gütersloh, 2011) 281–310, particularly 310.

Jesus Was a Man . . . —So What?

A Functional and Nonsexualized Understanding of Ministry in Anthropological Terms

Saskia Wendel

1. "Only men can act in persona Christi . . ."!?

"Only a baptized man (*vir*) validly receives sacred ordination" (CIC, can. 1024)—a plain and simple sentence that is explained in the *Catechism of the Catholic Church*: "The Lord Jesus chose men (*viri*) to form the college of the twelve apostles, and the apostles did the same when they chose collaborators to succeed them in their ministry. . . . The Church recognizes herself to be bound by this choice made by the Lord himself. For this reason the ordination of women is not possible" (1577).[1] It is an argument based on tradition or authority that is brought forward to justify the practice of exclusion, but the logical reasoning of such arguments is rather weak, given that the cited tradition has meanwhile been called into question by exegetes and church historians, and even been undermined by Pope Francis, who has recognized Mary Magdalene as the *apostola apostolorum.*[2] Nonetheless, it is quoted in numerous doctrinal statements when it comes to legitimizing the exclusion of women from the ecclesial ordained ministries,[3] or one argues from the perspective of legal positivism, not just according to the norm of the CIC that is quoted,

1. https://www.vatican.va/archive/ENG0015/__P4X.HTM.

2. The potentially explosive power of this decision may not yet have become clear. It means that Francis has officially abolished male exclusivity in the apostolic ministry.

3. Cf. CDF, *Inter Insigniores*.

but above all by attempting to interpret John Paul II's rejection of the ordination of women in *Ordinatio Sacerdotalis* as an infallible statement; however, this assessment, too, is the subject of great controversy among experts on canon law.

Alongside the well-known argument referring to tradition, there are also attempts to justify the practice of the exclusion of women from the ordained ministries with a systematic argument combining anthropological, christological, and ecclesiological positions and focusing on Jesus' masculinity. The priest acts *in persona Christi* as head and bridegroom of the church or congregation, which is understood as the "bride of Christ." Since Jesus was a man, he could also only be represented by men, and only men could assume the function of the bridegroom and counterpart of the (implied female) church.[4] However, it is not without a certain irony that the US-American feminist theologian Mary Daly made use of the same argument, albeit as justification for the fact that Christianity was irreparably patriarchal. Daly's core sentence, in which she thought she had summarized the central problem of Christianity, reads: "If God is male, then . . . the male must be God."[5] For Daly, it is particularly the belief in incarnation that means that God is male. The Logos becomes flesh in a male body, and through the Logos "becoming man," not just "becoming human," God communicates not just "something," but himself. According to (neo-)Chalcedonian Christology, the Logos bears both divine and human nature, and since, firstly, it has taken on masculine human nature and, secondly, the aspects of the one nature can be said to apply to the other one, masculine nature is embedded in the divine nature of the Logos. Now because the Logos is identical in origin and essence with the other two Persons of the Godhead, God himself is male. According to Daly this is the most important reason for the exclusion of

4. Cf. CDF, *Inter Insigniores* 5; on this cf. also G. L. Müller, Kann nur der getaufte Mann gültig das Weihesakrament empfangen? Zur Lehrentscheidung in Ordinatio sacerdotalis, in: Müller, ed., *Frauen in der Kirche—Eigensein und Mitverantwortung* (Würzburg, 1999) 278–356; Müller, Hat die Kirche die Vollmacht, Frauen das Weihesakrament zu spenden?, in: *Stimmen der Zeit* 230 (2012) 374–84.

5. M. Daly, Jenseits von Gottvater, Sohn und Co. Aufbruch zu einer Philosophie der Frauenbefreiung (4th ed., Munich, 1986) 33; English, *Beyond God the Father: Toward a Philosophy of Women's Liberation* (rev. ed., Boston, 1993).

women from ecclesial office, which represents Christ. Since he is male, only men can represent him.

Many find the thesis absurd that because Jesus was a man, only men can represent him and women cannot be admitted to ordained ministries. But it is not as ridiculous as many people think. It is the key element of justification in a hegemonic, excluding discourse, and it is also anything but irrational, but follows a certain logic. If one goes along with it, the argument even gains a disconcerting consistency. Whoever does not wish to tacitly accept the exclusion of women from ordination but is rather pushing for a change in this practice of exclusion, is forced to refute the argument, knowing full well that for the time being this theoretical undertaking will change nothing at all in practical terms. For power structures can only be changed by means of the performative construction of opposition on the level of practical action; but since we are talking here precisely about concrete discourses on power, it is also necessary to deconstruct these discourses and their narratives of legitimation. First of all, I will speak here about the premises and lines of argumentation[6] in order to go on to present a criticism of this argumentation.

2. The Components of the Argument "Jesus was a man . . ."

The argument that Jesus was a man, that therefore only men can represent him, and only men can act *in persona Christi*, is composed of the following preconditions and lines of argumentation:

First: The argument is founded on a substance ontological anthropology: everything that exists is determined in its specific difference to other things existing by an inherent unchangeable nature or substance; this also applies to the being known as "man."

Second: This substance ontology now also applies to sexual difference, which, according to the line of argumentation, is not an accidental supplement to human nature, but an essential element of it. Thus it is not so that only one human nature exists, but there is also an equally unchangeable, clearly defined male and female nature, also determined

6. I abstain from any judgment as to whether this argument is justified in referring to the tradition of the Church—such judgment lies in the field of patristicians and historians of theology. I simply refer to the argument put forward in *Inter Insigniores*, for example.

by substantial male and female characteristics, linked and related to anatomical characteristics.

Third: The traditional understanding of incarnation together with the doctrine of two natures is based on this anthropology of substance ontology, whereby the Logos, corresponding to the essential connection between human nature and sexual difference, assumes in the man Jesus of Nazareth not only human nature, but specific male nature.

Fourth: An understanding of the sacrament of holy orders is also derived from the anthropology of substance ontology. According to this, the person consecrated receives a special and ineradicable characteristic that is implanted into his general "human nature" and produces an ontological difference. Human nature is the carrier of this characteristic, but since it is always sexually differentiated, it not only based on "being human" but also on "being a man" or "being a woman." The *character indelebilis*, however, has not only a substance ontological but also a participation ontological component: it means that the consecrated person shares ontologically in another reality—that of Christ. The characteristic implanted into the consecrated body by the act of consecration implies the incorporation into another dimension of being, into the universal Corpus Christi.

Fifth: The body of Christ, in which the consecrated person shares, is on the one hand a universal saving space, that is to say, a kind of cosmic dimension in analogy to the saving space shared by all who have been baptized, and on the other hand the church, the mystical body of Christ. Furthermore, the consecrated person also participates in the individual body of Jesus, namely, with regard to the understanding of participation as representation. In his participation in the Corpus Christi, the consecrated person represents at the same time the individual Christ in his action of salvation and redemption. Representation here is an ontological, nonfunctional term: what is meant is real presence, not mere reference—presentation as a real symbol, not just a meaningful indication. The "Body of Christ," whether in the universal or individual sense, is now clearly configured as masculine, analogous to the masculine body of Jesus and to the essential masculinity of the Logos made flesh. The person who participates in it and represents it must correspond to this reality. The male Christ can therefore only be represented by a person corresponding to him in all his nature, that is, one who has not only a human nature but also a man's nature. Therefore, according to this logic, the consecration of women is considered *nullum*. Because, so to speak, the *character indelebilis* has the wrong carrier, it does not find its ontologically necessary foundation.

Sixth: But it is also important to see that the body of Christ is not connoted as entirely masculine. It is considered "male" in view of the activity of the consecrated person acting *in persona Christi*, but at the same time it is also connoted as female in view of the addressees of this action. This corresponds to the binary coding: active/male/form—female/passive/substance. "Male" is the head of the church and those who represent it, "female" are the members of the church, the congregation, or finally the church itself, insofar as it is not just the subject of saving action, but also a passive, receiving object. As such, the church is "Bride of Christ" and "Mother of all believers." Here again an anthropological aspect comes into play with regard to the question of ministry, this time with regard to the doctrine of creation "in the image of God" and its significance for the anthropology of the sexes. It is a question of the thesis of complementarity: as images of God, man and woman are basically equal in dignity and also equal in value, but not the same. According to this thesis, sexual difference marks an essential difference in the equality of the image of God: man and woman complement each other and need each other in their divergence from each other, and their differences are not interpreted as social but as natural and thus necessary and unchangeable.

What is regarded as anthropologically valid now also applies with respect to the ecclesial office. The promise of salvation with a male connotation needs to be correspondingly complemented and supplemented by the acceptance of salvation with a female connotation; the person acting *in persona Christi* (male, active) requires the complementary counterpart of the congregation (female, passive), and vice versa. Only in this way is it possible that they fit together in the presupposed complementarity: priest and congregation, bridegroom and bride.

The *conclusio* follows from the anthropological, Christological, and ecclesiological preconditions mentioned above. Only men can be consecrated, because only they bring with them the necessary ontological preconditions enabling them truly to act *in persona Christi*. With this systematically justified argument, the door to the opening of the ordained ministries to women, which seemed to have opened a crack because of the epistemological fragility of the tradition argument mentioned at the beginning and because of Mary Magdalene's recognition as "Apostle of the Apostles," now seems to be permanently closed. But the argument is not as convincing as it seems *prima facie*; on the contrary, its premises can be criticized, calling into question the validity of the conclusion drawn from them.

3. Criticism of the Argument

3.1 "Substance Ontology" and "Sexual Difference"

The entire argument is based on substance ontology, but this position is anything but self-evident; it had only attained such effectivity because Aristotelian Thomism has enjoyed priority in the thinking of Catholic fundamental theology and dogmatics. But there were also non-Aristotelian theological models in which substance ontology did not play a dominant role, such as Meister Eckhart's theory of the soul or the theology of the Cusanus, and substance ontology was philosophically criticized from various quarters. One may recall, for example, Immanuel Kant's reference to the involvement of substance metaphysics in the transcendental illusion of theoretical reason, or Martin Heidegger's renunciation of the abstract, eternal, and unhistorical essence in favor of the concrete, historical, relational existence of being. These criticisms deprive substance ontology of its alleged plausibility and make the arguments it presupposes vulnerable. Criticism of substance ontology now also has a particular influence on its reference to sexual difference; the "myth of what is obvious," namely, a given eternal and unchangeable "male" and "female" nature, connected with an equally eternal "human nature," becomes caught up in the transcendental illusion mentioned above, that is, the confusion of a thing in itself with its appearance. It also ignores the aspect that reality is not immediately recognized, but that this recognition only occurs in the interplay of receptive perception and spontaneous understanding and through the use of common language. Reality is not simply always existent, but it is also constructed or generated, and this also applies to sexual difference.[7] Furthermore, there is a

7. Cf. in detail S. Wendel, Sexualethik und Genderperspektive, in: K. Hilpert, ed., *Zukunftshorizonte katholischer Sexualethik* (Freiburg i.Br., 2011) 36–56; Wendel, Subjekt statt Substanz? Entwurf einer gendersensiblen Anthropologie, in: H. Landweer, C. Newmark, C. Kley, S. Miller, eds., *Philosophie und die Potentiale der Gender Studies. Peripherie und Zentrum im Feld der Theorie* (Bielefeld, 2012) 315–35.

naturalistic or biological fallacy between what is and what ought to be, if one deduces from anatomical features an unchangeable bisexual natural order, that is, if one attributes the binary code "male/female" entirely to an apparently given sexually differentiated substance together with corresponding natural characteristics. Thus there is more "gender" in "sex" than is often assumed; anatomical features are loaded to suit a binary coding and sociocultural characteristic of male/female, and conversely male/female are constructed as forms of power in discursive body practices. But if substance ontology does not apply, so that there is also no previous "human nature" or a "male or female nature," then the argument "Jesus was a man . . . " loses its supporting foundation. In addition, it loses its claim to universal validity, since other anthropological forms of thought also exist.

3.2 Gender Complementarity

Alongside substance ontology, the complementarity thesis is anthropologically and ecclesiologically significant for the argument. This presupposes, first, the above-mentioned binary code of bisexuality, underpinned by substance ontology, and second, in this thesis, difference is not only understood as diversity, but identified with inequality. This often leads to a problematic requirement that refers to Aristotle's notion of distributive justice, requiring that whatever is not equal should be treated unequally. According to this view, men and women are complementary to each other, but exactly for this reason they supplement each other in a relationship of matching and correlation; this alone is regarded as "natural" (or in theological terms as "God-given"), such as the apparently natural, given complementarity of sexual difference. They supplement each other by assuming different positions, functions, and tasks or roles, which are regarded as noninterchangeable, thanks to the natural condition of sexual difference to which they are attributed—equivalent, but not equal. The anthropological thesis of complementarity thus becomes the basis of an ethic that concludes from the alleged "being" of the "male/female" sexes in their complementary behavior that they "ought" to correspond to this being in their striving and desire and to fulfill it by their practice. According to this view, a person who does not conform to this behavior is intending, living, and acting "unnaturally"—in the eyes of religion in opposition to God's will in creation—and deliberately refusing to fulfill what "ought" to be done according to the "being," the natural, God-intended order. This is considered to be a wrong, misguided, "sinful" use of the freedom of will and action. If, on the other hand, it becomes clear that in spite of the existence of anatomical features (which no one denies, not even Butler[8]), no sexually differentiated "natures" and characteristics can be derived from them, then the complementarity thesis also loses its ontological basis—and thus also its plausibility.

3.3 "Male" Priest and "Female" Congregation in a Complementary Relationship and Partnership

Those anthropological positionings are also ecclesiologically relevant, because the construct described—a binary, complementary bisexuality reflecting socially dominant gender discourses and bodily practices—also establishes the traditional determination of the relationship between Christ and the church, thus also between clergy and laity, or priests and congregation, whereby here the organic model of the "members and body" analogy is virulent. Christ, configured as male, is the head of his body, but at the same time also the "bridegroom" of his "bride," the church. This model corresponds to the construct of a quasi-natural, God-given, matching, and yet complementary relationship between clergy and laity, between priest and congregation with their respective differing functions and tasks. The "female" congregation, so the idea goes, needs a "male" counterpart, for otherwise the complementary relationship cannot be achieved. But if the idea of a complementarity of the sexes ultimately relies on constructs of "male/female," then the assertion of a quasi-naturally given complementarity of (male) priest and (female) congregation collapses, especially since here again gender constructs are tacitly at work; this applies furthermore to constructs concerning the function of the ordained ministry and that of the congregation and the laity: "priest-active-shaping-speaking-male" versus "congregation-passive-accepting-listening-female."[9]

8. Cf. J. Butler, *Die Macht der Geschlechternormen und die Grenzen des Menschlichen* (Frankfurt a.M., 2009).

9. In this context, reference can also be made to the understanding of representation and thus also of the representative function of the ministry. Representation is not necessarily synonymous with ontologically graded participation in another reality, in other words, a Platonic understanding of representation, nor with the direct, unmediated and unbroken presence of one reality in another. Rather, representation

3.4 Incarnation in a "Male Nature"

The problem arising from the substance-ontologically determined construct of sexual difference and the thesis of complementarity now becomes particularly obvious with regard to the understanding of the ordained ministry and its restriction to men in the context of Christology, above all with respect to the understanding of incarnation. As already mentioned, Mary Daly had already pointed this out. Should both substance ontology and the complementarity thesis prove to be implausible, this has consequences for the classical formulations of Chalcedonian Christology, which are coded substance-ontologically or essentialistically: the Logos in Jesus of Nazareth assumed neither "human nature" nor "male nature," so that God's "becoming human" was not necessarily connected with a "being made man" either, regardless of its not only inspiratory but also incarnational character. This also applies to the aspect of embodiment in an individual body that, like all bodies, was determined and interpreted according to indubitably existent anatomical features with gender codes, that is, following the socially effective binary code "male/female." The inherent sexual difference of the body, and the fact that an identity of belonging or marking could be derived from it, is by no means "more original" or "more natural" than other determinations of belonging and identity markers, such as ethnic or social categories. "Gender" is one category of diversity (among others), not a definition of the essence of human nature—and that was the case with Jesus of Nazareth as with all human beings.

---

takes place in the mode of negative depiction and can never fully and completely represent what it wishes to demonstrate. It is necessary to relate this understanding of representation in the sense of a constantly "broken presence," a simultaneous presence and unattainability of the phenomenon to be represented, to the concept of the real symbol, which is applied mainly christologically, with corresponding consequences for the representative understanding of the church ministry. In addition, the concept of representation is deontologised insofar as it does not take place qua "being" but qua action, meaning as a practice, in this case a practice representing Jesus of Nazareth and corresponding to his actions. In addition, representation does not take place top-down, but bottom-up: Each and every one is capable of representing God and Christ, not only by the common priesthood of all believers founded in baptism, but already through the central characteristic of an existence that understands itself as God's creature, through the God-likeness to which each and every person is entitled.

In addition, the Logos, the Second Person of the Godhead, is not "male" either, even if this Person—strictly speaking in retrospect because of the incarnation as a man—is called "Son." God himself is neither "male" nor "female," and "father" and "son" are not determinations of being, but analogies and metaphors, culturally and linguistically formed and formulated, thus by no means to be testified eternally and necessarily. For if substance ontology is not valid, then this also applies to the determination of God, especially since God is not one being among others whose category of substance is described. God is neither masculine in himself, nor does he necessarily take incarnation in a man, nor does an incarnation as a man ascribe masculinity to God himself quasi-retroactively. Moreover, there is also the criticism of the concept of person employed in social theologies of the Trinity. According to relational Trinity doctrines, the three are not "persons" in the sense of three anthropomorphic individuals, but rather "distinct modes of subsistence" (K. Rahner), relationships of God to himself and to the creatures coming from God. In this respect, the Logos is also not a "person" to whom a sexualized nature (in this case the male one) may be attributed in analogy to a bodily individual, and who must then necessarily incarnate in a human individual of the same kind, namely a "man." Here residual anthropomorphisms in the understanding of God are at work that then take effect christologically and ultimately in the theology of ministry.

It remains to be stated that the argument "Jesus was a man" is by no means as irrefutable as it seems at first. Whether Jesus was a man or not is of no significance for the function of acting *in persona Christi.* But then, from a systematic point of view, nothing speaks against the fact that in principle all believers can act *in persona Christi*, irrespective of their ethnic, social, and sexual affiliation or identity. And since the argument from tradition is also not convincing, as we have seen, there is no legitimate basis for the prevailing practice of exclusion with regard to the admission to ordination to church ministry. But if this exclusion is continued unopposed and its lack of validity ignored, what is ultimately taking place, because it is desired and is possible, is arbitrary behavior. Such arbitrary action, however, throws a bad light on a community that claims to act in the name of Jesus and to represent him in this action.

(Translation from German by Neville Williamson)

Women in Church Ministries

Perspectives of a Theology of Ecclesiastical Offices after Vatican II and the Authority of Ordinatio Sacerdotalis

Margit Eckholt

1. "The door is closed, but not locked"—an Aporetic or Kafkaesque Situation with a View to the Debate on the Ordination of Women?

1.1 Ecumenical Perspectives: The Debate on Offices for Women in Christian Churches Has Gained Momentum

The documents released in the run-up to the 500th anniversary of the Reformation (1517–2017), entitled "From Conflict to Communion" (2013), on an international level and "Healing of Memories—Giving Witness to Christ" (2016) in the German context, pointed out the importance of commemoration on an ecumenical and international scale. Concurrently, they acknowledged that "despite all our ecumenical rapprochement, to this day we have not yet found common answers to fundamental questions concerning our understandings of Church and ministry."[1] One way to look at ministry from the Roman Catholic perspective is to focus

1. *Healing of Memories—Witnessing to Jesus Christ. A Joint Statement on the Year 2017*, September 17, 2016, ed. the Protestant Church in Germany and the Secretariat of the German Bishops' Conference, Joint Texts No. 24 (Hanover/Bonn, 2016) 60; see also *From Conflict to Communion. Lutheran-Catholic Common Commemoration of the Reformation in 2017. Report of the Lutheran-Roman Catholic Commission on Unity* (2nd ed., Leipzig/Paderborn, 2013).

on the episcopate, emphasize the threefold *ordo* as well as the apostolic succession based on the theology of ecclesiastical offices, and underline the "the sacramental identity of a priest and the relationship of the sacramental priesthood to the priesthood of Christ."[2] Although the Second Vatican council made the ecumenically relevant idea of "joint priesthood" fruitful for "people of God" ecclesiology, the results of Vatican II on ministry continue to be associated with a hierarchy between the common priesthood of all believers and the ministerial priesthood, as well as with the idea of a cultic-sacerdotal understanding of priesthood. On the other hand, the documents of Vatican II could pave the way for new ecclesiological perspectives and a new direction for the theology of ecclesiastical offices.[3]

In recent years, the Ecumenical Working Group of Protestant and Catholic Theologians (ÖAK) in Germany as well as ecumenical academic working groups have closely looked into the wording of the Second Vatican Council's Decree on Ecumenism, which maintains that the churches of the Reformation "have not preserved the proper reality of the eucharistic mystery in its fullness, especially because of the absence of the sacrament of Orders" (UR 22).[4] The working groups made it clear that the *defectus ordinis* does not mean absence but a shortcoming, and that, with a view to the principle of *Christus supplet* and the work of the Spirit of God, "the Church should look at the concept of the 'defectus ordinis' as a more or less realized *communio* and focus more on the pneumatological dimension in order to see whether the apostolic conti-

2. *From Conflict to Communion* 190, 77.

3. See also Hilberath, O. Hofius, E. Jüngel, M. Theobald, Tübinger Thesen zum Amt in der Kirche, in: *Ökumene vor neuen Zeiten. Für Theodor Schneider*, ed. K. Raiser and D. Sattler (Freiburg/Basel/Vienna, 2000) 261–91, especially B. J. Hilberath, IV. Das Amt in der Kirche nach (römisch-)katholischem Verständnis, 281–91, here 291. The difficulty of implementing the basic ideas of the Council becomes apparent in the document of the International Theological Commission, *Mysterium des Gottesvolkes* (Einsiedeln, 1985) No. 7.2.: "In order for Church life, for the Body of Christ to flourish, the common priesthood of all believers and ministerial priesthood or the hierarchical ministry must go hand in hand and relate to each other, but in a way that in terms of the ultimate purpose of Christian life and its fulfillment, the common priesthood is favored, while in terms of the visible organizational system of the Church and sacramental validity, ministry takes priority."

4. See Hilberath, Das Amt in der Kirche, 290.

nuity can only be guaranteed by the historical succession of bishops or by other essential signs of the *communio* as well."[5]

As recent exegetical and dogmatic-historical works show, it is indeed possible to continue the debate over the understanding of ministry and church based on the Bible. In a contribution for the Ecumenical Working Group of Protestant and Catholic Theologians dealing with the debate over church ministry and the apostolic succession, Otto Hermann Pesch underlines that "the development, consolidation and current change in the structure of offices undergone during the period starting after New Testament times and lasting until today with different situations in the churches, are the result of history."[6] This offers an essential foundation for the topic of women in church ministries as it needs to be discussed today. The office structures in the church have always been based on new "interpretations and applications"[7] of the biblical foundation, and therefore churches are free "to organize and reorganize offices and services according to today's requirements and, which always applies, according to the demanded unity in the apostolic faith, while preserving the New Testament's foundation and thus the churches' duty to serve the teachings of the apostolic Gospel and the apostolic faith."[8]

The Ecumenical Working Group did not consider the perspective of women's ordination.[9] If theological debates on offices really take the

5. See P. Walter, "Sacramenti Ordinis defectus" (UR 22,3). Die Aussage des II. Vaticanums im Licht des ökumenischen Dialogs. Zum Ergebnis der Studie von Pierluigi Cipriani, in: *Das kirchliche Amt in apostolischer Nachfolge III. Verständigungen und Differenzen. Für den Ökumenischen Arbeitskreis evangelischer und katholischer Theologen*, ed. Dorothea Sattler and Gunther Wenz (Freiburg i.Br., 2008) 86–101, 99f.

6. O. H. Pesch, Auf dem Weg zu einer "Gemeinsamen Erklärung zum kirchlichen Amt in apostolischer Nachfolge." Ein Plädoyer, in: *Das kirchliche Amt in apostolischer Nachfolge III*, 155–66, here 160.

7. Pesch, Auf dem Weg, 160: "That means: This office structure, or possibly just one of its existing forms, is not only based on the logical and consistent realization of the biblical example, but above all on constantly changing interpretations and applications of the Bible as a way of finding answers to constantly changing social, political and clerical challenges."

8. Pesch, Auf dem Weg, 161.

9. Ecumenical Working Group of Protestant and Catholic Theologians, concluding report, 167–267, here 180, No. 16: It is argued that the topic "could not have been adequately dealt with within the scope of this project."

historical development of official structures and the necessary reinterpretation and reapplication of the biblical foundation seriously, this perspective cannot be ignored by academic research. Certainly, the theological and ecumenical challenges regarding the understanding of church and office become more complex with the question of women in church office. But at the same time, the ecumenical perspective of the debate on the understanding of ministry within the Roman Catholic tradition can deliver a new dynamism and enhance the prospects for reforms as implied by Vatican II, particularly from the ecumenical point of view and considering the new worldview of the council. In the churches of the Reformation, the Anglican Church, and the Old Catholic Church, the ordination of women has been possible since the mid-twentieth century, even if it only resulted from the "need" of the parishes during the war and the postwar period and had to be fought for. The Orthodox Patriarchates of Alexandria and Jerusalem reintroduced the ordination of deaconesses in 2017, and in the Armenian Apostolic cathedral in Tehran, the twenty-four-year-old anesthetist Ani-Kristi Manvelian was ordained deaconess on September 25, 2017.[10]

Moreover, the ordination of three subdeaconesses by archbishop Wanda (diocese of Erbil/Iraq) in a migrant community of Chaldean Christians in Stuttgart-Bottnang on September 10, 2012 showed that the candidates are ordained by the laying on of hands, which underlines the apostolic succession and thus the representation of Christ in this office.[11] This is of central importance for the current debate on the female diaconate in the Roman Catholic Church.

In August 2016, Pope Francis convened a commission whose task is to examine the biblical, historical, and especially patristic reasonings concerning the ordination of women deacons. Today's discussions, whether they are in favor of the introduction of such an office or against

10. http://ostkirchen.info/teheran-weihe-einer-diakonin-fuer-die-armenisch-apostolische-kirche/.

11. See P. Hünermann, Zum Streit über den Diakonat der Frau im gegenwärtigen Dialogprozess – Argumente und Argumentationen, in: *Theologische Quartalschrift* 192 (2012) 342–78, esp. 376–78 (Ausblick: Die Tradition der Ostkirche—angekommen im Westen). Regarding the Orthodox theological discussion on the office, see the contribution of Thomai Chouvarda and Natallia Vasilevich in M. Eckholt, U. Link-Wieczorek, D. Sattler, A. Strübind, ed., *Frauen in kirchlichen Ämtern. Reformbewegungen in der Ökumene* (Freiburg i.Br., 2018).

it, clearly show that history-based argumentation alone is not sustainable, particularly given the wider historical manifestations of the office and the evolution of the ecclesiological foundations, and that the introduction of a female diaconate in the Catholic Church thus implies further theological considerations on offices and the sacraments as well as an open debate on current pastoral challenges. Neither can the topic be discussed without raising the question of establishing a presbyterate or episcopate for women. In a lecture before the spring plenary assembly of the German Bishops' Conference in Trier, Cardinal Walter Kasper proposed to appoint women parish deaconesses, a nonsacramental office. However, this would not do justice to the diaconal management tasks that women have de facto been fulfilling for many years, including in German churches. The consequence would be a hierarchy between the diaconate exercised by men and by women that would undermine the principle of gender equality repeatedly referred to in the German bishops' statements of the past years.[12] However, a decision in favor of a sacramental ministry, namely, the sacred order of the diaconate, runs contrary to the Code of Canon law, in which can. 1024 states that holy orders is reserved for baptized men. Referring back to *Inter Insigniores* of October 15, 1976, Pope John Paul II reaffirmed this position in his Apostolic Letter *Ordinatio Sacerdotalis* issued on May 22, 1994 as a binding magisterial statement, thus declaring the debate over priestly ordination for women concluded: "Wherefore, in order that all doubt may be removed regarding a matter of great importance, a matter which pertains to the Church's divine constitution itself, in virtue of my ministry of confirming the brethren (cf. Lk 22:32) I declare that the Church has no authority whatsoever to confer priestly ordination on women and that this judgment is to be definitively held by all the Church's faithful" (OS 4).

12. See the lecture of Cardinal Kasper on the occasion of the study day "Das Zusammenwirken von Frauen und Männern im Dienst und Leben der Kirche" at the spring plenary assembly of the German Bishops' Conference on February 20, 2013 in Trier, http://www.dbk.de/fileadmin/redaktion/diverse_downloads/presse_2012/2013-035-Studientag-FVV-Trier_Vortrag-K-Kasper.pdf; for gender equality, see the German Bishops' statement published in 1981: *Zu Fragen der Stellung der Frau in Kirche und Gesellschaft*, ed. Secretariat of the German Bishops' Conference (Bonn, 1981).

1.2 The Debate over the Authority of Magisterial Statements on Women's Ordination

In the context of systematic theology and canon law, it has been discussed whether *Ordinatio Sacerdotalis* is binding or not, and the authority of this document as well as can. 1024 of the Code of Canon Law will be reexamined along with the fundamental questions of sacramental theology, offices, and the theological controversy regarding the *ordo*, which equally concerns the theology of the permanent diaconate[13] that is based on the results of Vatican II. The possibility of establishing a female diaconate will be part of this discussion. In this respect, another issue will have to be addressed, that is, the question of a renewed vision of the authority of the papal office, which cannot be answered by relying on the literal sense of the pope's words, which are always subject to error, but by courageously giving room to the work of God's Spirit, thus paving the way for new paths. This is exactly what it takes to make a fundamental decision about women's ordination and recognize women as witnesses to the message of the resurrection, standing in apostolic succession, sent for the proclamation of the Gospel.

In an analysis of the binding nature of *Ordinatio Sacerdotalis*, the Dominican priest Jean-Pierre Torrell pointed out that "the possibility of future progress was not completely excluded"[14] and that "the credibility of tomorrow's magisterium was at stake." Peter Hünermann maintains in his text analysis that an apostolic letter does not have absolute authority: "In formal terms, the Pope does not deliver an infallible, dogmatic definition. This is what the genus litterarium, the carefully delimited choice of words depicting the character of the Papal authority and the act of the declaration itself, indicates. The Pope, however, considers this teaching as a matter of faith authentically taught by tradition and the College of Bishops, thus creating an obligatory character that is definite."[15] Accord-

13. Concerning the debate on the Permanent Diaconate, see P. Hünermann, Anmerkungen zum Motu proprio "Omnium in mentem," in: *Theologische Quartalschrift* 190 (2010) 116–29; R. Hartmann, F. Reger, S. Sander, eds., *Ortsbestimmungen: Der Diakonat als kirchlicher Dienst* (Frankfurt a.M., 2009).

14. J.-P. Torrell, Die Verbindlichkeit von "Ordinatio sacerdotalis." Zur Hermeneutik lehramtlicher Dokumente, in: G. L. Müller, ed., *Frauen in der Kirche. Eigensein und Mitverantwortung* (Würzburg, 1999) 357–79, here 375.

15. P. Hünermann, Schwerwiegende Bedenken. Eine Analyse des Apostolischen Schreibens "Ordinatio sacerdotalis," in: W. Groß, ed., *Frauenordination. Stand der Diskussion in der katholischen Kirche* (Munich, 1996) 120–27, here 123.

ing to *Ordinatio Sacerdotalis*, the issue of women's ordination therefore cannot be discussed arbitrarily ("disputabilis").[16] As a consequence, faithful Catholics are facing an "aporetic" situation, as Peter Hünermann puts it, not because of the impossibility of establishing women's ordination right away or the diverging views within the universal church when it comes to female ministry or else the difficult dialogue with the oriental churches, but specifically because of the "authority of the office."[17] This aporia increasingly reveals itself in the words of Pope Francis when he comments on the statement of John Paul II.

On his return flight from the ecumenical encounter in Lund on November 1, 2016,[18] Pope Francis said in an interview that the door was closed for the issue of women's ordination. This strict referral to the authority of one of his predecessors is striking, particularly in view of the new "pastoral" way in which he assumes the magisterium and his references to synodal structures, the necessity of comprehensive and participatory consultations in controversial ecclesiastic and pastoral matters as laid out in the two-stage process, including the Synod on the Family (2015), and the subsequently published Apostolic Exhortation *Amoris laetitia* (2016). Pope Francis is aware of the competent theological work done by women. When he served as Archbishop of Buenos Aires, he supported the Argentine women theologians' network Teologanda, he sees the necessity of promoting women, in *Evangelii Gaudium* he pointed out the need to qualify women also for management tasks in the church,[19] and in his speeches he encourages

16. Hünermann, Schwerwiegende Bedenken, 122.

17. Hünermann, Schwerwiegende Bedenken, 126.

18. http://www.katholisch.de/aktuelles/aktuelle-artikel/papst-erteilt-frauenpriestertum-erneut-absage: "Pope Francis once again rejects priestly ordination for women in the Catholic Church. The last word on the matter of female ordination was spoken quite clearly by his predecessor John Paul II, Francis said on Tuesday on the return flight from his two-day trip to Sweden. 'And this remains valid.' Francis was referring to the Papal Letter *Ordinatio Sacerdotalis* from 1994, in which John Paul II (1978–2005) ruled out women's ordination in the Catholic Church. The Pope from Poland argued that Jesus had appointed only men as apostles and put forward ecclesiastical tradition."

19. Pope Francis, Apostolic Exhortation *Evangelii Gaudium* on the Proclamation of the Gospel in Today's World, November 24, 2013, http://www.vatican.va/content/francesco/en/apost_exhortations/documents/papa-francesco_esortazione-ap_20131124_evangelii-gaudium.html: "But we need to create still broader opportunities for a more incisive female presence in the Church. . . . and in the various

especially women religious to empower themselves and shake off their subservient attitude.[20] Considering the way Pope Francis attends to the pastoral magisterium, and in view of the reform processes he initiated, one might ask if he could, in a certain way, rise above his predecessors' statements on women's ordination and open up new perspectives for the concept of authority in the Catholic Church. Francis clearly perceives the papal office in a new communicative way, consistently calling for *metanoia,* the conversion to the Gospel, and also learning from others, in awareness of the guilt the church has burdened itself with over the centuries. As far as the participation of women is concerned, the church, or rather the magisterium, can only find answers by taking a close look at the women and learning from them. The shift away from "self-referentiality" Pope Francis calls for in his speeches and sermons particularly concerns the self-referentiality of a church led exclusively by men, a church that clings to the idea that only men can act "in persona Christi."

1.3 Kafkaesque Situation?

With Francis maintaining the ideas of one of his predecessors on women's ordination, the situation of the pontificate of Francis seems to be more than aporetic; one might even call it "Kafkaesque": The man before the law[21] is waiting by a closed door; as the years go by he recognizes an

---

other settings where important decisions are made, both in the Church and in social structures" (EG 103). See also https://es.aleteia.org/2018/01/05/necesitamos-mujeres-lideres-ensena-el-papa-francisco (15.2.2018). See also Pope Francis, *Keine Kirche ohne Frauen*, introduced and ed. Gudrun Sailer (Stuttgart, 2016).

20. See Vatican Radio, news of the day, October 12, 2013: Francis: "Women are called to service, not servitude": The role of women in the church may not be limited to menial services. This is what Pope Francis told all men and women participating in a congress celebrating the 25th anniversary of the papal document *Mulieris dignitatem*. Deviating from the script for his speech, the Pope acknowledged: "I suffer—speaking truthfully!—when I see in the Church or in some ecclesial organizations that the role of service that we all have, and that we must have—but that the role of service of the woman slips into a role of 'servidumbre' [Spanish: servitude] . . . when I see women that do things out of 'servitude' and not out of service. . . . And that it is not understood well what a woman ought to do. Can she be valued more?" Quoted from: http://www.radiovaticana.va/proxy/tedesco/tedarchi/2013/Oktober13/ted12.10.13.htm.

21. F. Kafka, Im Dom, in: *Der Proceß*, ed. Malcolm Pasley (Frankfurt a.M., 2002) 270–304.

increasingly shining light behind the door, and at the end of his life, the gatekeeper will tell him that this was his door and that he could have walked through. Kafka's text has been interpreted in many different ways, and therefore it is irrelevant whether the pope himself or we, the women, wait by the door. The important thing is the light behind it shining brighter and brighter. With a view to the magisterial statements, the door to women's ordination is certainly closed, but it is not locked, and there is a light shining behind that door, inspired by a rich history, by the Gospel of Jesus Christ. This is exactly what the Second Vatican Council commemorated when it named evangelization as the primary mission of the church, and all its actions should be based on it (see LG 1). Fifty years after the council, Pope Francis stands for an *aggiornamento* of the council's reform movement in the spirit of the Gospel, supporting a lively commemoration of the spiritual and universal shifts initiated by the council.[22]

When rereading the Vatican II documents, we must also commemorate the women who accompanied the council process, were appointed auditors in consultation processes (especially on the decree on the Apostolate of Lay People and the Pastoral Constitution) and contributed to the reception of the council on various levels: in the parishes, giving pastoral care to women, with their theological work, and as consultants to the bishops.[23] Women's ordination was one of the suggested themes for Vatican II, and at the council, open-minded bishops asked whether women should be granted equal access to ministries.[24] After the council, academic studies, mainly in the fields of canon law and biblical theology, saw the light and started a debate on women's ordination. *Inter Insigniores*, published in 1976, can certainly be considered as a direct response to the acceptance of women to ministry in member churches of the Anglican

22. See M. Eckholt, Der Papa-pastor. Lateinamerikanische Prägungen eines fünfjährigen Pontifikats, in: *Stimmen der Zeit* 236 (2018) 155–65.

23. See the most recent publication: R. Heyder, G. Muschiol, eds., *Katholikinnen und das Zweite Vatikanische* Konzil (Münster, 2018); see also the reports by contemporary witnesses compiled in the AGENDA publication: M. Eckholt, S. Wendel, eds., *Aggiornamento heute. Diversität als Horizont einer Theologie der Welt* (Ostfildern, 2012) 51–109.

24. E. Jung-Inglessis, Women at the Council. Spectators or Collaborators, in: *Catholic World* 200 (1965) 277–84, here 279f.; J. A. Komonchak, Unterwegs zu einer Ekklesiologie der Gemeinschaft, in: *Geschichte des Zweiten Vatikanischen Konzils (1959–1965)* vol. 4, ed. G. Alberigo, G. Wassilowsky (Mainz/Leuven, 2006) 1–108, esp. 22–31, here 24.

Communion, but at the same time it mirrored the discussion within the Catholic Church and in-depth theological studies on the subject.

Sister Mary Luke Tobin, President of the Leadership Conference of Women Religious in the US during the council, was appointed one of the first women auditors of the council by Paul VI in 1964 and served as advisor to the US Women's Ordination Conference after the council. Despite how things turned out, she continued to point out that with the paradigm shift in revelation theology and ecclesiological matters caused by Vatican II, the door to the house of the church had been opened and could not be shut again.[25] The following considerations are based on this statement of one of the brave women of the council and its aftermath. The vivid memory of the reform movement of Vatican II and the impulses the council gave for ecclesiology and the theology of ecclesiastical offices (as laid out in the second part of this article) place the question of the authority of *Ordinatio Sacerdotalis* in a wider context and, from a spiritual perspective, point to the fact that the light shines brightly behind the closed door and that it cannot be locked. This is why new debates are needed, and why today's women theologians refer back to the largely rejected theological and canonical studies on women's ordination as they were submitted since the time of the council by women like the canonist Ida Raming, who took up the atmosphere of change arising from the council. Such an approach to Vatican II, based on the spiritual depth of the council, calls for the realization of the radical transformation processes initiated by John XXIII and the council as well as for the necessity of dealing with misguided decisions and therefore of admitting guilt. The church, too, is continuously called to conversion and to follow the path of the poor Jesus (see LG 8). This spiritual dynamism is fundamental to the council documents and has accompanied the reception process of the council in the universal church. According to the Spanish Jesuit Santiago Madrigal, the pontificate of Francis stands for this kind of "mystagogical rereading" of the council.[26] The third section of this article, which looks

25. See C. E. McEnroy, *Guests in Their Own House. The Women of Vatican II* (New York, 1996) 270: Carmel McEnroy quotes the US-American Council auditor Mary Luke Tobin. See M. L. Tobin, *Hope Is an Open Door*, Journeys in Faith (Nashville, 1981).

26. See S. Madrigal, El Concilio Vaticano II: Remembranza y actualización, in: *Teología* 117 (2015) 131–54.

ahead rather than offers a conclusion, will therefore take a glance at Pope Francis's pastoral magisterium: how, in times of the various challenges the church faces in its mission to proclaim the Gospel of Jesus Christ and to represent a "sign" of salvation for the people, he promotes the council's reform process driven by the Spirit of God by exploring different directions in order to be able to represent the kind of church of Jesus Christ that goes back to its origin—Jesus' proclamation of God's kingdom and the testimony of the apostles, male and female. The question of women's rights, which John XXIII already in 1963 called a sign of the times in *Pacem in Terris*, is one of the directions taken. The church has always been a church that includes women, and therefore the magisterium cannot turn down the invitation to discuss the question of offices for women in the church with women and female theologians and to listen to and learn about new perspectives such as the gender perspective, new approaches to theological anthropology, and a new way to look at Mary. For this reason, the concluding idea will be whether the pope may be a Kafkaesque gatekeeper who points his confreres in the episcopates as well as male and female theologians and Catholics in general to the door through which we can in fact walk, for it is not locked but only closed, because he is aware of the light shining ever more brightly behind the door, arising from the depth of God's story and his Gospel.

2. The Score of the Council: Mission, Communication, and Sacramentality

The score of the council documents comprises the theological-ecclesiological foundations for the spiritual process of renewal and, subsequently, "structural changes" in the church, allowing it to live up to its mission of proclaiming the Gospel in accordance with the "signs of the times." In this respect, one needs to investigate the statements of the magisterium regarding church ministries for women in order to reevaluate to what extent they are binding. The concepts of *aggiornamento* and *ressourcement* coined by the council are a reminder of the fact that faith is a dynamic process based on the profundity of the Gospel and Jesus' proclamation of the reign of God and implies a continuous conversion to the Gospel. This dynamic process accompanies the people of God on its way through time that is an integral part of what concerns people and the world. The council refers to the "signs of the times" marking the process of becoming a universal church (*Welt-Kirche-Werden*), that is, to become a church that serves life, shoulder to shoulder with the poor, the hungry, the mourning, the imprisoned, and the excluded. And in order to make this service possible, the church must also rethink its own structures in the process of reorientation toward the Gospel (see LG 8). The question of gender equality, described as a "sign of the times" by John XXIII, was one of the themes of Vatican II,[27] and therefore the authority of the statements on women's ordination must be measured by this dynamism.

In view of argumentation patterns that also show up in Pope Francis's statements on women in church ministries, focusing on Mary and promoting a Christ-church relationship "charged" with gender typologies, it is important to refer back to the council documents. Bible-based arguments are decreasingly significant, the International Biblical Commission having repeatedly pointed out[28] that women could not be excluded from apostolic ministry and that the idea of the mission was by no means to be limited to men. In the interview on his return flight from Lund on November 1, 2016, Pope Francis briefly referred to Mary, maintaining that she received neither the mission proper to the apostles nor the ministerial priesthood (see also OS 3) and that she represented the female soul of the church, while Jesus, as a man, stood opposite to this church, his "bride." "Who is most important in theology and in the mystic[s] of the Church: the apostles or Mary on the day of Pentecost? It's Mary! . . . the Church is a woman! It's 'la Chiesa' (in Italian), not 'il Chiesa' . . . it's 'la Chiesa' and the Church is the spouse of Christ. It's a spousal mystery. And in light of this mystery you will understand the reason for these two dimensions. The Petrine dimension, which is the bishops, and the Marian dimension, which is the maternity of the Church . . . but in the most profound sense. A Church doesn't exist without this feminine dimension, because she herself is feminine."[29]

27. M. Eckholt, *Ohne die Frauen ist keine Kirche zu machen. Der Aufbruch des Konzils und die Zeichen der Zeit* (Ostfildern, 2012).

28. See W. Gross, Bericht der Päpstlichen Bibelkommission, 1976, in: W. Gross, ed., *Frauenordination. Stand der Diskussion in der katholischen Kirche* (Munich, 1996) 25–31.

29. https://www.catholicnewsagency.com/news/full-text-pope-francis-in-flight-presser-from-sweden-66035 (23.2.2018).

In the introduction to the collection of texts *Empfänger des Weihesakraments* (Recipients of the Sacrament of Holy Orders), Gerhard Ludwig Müller refers to the "difficulty of agreeing on the sacramental nature of ministry" and holds a similar opinion on the relation between Christ and Mary: "The sacramental understanding is the reason and a criterion for the question of who receives holy orders in the stage of episcopate, priesthood and diaconate. This raises the question whether the significance of the relational incarnation, which, with reference to the relationship between man and woman, shows the relation of Christ to the Church either as head of the body or as a groom to his bride, defines the sacrament of holy orders and whether it is therefore imperative for the priest representing Christ sacramentally to be male in order to validly receive the sacrament of orders. The alternative explanation for the existing practice of the Church would be that it is merely the reminiscence of an outdated social structure."[30]

This pattern of reasoning describing Christ's relation to the church in connection with a gender typology and anthropology that is characterized by a male-female polarity deriving from romantic ways of thinking does not take into account the ecclesiological paradigm shift achieved by the council and instead takes up the sacerdotal understanding of ministry of the scholastic and Tridentine traditions. It rules out any further female participation in the church and its official structure. For this precise reason it will be useful to look at the council's groundwork in terms of revelation theology and ecclesiology and consider the Mariological perspective of the Constitution on the Church, which allows for a new understanding of Mary as a woman of the people, under the headings of mission, communication, and sacramentality.

2.1 Communication and Mission

The theological and ecclesiological paradigm shift caused by the council is based on a new understanding in the field of communication theory as to what revelation means. God, with his unfathomable love, addresses people as friends and, through the work of his Spirit throughout history, enables them, the children of God, to respond to this Word that

30. G. L. Müller, *Der Empfänger des Weihesakraments. Quellen zur Lehre und Praxis der Kirche, nur Männern das Weihesakrament zu spenden* (Würzburg, 1999) 28.

creates life and represents reconciliation.[31] Everybody, men and women, laypeople and office holders, responds to this calling of God in the same way. Before God, we are all children of God, who were baptized to bear witness to the Gospel of life.

According to *Lumen Gentium*, "[t]he holy People of God shares also in Christ's prophetic office: it spreads abroad a living witness to him, especially by a life of faith and love and by offering to God a sacrifice of praise, the fruit of lips praising his name (cf. Heb. 13:15)" (LG 12). *Lumen Gentium* conveys that this is a testimony of the entire people of God by pointing to the *sensus fidelium*, the "discernment in matters of faith . . . aroused and sustained by the Spirit of truth" (LG 12) for the welfare of the whole people of God.[32] The quote "neither Jew nor Gentile, neither slave nor free, nor is there male and female" (Gal 3:28) applies here; it is "a fundamental statement of the Church from Vatican II," Peter Hünermann writes in his interpretation of *Lumen Gentium*.[33] The "equality and dignity of all church members constitutes the fundamental behavioral norm for Christians among one another."[34] Women are equal members of the people of God; this is why they enjoy "true Christian dignity." They are part of the "royal priesthood" (LG 10) and the "chosen people," and their "appreciation of the faith" (LG 12) contributes to defining the prophetic office of Christ, which, in the chapter

31. See H. Hoping, Theologischer Kommentar zur Dogmatischen Konstitution über die göttliche Offenbarung *Dei Verbum*, in: *Herders Theologischer Kommentar zum Zweiten Vatikanischen Konzil*, ed. P. Hünermann and B. J. Hilberath, vol. 3 (Freiburg/Basel/Vienna, 2005) 695–831, here 739–42 (Kommentar zu DV 2).

32. "By this appreciation of the faith, aroused and sustained by the Spirit of truth, the people of God, guided by the sacred teaching authority (*magisterium*) and obeying it, receives not the mere word of men, but truly the word of God (cf. 1 Th. 2:13), the faith once for all delivered to the saints (cf. Jude 3). The People unfailingly adheres to this faith, penetrates it more deeply with right judgment, and applies it more fully in daily life" (LG 12). See: *Sensus fidei* und *sensus fidelium* im Leben der Kirche. Der Text der Internationalen Theologischen Kommission von 2014, in: Th. Söding, ed., *Der Spürsinn des Gottesvolkes. Eine Diskussion mit der Internationalen Theologischen Kommission* (Freiburg/Basel/Vienna, 2016) 13–76.

33. P. Hünermann, Theologischer Kommentar zur dogmatischen Konstitution über die Kirche *Lumen Gentium*, in: *Herders Theologischer Kommentar zum Zweiten Vatikanischen Konzil*, vol. 2, ed. P. Hünermann, B. J. Hilberath (Freiburg/Basel/Vienna, 2004) 263–582, here 467.

34. Hünermann, Theologischer Kommentar . . . *Lumen Gentium*, 330.

on the lay apostolate, is described as follows: "[T]he laity can be called in different ways to more immediate cooperation in the apostolate of the hierarchy, like those men and women who helped the apostle Paul in the Gospel, laboring much in the Lord (cf. Phil 4:3; Rom 16:3ff)" (LG 33).

The idea of the mission is rooted in God's communication itself, shapes the people of God, and defines it through communication and participation among the people of God. The church is based not only on the events of Holy Thursday, the Last Supper Jesus shared with his apostles, but also on the mission arising from the encounter with the resurrected Jesus that both men and women received in the same way. In June 2016, Pope Francis provided the feast day of Mary of Magdala with a liturgical upgrade.[35] Mary, just like Peter or John, witnesses the Easter event, and in the moment of her conversion at the tomb (Jesus, whom she first takes for the gardener, calls her by her name, and she says "Rabboni" and receives the word of the mission), she is called to proclaim the Gospel to her "brothers" (John 20:16–17). From this "conversion" to life, the event of the resurrection, arises the church, as the gospels, the epistles, and the Acts of the Apostles testify in various ways. These testimonies stem from the encounter with the resurrected Jesus and his mission targeting the brothers and sisters and, far beyond that, the peoples (this is what the mission of Paul and his male and female coworkers stands for). For this very reason, the council describes the church as "by its very nature missionary" (AG 2) in the Decree on Missionary Activity *Ad Gentes*: "The Church on earth is by its very nature missionary [i.e., acting as a messenger], since, according to the plan of the Father, it has its origin in the mission of the Son and the Holy Spirit" (AG 2).[36] It renews itself in the encounter with the risen Christ and thus gains the strength to break

35. The preface of the "feast" on July 22 puts Mary of Magdala on the same level as the apostles. In the Latin text, she is expressly introduced as a "paradigm for the ministerium of women in the Church." First and foremost, magisterium means "service," but in some languages the translation "office" is also implicit. The revised version of the preface (the introductory words to the prayer on her feast) states that Christ "honored her with the task of being Apostle to the Apostles." See http://de.radiovaticana.va/news/2016/06/10/liturgie_maria_magdalena_wird_den_aposteln_gleichgestellt/1236162.

36. Second Vatican Council, Decree *Ad Gentes* on the Missionary Activity of the Church, in *Vatican Council II: The Conciliar and Postconciliar Documents*, new rev. ed., Austin Flannery, OP, ed. (Collegeville, 2014) 814.

down barriers, admit guilt (LG 8), and embark on new paths. In the last chapter of his Apostolic Exhortation *Evangelii Gaudium*, Pope Francis attaches great importance to the working of the risen Christ when he refers to the sermon of the very first disciples: " '[T]he Lord worked with them and confirmed the message' (Mk 16:20). The same thing happens today. We are invited to discover this, to experience it. Christ, risen and glorified, is the wellspring of our hope, and he will not deprive us of the help we need to carry out the mission which he has entrusted to us" (EG 275).[37] This mission always has transforming power as it is based on the event of the resurrection (see EG 275).

> [I]t contains a vital power which has permeated this world. . . . It is an irresistible force. . . . But it is also true that in the midst of darkness something new always springs to life and sooner or later produces fruit. On razed land life breaks through, stubbornly yet invincibly. However dark things are, goodness always re-emerges and spreads. Each day in our world beauty is born anew, it rises transformed through the storms of history. Values always tend to reappear under new guises, and human beings have arisen time after time from situations that seemed doomed. Such is the power of the resurrection, and all who evangelize are instruments of that power. (EG 276)

2.2 Sacramentality and Kenosis

The idea of the mission also defines the meaning of sacramentality.[38] The church, in all its activities in liturgy, deaconry, and proclamation, is called to announce the Gospel and to base its existence and actions wholly on this Gospel. On that note, it is a mystery and in Jesus Christ it is "in the nature of a sacrament—a sign and instrument, that is, of communion with God and of unity among all men" (LG 1). The church's task is to illustrate

37. Pope Francis, Apostolic Exhortation *Evangelii Gaudium*, http://www.vatican.va/content/francesco/en/apost_exhortations/documents/papa-francesco_esortazione-ap_20131124_evangelii-gaudium.html#The_mysterious_working_of_the_risen_Christ_and_his_Spirit.

38. See the contribution of M. Eichinger, Zur Sakramentalität von Welt und Menschheit nach dem Zweiten Vatikanum. Anmerkungen zu einer postkonziliar vergessenen Thematik, in: W. Geerlings, M. Seckler, eds., *Kirche sein. Nachkonziliare Theologie im Dienst der Kirchenreform. Für Hermann Josef Pottmeyer* (Freiburg/Basel/Vienna, 1994) 181–98.

God's love and mercy, the foundation of its very nature, to the believers and with them to the whole world, a love that finds its ultimate expression in the self-offering of Jesus on the Cross. Therefore, the "kenotic" structure is inherent in all church activities through the imitation of the "poor Jesus" (LG 8)[39] and God's Word offering itself completely, even unto death. The redeeming love of Christ must be given a concrete appearance, but one that is always subject to change. This is the very essence of a sacramentality and, in this sense, representation of Christ that comes first before all individual sacraments, even the sacrament of holy orders. Consequently, Christ does not stand "opposite" the church. In accordance with the christological decision made by the Council of Chalcedon (451), the relation between Christ and the church is in fact "perichoretic,"[40] which means that Christ is made present sacramentally in all activities, particularly in accompanying the suffering and the poor and in comforting those who suffer violence and distress. Such a definition was formulated, for example, in the ecclesiological concepts of liberation theology after the council.[41] Liberation theology even goes one step further, pointing out that the church is the sacrament of salvation precisely when it "makes an option for them, lives for them, and is persecuted for their sake . . . , but mainly in the sense that it arises from them, from their believing response, and that thus they come to be the authentic and first subject of ecclesial life and structure."[42] Therefore, Jesus Christ cannot be "illustrated" or "represented" by the office holder alone, for Christ is represented through all church activities as a response to God's call inviting us to proclaim

39. "Christ Jesus, 'though He was by nature God . . . emptied Himself, taking the nature of a slave' (Phil 2:6, 7), and 'being rich, became poor' (2 Cor 8:9) for our sake. Likewise, the Church, although she needs human resources to carry out her mission, is not set up to seek earthly glory, but to proclaim, and this by her own example, humility, and self-denial. . . . she recognizes in those who are poor and who suffer, the image of her poor and suffering founder" (LG 8).

40. In this sense, the church is not considered the "living Christ"; the Gospel is always the primary instance; if there can be talk of Jesus being the counterpart to the church, it implies that God's grace is the primary instance.

41. See, e.g., L. Boff, Ecclesiogenesis: The Base Communities Reinvent the Church (Maryknoll, 1986).

42. A. Quiroz Magaña, Ecclesiology in the Theology of Liberation, in: I. Ellacuría, J. Sobrino, eds., *Mysterium Liberationis. Fundamental Concepts of Liberation Theology* (Maryknoll, 1993) 194–209, here 202.

the Gospel, alleviate human suffering, give people the recognition they deserve, and care for the "common home of the creation" (see *Laudato si'*), wherever misery cries out for us, people are excluded, or the dignity of the creation is spurned. Whenever the concept of kenosis is applied, when the "poor Jesus" is thus made present sacramentally, there is also *ecclesiogenesis* and the people of God are growing as a sign of salvation for the peoples. All baptized people contribute to this. As the Ecumenical Working Group of Protestant and Catholic Theologians puts it, "all Christians are called to fulfill the apostolic succession," "since the vocation to Christianity through baptism (strengthened by confirmation) is by its nature also a calling to the apostolate, i.e. 'the salvific mission of the Church itself' (LG 33), which the Church is required to fulfill from its apostolic origin with the help of all its members."[43]

2.3 Theology of Ecclesiastical Offices and Its Consequences

Based on the idea of the people of God and the way communication theory understands revelation, the council paved the way for the development of a new understanding of ministry that has remained controversial until today, although there were certainly ambiguities considering the disputes, especially about the understanding of ministry,[44] between the council's minority and majority groups. Ministry must serve the apostolic mission and should be understood based on this mission.[45] This is how

43. Ecumenical Working Group of Protestant and Catholic Theologians, *Abschließender Bericht* (Final Report), 167–267, here 255.

44. See O. Fuchs, P. Hünermann, Theologischer Kommentar zum Dekret über den Dienst und das Leben der Presbyter, in: *Herders Theologischer Kommentar zum Zweiten Vatikanischen Konzil*, ed. Peter Hünermann and Bernd Jochen Hilberath (Freiburg/Basel/Vienna, 2005) 337–580.

45. Vgl. M. Theobald, Die Zukunft des kirchlichen Amtes. Neutestamentliche Perspektiven angesichts gegenwärtiger Blockaden, in: *StZ* 216 (1998) 195–208: Michael Theobald puts the result of the exegetical studies in a nutshell. Ministry should be understood on the basis of the mission, not from a cultic-sacerdotal perspective. With reference to Eph 4:11 he writes: "And he himself (the exalted Christ) gave (i.e., to the Church as a present) some as apostles, others as prophets or as evangelists, shepherds and teachers, to equip the saints for the work of ministry, for building up the body of Christ" (197). He also refers to Rom 10:14f. and Eph 4:11: "If anywhere, a theology of ecclesiastical offices has to start here, i.e. with the idea of an individual mission to proclaim the Gospel" (198).

the New Testament exegete Michael Theobald summarizes the findings of recent exegetical studies. "If anywhere, a theology of ecclesiastical offices has to start here, i.e. with the idea of an individual mission to proclaim the Gospel," he states with reference to Rom 10:4f and Eph 4:11.[46] His views are in line with the direction given by the council. According to the guiding perspective of *Lumen Gentium* in the chapter on the episcopate, church office is supposed to "illustrate" and "represent" Jesus Christ in a way that the people of God can live up to the expectation that it proclaim the Gospel and let the communion with God and among one another grow: "In order to shepherd the People of God and to increase its numbers without cease, Christ the Lord set up in his Church a variety of offices which aim at the good of the whole body. The holders of office, who are invested with a sacred power, are, in fact, dedicated to promoting the interests of their brethren, so that all who belong to the People of God, and are consequently endowed with true Christian dignity, may, through their free and well-ordered efforts towards a common goal, attain to salvation" (LG 18). Ministry is a central "pastoral service," "*Hirtendienst*" for the "common good of the whole body of the Church."[47] The office holder's task "as a public witness to the Gospel" is to "grant all baptized people their 'royal priesthood' through word and sacrament, to protect and witness it." On the other side, the congregation of the "royal priesthood" is obligated to "support the holders of ecclesiastical offices in their work should the latter fail to bear testimony, if necessary causing a dispute within the boundaries of Christian standards."[48] If, as pointed out by the dogmatic theologian Guido Bausenhart, one attaches importance to the active voice expressed in *perveniunt*: "in order that the members of the People of God attain salvation": "With the help of its own (given) strength, the People of God makes its way through history until its eschatological fulfillment as the Kingdom of God . . . "[49], this

46. Theobald, *Die Zukunft des kirchlichen Amtes*, 198.

47. Hünermann, *Theologischer Kommentar zur dogmatischen Konstitution über die Kirche* Lumen Gentium, 406.

48. Pesch, Auf dem Weg, 164.

49. G. Bausenhart, IV. Im Dienst der Evangelisierung, in: *Herders Theologischer Kommentar zum Zweiten Vatikanischen Konzil*, ed. P. Hünermann and B. J. Hilberath, vol. 5, *Die Dokumente des Zweiten Vatikanischen Konzils: Theologische Zusammenschau und Perspektiven* (Freiburg/Basel/Vienna, 2006) 287–95, here 288.

means that a variety of vocations including sacramental ministry can develop from the service of evangelization and the empowerment of all the faithful, made up of men and women. The result is not a sacramental ministry existing "opposite" the people of God but one that develops from the sacramental service of the entire people of God, proclaiming and "illustrating" the Gospel of Jesus Christ; and as the council repeatedly underlined, this is a mission men and women are equally called for. The "distinction between the ordained as the *teaching* Church and laypersons as the *listening* Church may therefore be considered obsolete." "Everyone is the teaching as well as the listening Church, regardless of any specific understanding of the teaching part."[50] Consequently, the cultic-sacral understanding of ecclesiastical offices—which developed through scholastic theology particularly in the context of the Council of Trent and the Tridentine Church's understanding of priesthood, which has been valid until recently—is also obsolete.[51]

The council names a multitude of *ministeria*, or offices, necessary for the church to comply with its task of evangelization. Jesus Christ instituted "a variety of ministries" (LG 18), all based on the welfare service the church is obliged to offer in the imitation of Christ. According to Peter Hünermann, unity is mirrored in the "richness of episcopal ministry, in its ordination authority, in the way all services aim at the salvation of the People of God and in the fundamental fact that all services

---

Bausenhart points to the active voice in "perveniunt" (291), "in order that the members of the People of God attain salvation": "With the help of its own (given) strength, the People of God makes its way through history until its eschatological fulfillment as the Kingdom of God."

50. Hilberath, Das Amt in der Kirche, 285f.

51. See M. Theobald, III. Thesen zur neutestamentlichen Begründung des kirchlichen Amtes, Tübinger Thesen zum Amt in der Kirche von B. J. Hilberath, O. Hofius, E. Jüngel, M. Theobald, in: *Ökumene vor neuen Zeiten. Für Theodor Schneider*, ed. K. Raiser and D. Sattler (Freiburg/Basel/Vienna, 2000) 275–79, here 279f. If the "perichoretic" relation between Christ and the church in line with the council's idea of the People of God is not taken into account, ministry might falsely be considered as existing "opposite" the church, which is often the echo of a cultic-sacerdotal understanding. See W. Kasper, *Die Kirche und ihre Ämter. Schriften zur Ekklesiologie II* (Freiburg/Basel/Vienna, 2009) 299: "Ministry stands for the inner-world, underivable nature of mercy and consolation attributed to salvation. It bears testimony of Jesus Christ's being 'ahead' and the anticipating character of His work of salvation."

make Christ present sacramentally" (cf. LG 28).[52] Jesus, as the one who institutes them, legitimizes the authority of the *ministeria* and "qualifies the power and thus the service sacramentally (*sacra potestas*),"[53] Guido Bausenhart states in his analysis of the conciliar theology of ecclesiastical offices. "The 'populus Dei' for its part experiences the service of the 'ministri' as support in its endeavors (conspirantes) to attain salvation (salus) in the encounter and communion with the Lord, so that it can freely (libere) expose itself to their work and seek their effectiveness, wherein the 'ministeria' again find recognition and legitimization."[54] As a consequence, Bausenhart continues, "we are in need of a concept of the ecclesiastical office . . . that has not been created at the cost and expense of the community or rather all baptized people . . . , rather of one framed 'in proportion' to them: The relationship between ministry and the community/the baptized is not one-sided but characterized by a perichoretic relation of mutual exchange."[55] In this sense, Bausenhart refers to the "pastoral sacramentality" of the office and its "relativity" to the people of God at the service of evangelization. Ministry is always *pro aliis*,[56] and therefore "its relation to the 'populus Dei' is essential when defining [it]."[57] "The 'ministri' belong *in* the Church and their work

52. P. Hünermann, "Die Kirche braucht auch . . . Frauen im kirchlichen Amt," in: M. Heimbach-Steins, G. Kruip, S. Wendel, eds., *Kirche 2011. Ein notwendiger Aufbruch. Argumente zum Memorandum* (Freiburg/Basel/Vienna, 2011) 189–97, here 194; regarding the unity of the Ordo see also R. Radlbeck-Ossmann, Das Argument von der Einheit des Ordo. Fundament für die Ablehnung eines Diakonats der Frau?, in: D. Winkler, ed., *Diakonat der Frau. Befunde aus biblischer, patristischer, ostkirchlicher, liturgischer und systematisch-theologischer Perspektive* (Vienna, 2010) 119–34; S. Demel, *Frauen und kirchliches Amt. Vom Ende eines Tabus in der katholischen Kirche* (Freiburg/Basel/Vienna, 2004) 73–75.

53. G. Bausenhart, IV. Im Dienst der Evangelisierung, 288.

54. Bausenhart, IV. Im Dienst der Evangelisierung, 288, with reference to LG 18: "The holders of office, who are invested with a sacred power, are, in fact, dedicated to promoting the interests of their brethren, so that all who belong to the People of God, and are consequently endowed with true Christian dignity, may, through their free and well-ordered efforts towards a common goal, attain to salvation."

55. Bausenhart, IV. Im Dienst der Evangelisierung, 291.

56. Bausenhart, IV. Im Dienst der Evangelisierung, 288.

57. Bausenhart, IV. Im Dienst der Evangelisierung, 290. The concentration on the Tridentine definition of the "potestas conficiendi corpus eucharisticum" is thus obsolete (see also 288).

relates to it. It is a relation with sisters and brothers . . . , characterized by something all people (omnes) in Church have in common: 'vera dignitas christiana,' meaning that the 'ministri' belong to the 'populus Dei' as well."[58] Otto Hermann Pesch phrases it similarly for the Ecumenical Working Group of Protestant and Catholic Theologians: "As a Christian, the office holder's life does not differ from the one of all other Christians in and resulting from the personal relation to God. As an office holder, he distinguishes himself substantially through his 'function,' but this function again stands for a two-sided personal relation, which he is devoted to for life in a particular relation with Christ, being his 'tool,' and with the Church/the community, which he serves and which in itself is a 'relational reality.' "[59] For the sacral office, however, this does not mean, according to Bernd Jochen Hilberath, that the ordained office holders "are changed, glorified etc. in their personal 'being' or ontological status." "The alternative of function and being is to be exposed as illusory, just as the alternative between functional and ontological."[60] What is fundamental is the common participation of "ordained" and "laypersons" in the sacramental mission of the people of God. The entire priestly people of God "takes part in the three offices of Christ in an official way, in that they represent the office of Jesus Christ *in* and *towards* the community by referring to Him."[61] These fundamental findings are groundbreaking for the involvement of women in church and their full access to the various church offices.

2.4 Mary, the Church, and Gender Perspectives

In the short interview given on his return from Lund, Pope Francis juxtaposed Christ and Mary as well as ministry and the church when asked about women in ecclesiastical offices, thus providing a reason for the exclusion of women from ministry. In the light of the line of thought proposed in the council documents, it becomes clear that such a juxtaposition corresponds neither with the idea of the people of God nor with the

58. Bausenhart, IV. Im Dienst der Evangelisierung, 287.

59. O. H. Pesch, Auf dem Weg, 166, n. 17: Pesch refers to the comprehensive study in biblical theology by Th. Ochs, *Funktionär oder privilegierter Heiliger? Biblisch-theologische Untersuchungen zum Verhältnis von Person und Funktion des sakramental ordinierten Amtsträgers* (Würzburg, 2008).

60. Hilberath, Das Amt in der Kirche, 286.

61. Hilberath, Das Amt in der Kirche, 283.

perichoretic relation of call and response that characterizes the mission and manifests itself in church through a multitude of *ministeria*. On the one hand, the latter belong "in" the church; on the other, they must be seen in relation to the people of God because they are called by Jesus Christ. The council fathers concluded the Constitution on the Church with a chapter about Mary, describing her as a "woman of the people" who symbolizes the people of God responding to God's call as well as the church that gives concrete shape to the people of God.[62] The constitution begins with a look at Jesus Christ. The church is based on him alone, who is "the light of humanity" (LG 1). This universal perspective forms the constitution's framework. Through Jesus Christ we can experience the meaning of God's friendship and grace and the gift of his love. The constitution concludes with the statement that Mary is "the sign of created hope and solace to the wandering people of God" (LG 68). Her example shows people what redemption and promise mean and what it is like to have God's love embedded in their hearts again despite all the world's brokenness and the contingency of time. The church penetrates her nature through lively communion and the power of faith. By responding to the gift of friendship that God revealed through Jesus Christ, various forms of life arise whose "model" is Mary. All possible responses are embedded in this model, including official and charismatic structures. In this sense, Christ and Mary do not stand opposite each other. They are, rather, a symbol of the friendship with God that, through God's ever present mercy, characterizes a human being's friendship with God. Mary stands for these responses made possible by the mission given by Jesus Christ, including the official as well as the charismatic structures of the church.

The image of the Virgin Mary as described by Pope Francis has been based on a patristic and scholastic mindset following a gender anthropology reminiscent of a romantic way of thinking and marked by male-female polarity and complementarity, which again hark back to the symbolism of the biblical-patristic bridal mysticism. Hans Urs von Balthasar based his ecclesiological ideas on this gender typology[63] and

62. See M. Eckholt, *Frau aus dem Volk. Mit Maria Räume des Glaubens öffnen* (Innsbruck, 2015).

63. See H. U. von Balthasar, Welches Gewicht hat die ununterbrochene Tradition der Kirche bezüglich der Zuordnung des Priestertums an den Mann?, in: G. L. Müller, ed., *Frauen in der Kirche. Eigensein und Mitverantwortung* (Würzburg, 1999) 252–58, here 256: "For the major ecclesiastical meditation, solidly based on statements of the

influenced many magisterial texts, which is mirrored in the interview given by Pope Francis. The ontological theory of male-female complementarity that prevailed during the nineteenth-century Romantic movement entailed a mythification as well as a stigmatization of femaleness, resulting in a gender-specific distribution of work and a social construction of gender models that to some extent still lingers today.[64] When Pope Francis looks at Mary, he certainly shows that he holds women in high regard. By referring to a polar gender anthropology, however, he also fosters the argumentative structure of Christ and the church existing opposite each other, which does not live up to the people-of-God-ecclesiology of the council and instead continues the sacerdotal understanding of offices that derive from the scholastic and Tridentine tradition.

The documents of the Second Vatican Council look at Mary from a different angle. She is the "woman of the people," an idea that developed above all in the Mariological concepts of liberation theology. Alvaro Quiroz Magaña states in his contribution on ecclesiology as viewed by liberation theology that Mary is the "ordinary woman of the people," the "mother of Jesus, the carpenter's son," who showed "solidarity with her folk and with the hopes of her people," "handmaid of that Lord who topples the mighty from their thrones and exalts the humble, who fills the poor with good things and sends the rich empty away. In this woman, who is blessed because she accepts and performs the will of God and maintains her fidelity to the last, her son's cross, in this nurturing mother of the nascent church gathered in the faith of the Risen One, liberation ecclesiology has found strength for the endorsement of the Latin American woman—doubly oppressed, as poor and as woman. It has found the thrust to acknowledge and foster their participation in the management of the church, their role in the journey of a poor people, who now burst upon history. In Mary, ecclesiology finds the creativity it needs to pursue the needed evangelization of popular religion."[65] Mary

---

New Testament, this femaleness of the Church is in fact an equally integral part of the tradition as the attribution of the apostolic office to men."

64. See the (ironic) critical analysis of this tradition in Th. Heimerl, *Andere Wesen. Frauen in der Kirche* (Graz, 2015) 97–102 (Thomas of Aquinas meets Judith Butler).

65. Q. Magaña, Ecclesiology in the Theology of Liberation, 205; a work on liberation Mariology has been published by I. Gebara, M. C. Lucchetti, Maria Bingemer, *Mutter Gottes und Mutter der Armen* (Düsseldorf, 1991).

has been an example and consolation for women in the history of Christian faith because she opened a room of wisdom and theology of and for women, even though, until the twentieth century, this room has occupied a marginal position behind the scenes of the "official" theology, not recognized or explored for the analysis of the faith and even less for ecclesiological perspectives. Mary has accompanied and guided women toward a wisdom-filled and prophetic theology, integrated into the various practices of life, prayer, community and the care for the respective "signs of their times," especially for places accessible to women in church and society. She thus represents a feminist "theology of the people," as one can call it with reference to the theology of Argentina, home country of Pope Francis.[66] This theology must be taken into consideration when discussing the question of women in church offices in a theological context.

2.5 Conciliar Reform Processes without Women?

As to the new paths drawn in the council documents in terms of theology of grace, ecclesiology, the sacraments, and the theology of ecclesiastical offices, the reception of the council barely complied with the tenor of the council's score regarding women in church offices, and whenever there were attempts to pose the question of women's participation and to answer it in a way that corresponded with the council's view that the "equality and dignity of all Church members . . . constitutes the fundamental behavioral norm for Christians among each other,"[67] the performance was interrupted.

The issue of women in church ministries was discussed in the context of the council, but it was never at the center of debates in the commissions. In their propositions to the council, Ida Raming, Iris Müller, Gertrud Heinzelmann, and Josefa Theresia Münch requested complete equality for women in the church and hence access to all ecclesiastical offices.[68] Catholic women's organizations discussed the question of a

66. See, e.g., V. Azcuy, M. García Bachmann, Nancy Bedford, *Teología feminista a tres voces* (Santiago de Chile, 2016).

67. Hünermann, *Theologischer Kommentar zur dogmatischen Konstitution über die Kirche* Lumen Gentium, 330.

68. See G. Heinzelmann, *Frau und Konzil. Hoffnung und Erwartung. Eingabe an die hohe vorbereitende Kommission des Vatikanischen Konzils über Wertung und Stellung der Frau in der Römisch-katholischen Kirche* (Zürich, 1962); Heinzelmann,

female diaconate, although no such proposition reached the council.[69] The topic is part of the reception of the council in the local church in Germany, but the vote of the Würzburg Synod for the introduction of the female diaconate still remains unanswered.[70] Consequently, the issue of women in church ministries will continue to be part of the process of reception following the Vatican II. It is therefore in this context that the question of the authority of *Ordinatio Sacerdotalis* and other magisterial documents needs to be discussed. The universal church has not yet started to deal seriously with the question of offices and the sacraments based on the score of the council on an academically sound theological and ecclesiological level and in the name of a church that considers itself the people of God, a church that refers to Gal 3:28 and the equal dignity of men and women due to their God-likeness. In particular, a satisfactory clarification of the "relativity" of ministry, its integration into the different communication channels inside and outside the church, is still overdue.

What is needed is not the mere annulment of can. 1024 of Canon Law but a theological reflection process revolving around ministry and involving the entire people of God. Women are not willing to insert themselves into the existing clerical and kyriarchal structures, as Rosemary Radford Ruether puts it,[71] but they strive to reorganize, together with those who

---

Wir schweigen nicht länger! Frauen äußern sich zum 2. Vatikanischen Konzil (Zürich, 1964); Heinzelmann, *Die getrennten Schwestern. Frauen nach dem Konzil* (Zürich, 1967). The canonist Ida Raming wrote the following study: *Priesteramt der Frau. Geschenk Gottes für eine erneuerte Kirche. Erweitere Neuauflage von "Der Ausschluß der Frau vom priesterlichen Amt" (1973) mit ausführlicher Bibliographie (1974–2001)* (Münster, 2002).

69. On this subject see R. Heyder, "Ein Sprung nach vorn." Der Beitrag deutscher Katholikinnen zum Konzil, in: Zentralkomitee deutscher Katholiken, ed., *Einen neuen Aufbruch wagen. 98. Deutscher Katholikentag, Mannheim 16.-20. Mai 2012. Dokumentation* (Kevelaer, 2013) 104–9; see also Heyder, Muschiol, eds., *Katholikinnen und das Zweite Vatikanische Konzil.*

70. See M. Eckholt, Den Frauendiakonat weiter in die Diskussion bringen! Anmerkungen anlässlich der Relektüre von zwei Aufsätzen des italienischen Camaldulenser Paters Cipriano Vagaggini, in: *ET Studies* 6 (2015) 335–44; Eckholt, Frauendiakonat—neue Bewegung?, in: *ThPQ* 165 (2017) 266–75.

71. On the concept of "kyriarchy" see R. Radford Ruether, Frau und kirchliches Amt in historischer und gesellschaftlicher Sicht, in: *Concilium* 12 (1976) 17–23; E. Schüssler Fiorenza, *Grenzen überschreiten. Der theoretische Anspruch feministischer*

bear responsibility in church, the institutional structures in the spirit of the "diaconal" church of Vatican II that is devoted to the needs and joys of all people and the world.[72] There are certainly, and luckily, best practices of new forms of communion and cooperation and a participatory exercise of ministry by bishops, priests, and deacons in Germany and the universal church. However, they are fragile for not being supported by dogmatic theology or canon law. If one does not take into account the practical experience of female parish expert workers and many other women who serve the church, including those who serve on a voluntary basis, and if one does not include the academic work of female theologians and canonists in an enhanced, large-scale ecclesiastical process of discussion and decision-making, the sound of the council score cannot be heard in all its fullness. The further reception of the council and the intended reform processes in the church cannot abandon the competencies and charisms of half the people of God. God's call addresses every single man and woman of the people of God. Their freedom to respond to this call, in accordance with the dynamism of faith in communication as part of Vatican II's Constitution on Divine Revelation, is curtailed if women are denied access to ministry.[73] From an ecumenical point of view it is, moreover, offensive to all the women holding different offices with God's blessing in the churches of the Reformation, the Anglican Church, and the Old Catholic Church.

Theologie (Münster, 2004); Schüssler Fiorenza, Sprache und Herrschaft. Feministische Theologie als Kyriarchatsforschung, in: R. Jost, K. Raschzok, eds., *Gender, Religion, und Kultur. Biblische, interreligiöse und ethische Aspekte* (Stuttgart, 2010) 17–35.

72. See also the contributions on women in church offices in: Sr. I. Grave, Sr. J. Schmidt, Sr. M. Zangerle, eds., *Frauen in der Kirche? Unverzichtbar* (Freiburg/Schweiz, 2015).

73. See I. Raming, Priesteramt für Frauen. Eine Forderung der Gerechtigkeit und Anerkennung ihres Christseins, in: *KatBl* 120 (1995) 296–99. Ida Raming refers to the Council, to Gal 3:28, the free choice of vocation (CiC c. 219), the meaning of sensus fidelium, the mystical relationship of each (male and female) Christian to Christ. The ordination of women implies the "recognition of women as faithful human beings, as Christians" (297), which is being fundamentally contested as long as ordination is denied.

3. Pope Francis—a Kafkaesque Gatekeeper? Venturing onto New Paths

More than fifty years after the council, Pope Francis builds on the spiritual dynamism and the reform movement that it engendered. Such documents as *Evangelii Gaudium* are characterized by a spirit of conversion and a genuine struggle to increase the credibility of the proclamation of the Gospel in times when, on the one hand, ties with the church keep dissolving and ecclesiastical positions are marginalized, but on the other hand, the Gospel's message of peace is more popular than ever. Pope Francis assumes the responsibility of the office to find new paths for the proclamation of Jesus Christ. He knows of the "capillary spread"[74] of faith, a phenomenon similar to the situation in early Christian missionary times, and is aware that this context implies an identity crisis for the ministry in its current form, but that it therefore also represents an opportunity for renewal rooted in the origin of the mission given by Jesus Christ.[75] The growing controversy about the pontificate illustrates the importance of the reform process initiated by Francis. This process originates from the dynamisms of faith and the processes of reorientation that come along with it and inevitably includes a structural change. Consequently, there should be constructive discussions on the authority of magisterial decisions given a pastoral magisterium that considers the church "which goes forth" and gains credibility by preserving the tradition in a creative way that embraces new paths. On the occasion of a Reformation commemoration ceremony in Osnabrück on October 31, 2017, the Catholic bishop of Osnabrück, Dr. Bode, stated in a dialogue sermon together with his Protestant counterpart Dr. Klostermeier: "Since in the Catholic Church, we are often tempted to preserve structures and laws in a way that threatens to limit the space for the spirit, the impulse of the Reformation from Luther's personal experience is so important for us. We must be challenged by it like by a thorn in our flesh so that overly earthly ideas will not keep us from tackling the challenge."[76] This should also be a guideline for structural changes

74. M. Sievernich, *Die christliche Mission. Geschichte und Gegenwart* (Darmstadt, 2009) 28ff.

75. This identity crisis is discussed by Radford Ruether, Frau und kirchliches Amt in historischer und gesellschaftlicher Sicht, 22.

76. See https://bistum-osnabrueck.de/antwort-von-bischof-franz-josef-bode-zu-roemer-321-28 (23.02.2018).

regarding church offices for women, where ecumenical solidarity has the potential to encourage the process.

Therefore, the door leading to a debate on ecclesiastical offices for women cannot be entirely locked. Those who wait in front of the door, that is, the pope and with him many men and women, see the light shining ever more brightly in the room behind the door, and this light spreads by means of the new communication structures implemented by Francis through the synodal principle that he writes in the heart of a Church "which goes forth," especially by focusing on the other men and women who walk this path together with him. In *Evangelii Gaudium* Francis points out: "[I]t means learning to find Jesus in the faces of others, in their voices, in their pleas. And learning to suffer in the embrace of the crucified Jesus whenever we are unjustly attacked or meet with ingratitude, never tiring of our decision to live in fraternity [or sisterhood]" (EG 91). If bishops take this seriously, if they respect the religious seriousness of women in their discussions on women in church offices, it will cause a process of change. And in a profoundly religious sense it has to do with what Francis calls "true healing": "There indeed we find true healing, since the way to relate to others which truly heals instead of debilitating us, is a *mystical* fraternity, a contemplative fraternity. It is a fraternal love capable of seeing the sacred grandeur of our neighbour, of finding God in every human being, of tolerating the nuisances of life in common by clinging to the love of God, of opening the heart to divine love and seeking the happiness of others just as their heavenly Father does" (EG 92). Listening to others implies being aware of points of disagreement; it requires patience, waiting, and the discernment of spirits, and as far as the question of women in church offices is concerned, it also means losing one's fear and freeing oneself from the taboo of discussing the topic of women's ordination. The locked door represents the approaching end of an era for a church unwilling to move forward in the spirit of the Gospel and the Second Vatican Council. Then the church will fully develop into the people of God, "in accordance with the great plan of his fatherly love," and it will be "a place of mercy freely given, where everyone can feel welcomed, loved, forgiven and encouraged to live the good life of the Gospel" (EG 114).

Such a vivid memory of the Gospel of Jesus Christ, or, putting it figuratively, this Kafkaesque scenery, will break up the "aporetic situation" described by Peter Hünermann with regard to the binding nature of *Ordinatio Sacerdotalis*, giving the magisterium and consequently the church new credibility. Certainly, the magisterium is supposed to establish unity, it is one of its key services,[77] and in view of the structural change that goes along with women's ordination, it is often the points of disagreement in the different world contexts that are brought to attention. In an increasingly plural universal church, however, unity can only be built in a way similar to the missionary situation of the first Christian centuries, which has always included arrangements and decisions taken and tested at a local level. Pope Francis relies on the importance of the synod, shared conversations, and theological discourses as well as on the analysis of pastoral activity with all its points of disagreement. The magisterium will gain credibility by allowing for statements like those in *Ordinatio Sacerdotalis* to be put into perspective in a synodal process involving women from all continents and by leaving more room for good academic discourse in theology and canon law on anthropology, the doctrine of God, ecclesiology, and the question of women's ordination, just as they have been submitted by women (and men) since Vatican II. A church "in motion" and "which goes forth" will leave doors open while thinking of those who arrive unexpectedly and wish to come in.

(Translation from German by Maren Thölking)

77. John Paul II, *Ut unum sint*. On Commitment to Ecumenism, May 25, 1995, http://www.vatican.va/content/john-paul-ii/en/encyclicals/documents/hf_jp-ii_enc_25051995_ut-unum-sint.html.

Apostolicity—A Vocation Founded in the Resurrection Christ Event

Dorothea Sattler

Introduction

Let me begin with my conviction based on theology.[1] In this lecture I am arguing in favor of allowing both women and men to participate in the apostolic ministry, which is founded on the divine commission to the effective, transforming representation of the redeeming Christ event in word and sacrament.

Ecumenical theology provides a rich source of academically proven expertise distinguishing between the one divine foundation and the many, historically conditioned forms of the churches. To a high degree, there is agreement that official church ministry must be conferred according to a proper order, the conditions of which should be defined in accordance

1. In the written version of my short lecture, I have for the most part retained the spoken word. In this way I would like to signal that the text represents my personal opinion. For thematic reasons, I have also left those passages in the text which result from the date the lecture was given, December 8. I deliberately refrain from detailed references to literature. One can find a great number of references in: M. Eckholt, Ökumenische Herausforderung. Frauen in kirchlichen Ämtern in der römisch-katholischen Kirche, in: Ökumenische Rundschau 66 (2017) 477–489; S. Demel, Frauen im kirchlichen Amt—eine Geschichte von Schuld und Verantwortung, in: L. Ackermann, H. Unger, eds., *Unser Pfarrer ist eine Frau. Erfahrungen und Konsequenzen. Eine ökumenische Standortbestimmung* (Freiburg/Basel/Vienna, 2012) 227–61; W. Groß, ed., *Frauenordination. Stand der Diskussion in der Katholischen Kirche* (Munich, 1996).

with theological criteria.[2] Every social institution needs agreed management structures. Disorder leads to arbitrariness. However, order has no meaning of itself. It may on no account stand in manifest contradiction to theological insights proved jointly in fellowship. The exercise and defense of claims to power based on tradition must be subject to a spiritual judgment. Order—the form of church existence—always has to serve the reason and purpose of the institution.

Against the background outlined above, it is my conviction that the necessary distinction between the justification and the form of church ministries requires a soteriologically focused perspective on the aims intended by the formation of ministries. What is the purpose of ecclesial offices and services? How does God want to use people to demonstrate things, to enable experience, to give proof of the truth? In searching for a theologically appropriate definition of the meaning of ministries, how important is the question of whether the person called by God is a man or a woman? In spite of every possible openness for different positions on this topic, I am faithfully confident of one thing: no ecclesiastical order will endure forever if it contradicts God's intended goal with his creation. However closely, from a human perspective, a church order may currently be determined, it is always subordinate to God's commandment. I therefore explicitly demand respect for the *ius divinum*—for divine law in the order of ecclesiastical offices. I have faith in God. What does God want? That is the crucial question to be posed in our context, which entails further questions: who is able to recognize what God wants? Who can be involved in the search for an answer to this question? Who may participate in which churches in the processes of binding decision-making? What value is accorded to theological argumentation in our topic? If the question has such far-reaching significance, are church officials ever entitled to prevent the open-ended search for a truth that is justified theologically?[3]

2. Cf. Ökumenischer Arbeitskreis evangelischer und katholischer Theologen. Abschließender Bericht, in: D. Sattler, G. Wenz, eds., *Das kirchliche Amt in apostolischer Nachfolge*, vol. 3, *Verständigungen und Differenzen* (Freiburg/Göttingen, 2008) 167–267.

3. Cf. P. Hünermann, Dogmatische Reflexion anlässlich der Antwort der Glaubenskongregation vom 28. Oktober 1995. "Zur Frage der dogmatischen Verbindlichkeit des Ausschlusses von Frauen von der Priesterweihe," in: W. Groß, ed., Frauenordination, 129–46.

I will go on to speak of the differentiations that are necessary for theological reasons (section 1), then I will try to go deeper into the subject in particular cases (section 2), and in conclusion (section 3) I will address the basic attitudes I consider to be necessary today, when obviously disagreements still exist when answering our question for clergy—for the baptized—and for our dealings with one another.

1. Differentiations

There are, in my view, differentiations that are necessary with regard to the question of how God deals with his people in order to achieve the goal of his mission, namely, to bring people to believe in redemption from sin and death. I would like to begin with a distinction that may seem unusual in our context, but seems to me to be very relevant, not only on this feast day—December 8: I will start with the distinction between election and vocation.

1.1 Election and Vocation

God chooses individuals in order that their lives may serve to affirm in exemplary fashion his will to save and fulfill his creation. On December 8 the Roman Catholic calendar celebrates the Immaculate Conception, the remembrance that the Virgin Mary was preserved free from the stain of original sin.[4] In spite of all the questions on this dogma of 1854 that exist from a theological point of view, and not only from an ecumenical perspective, I would like to make one important point: God chooses a woman's form in order to give the whole world a symbol of the new creation. In ecumenism we have learned to understand the mystery of today's feast in a typological sense: it is not a matter of absolving an earthly woman of personal sin. It is a question of basic soteriological contexts. With the Christ event, God makes a new start with his sinful creation. God cannot take the path of redemption without the free affirmation of a human. Mary—a woman gives her *fiat*: "Yes, I am ready,

4. Cf. in more detail: D. Sattler, Maria als Sinnbild der erlösten Schöpfung. Einübung in eine ökumenisch sensibilisierte Dogmenhermeneutik, in: D. Sattler, K. Raiser, eds., Ökumene vor neuen Zeiten. FS für Theodor Schneider (Freiburg/Basel/Vienna, 2000) 225–44.

let it be done." The divine promise to free all creation from the clutches of sin is made concrete in the election of the woman Mary, the new Eve.

The topic of the divine election of special people to fulfill God's ways with his creation has to be clearly distinguished from questions of the calling of individual people into the service of public witness for God's action. The decision about who can and may be called by God is taken by humans with their limited insights. It is very painful to hear the innumerable life stories of women who are, at the decision of human authorities, denied the right to experience God's call to an ecclesiastical ministry. Vocation—this, too, is a divine action, but humans participate in the selection of those who may be considered called. Humans determine the criteria and ensure that they are followed. Humans, however, are capable of error. I consider it important that the churches enter into dialogue with one another to consider which qualifications are required in order to experience God's call to a sacramental ministry.

1.2 The Twelve and the Apostles

Over and over again, exegetical contributions remind us of long familiar insights. The New Testament Scriptures legitimize existing structures of authority; they intend to ensure that Christianity remains connected to the Jewish tradition, and they remain embedded in the framework of social conditions at that time. Anyone who reads the New Testament Scriptures comes to the conclusion that, taking the entire tradition to be found in the Bible, the number of apostles was higher than twelve. The criterion named in the entirety of biblical tradition concerning participation in the apostolate is testimony to the risen Christ Jesus. That is what matters: who was commissioned by Jesus Christ himself to bear witness to his risen life, to his resurrection into eternal life? Sometimes it seems to me a kind of miracle that God himself, through his Holy Spirit, managed to ensure that the women were not forgotten by those in the early church who remembered Jesus and wrote about him in the Gospels. Mary Magdalene, the *apostola apostolorum,* has been venerated for a long time; in the pontificate of Francis she has come to gain new esteem. The apostolic ministry consists in public witness to the risen Christ. Women are called to do this, and are willing to do so, then as now.

1.3 Scripture and Tradition

In the twentieth and twenty-first centuries many ecumenical bodies around the world have worked intensively on the relationship between

Scripture and tradition. From the multitude of possible references to our topic I can mention only a few.[5]

In ecumenism we agree that Scripture is a result of tradition. The oral tradition in the local churches predates the scriptural versions. From a scientific perspective, a verbal inspiration—or even the idea that in this way historical facts had possibly been held fast—is out of the question. The written testimonies are also formulated in accordance with their time, culturally related to the thought and language of their surroundings, located in the situation and context of their origin.

At the same time, in ecumenical theology we do not abandon the idea of achieving knowledge of the one center of the biblical Scriptures, thanks to the working of God's Spirit in all of us in common, so that the importance of individual themes can be assessed in their relative significance. Every interpretation of Scripture can be measured by the degree in which it promotes the knowledge of Jesus Christ. Nowadays, in Christian ecumenism, we are therefore by no means skeptical that we can name jointly the criterion that must guide every interpretation of Scripture, namely, its testimony to God's willingness to turn to sinners in his gracious mercy. The exercise of the apostolically founded ministry of witnessing to Jesus Christ is subject to a criterion of content. The preaching ministry must be oriented to the content of the Gospel.

2. Going Deeper

2.1 Faithfulness to the Apostolic Origin

Christianity has its origin in the liberating message proclaimed by God in Jesus of Nazareth, which remains present through God's Holy Spirit in time and history. In short, I would define the content of the criterion for this faithfulness to the apostolic origin as follows: It is the human witness to God's readiness to reconciliation despite all sin. God upholds for sinful creation his merciful willingness to continue to relate to it. Sin and death cannot unfold their destructive power where God is experienced as the source of reconciliation and of life that cannot be

5. Cf. Ökumenischer Arbeitskreis evangelischer und katholischer Theologen, Schriftverständnis und Schriftgebrauch. Abschließender Bericht, in: Th. Schneider, W. Pannenberg, eds., Verbindliches Zeugnis, Bd. 3: Schriftverständnis und Schriftgebrauch (Freiburg/Göttingen, 1998) 288–389.

lost. People who are called to apostolic ministry have to proclaim this in word and deed.

In ecumenical conversations it has often been considered that it makes little sense to separate the question of the people, those persons who guarantee faithfulness to the apostolic origin (*successio personae*), from the question of the contents, the preservation of the message of the Gospels (*successio verbi*). Where it succeeds, the apostolic succession relates to both realities: People serve the proclamation of God's Gospel. Christ Jesus is God's last word of reconciliation with his creatures, valid for all ages. Many ecumenical dialogues establish that the churches' upholding of the apostolic tradition is not guaranteed by an order of ministries that appeared meaningful for human reasons at that time; it is rather God's Spirit alone who guarantees that they remain in the apostolic tradition. God's Spirit is the guarantor of the continuity of present-day churches with the apostolic origin of the one church. When women began to preach in public in the context of churches influenced by the Reformation, there was a connection with movements noticeably marked by revival through the work of the Spirit of God. This brought about a renewal of tradition. Without pneumatological argumentation based on present-day experiences of the Spirit, we cannot make any progress in ecumenism on the question of the recognition of ministries. I am confident that the *via empirica*—telling each other of our experiences—will bring us closer to the goal that the factual effectiveness of church ministries exercised by women, too, will find recognition as having been worked by God's Spirit.

2.2 Bearing Witness to Paschal Hope

The category of witness is very important in ecumenical theology of ministries. There is the ecumenism of the martyrs, which has often been actively encouraged by popes in recent times, beginning with John Paul II. The memory of the Lübeck martyrs has become a source of ecumenical hope. The international Community of Sant' Egidio repeatedly recalls people of all denominations who lost their earthly lives because they held steadfastly to their faith. The memory of people of all denominations martyred for Jesus Christ, and the lively hope of eternal life for those righteous believers who were killed, ties us firmly together in ecumenism today. We suffer jointly from the knowledge that we have made martyrs on both sides. We respect all martyrs for Jesus Christ in deep ecumenical solidarity with one another. Who would wish to deny that Dietrich Bonhoeffer was properly called to his office as pastor? From the official church point of view, it is not only the ministry of Protestant women that is not recognized by the Roman Catholic side as apostolically justified, but also the ministry of the men ordained in Protestant churches. This has consequences for the question of communion at the Lord's Supper and the Eucharist. It is a cause of great pain. In my opinion, ecumenism demands a reflection on the nature of the apostolicity of the churches, which sees the practical testimony to Jesus Christ as the decisive criterion.

2.3 Living Mission Holistically

Apostolicity means mission—mission as the living proclamation of the Gospel. The vocation to apostolic service is not limited to a ministry connected with the public proclamation of the Word of God and the celebration of the sacraments. Living a missionary life means witnessing to Jesus Christ in everyday life; saying the first word after a long silence, or at least reaching out a hand if no words of reconciliation can be found; listening attentively even when we are in a hurry and the conversation does not appear to be leading anywhere; making up for damage, even if we are not ourselves responsible for it; getting up in the morning over and over again in order to take care of one another from day to day, even when it is sometimes so burdensome.

For thousands of years, women—and men as well, of course—have rendered such apostolic services. Whatever happens in love is of lasting value. At the same time, in our time there is a need for women gifted with God's Spirit, who preach in public after studying Holy Scripture, who speak of their faith convictions and inspire others to do the same. We need the ordained ministry of women, too, so that the whole of baptized Christianity can live its apostolic mission and at least be encouraged to do so and be consoled if, once again, it does not succeed. An ecclesial office serves all baptized Christians. Discovering talents, promoting them, encouraging people to do good—that is a challenging task when following Jesus Christ.

3. Basic Attitudes

3.1 Responsibility before God

In my view it is helpful, in spiritual discernment, to be responsible to God himself when convinced of one's vocation to the ordained ministry. What may lead people to have doubts is not necessarily called into question by

God in the same way. When it comes to the question of women's participation in the sacramental ministry, I await God's judgment with confidence.

3.2 Readiness for People

The willingness to stand by people in their needs and worries should always be in the foreground of church action. All church ministries need to be diaconally orientated. The office of diaconate also serves others, and is as such a leadership task, not merely a benediction for one's own diaconal action.

3.3 Ability to Suffer in One's Lifetime

From my point of view, the awareness of one's own span of life is just one aspect in our range of topics. I hope that the Osnabrück Theses will not go unheard. Information is a prerequisite for contradiction. I do not expect decisive changes in the Roman Catholic Church in my own lifetime. Much has already happened. May we at least make progress on the question of women's participation in processes of decision-making.

Every day demands from us the readiness to endure suffering. We women are well trained in this, so that we are truly a sacramental image of Jesus Christ.

(Translation from German by Neville Williamson)

Equality in the Church—But Stopping Short of the Sacrament of Ordination?

On the Binding Nature of Dogma and Processes of Decision-Making in the Church with Regard to Ecclesiastical Offices for Women—From the Perspective of Canon Law

Sabine Demel

Introduction

How far can the promotion of women go in the Catholic Church? Female counselors, theology professors, and department heads in the episcopal curia are now well established. Since 1983, that is, since the 1983 Code of Canon Law came into force, almost all ecclesiastical ministries and offices that are open to lay people can also be occupied by women. So where is the problem here? Or is there no problem anymore? Does the question of ecclesiastical offices for women only concern the admission of women to the sacrament of ordination in its three forms of ordination to deacon, priest, and bishop? And is it conceivable that there might be a change in the ecclesiastical regulation that has hitherto excluded women from consecration? Or is this door closed forever?

From the specific perspective of canon law, there are three aspects of these questions that have to be considered above all:

1. Women are also underrepresented in ecclesiastical offices other than the sacrament of ordination.

It is incomprehensible why it was not until 2017 that it could be proudly proclaimed that the quota of women in the upper-level diocesan ministry for Pastoral Care in the area of the German Bishops' Conference (DBK) had meanwhile reached 40 percent, of which 13 percent were even in leadership positions.[1] Why has it taken so long to make decisions in the individual German dioceses and at the level of the DBK? After all, the legal basis for this was already in place in 1983. For the Code of Canon Law of 1983, which is still in force today, introduced potentially momentous innovations, namely, that lay people can also hold ecclesiastical offices (can. 228 §1 in conjunction with can. 145f CIC) and that—with one exception[2]—there is no longer any distinction between women and men, that is, there are no longer any male privileges (can. 208 CIC).

Theoretically, equal rights for women in the Catholic Church have been largely guaranteed since 1983, but in practice and structure this fact has for decades not been implemented very effectively. If at all, women appear only very occasionally in positions of ecclesiastical leadership or authority, such as department heads in an episcopal ordinariate, theology professor, director of an academy, or head of a Catholic office. Thus it is here the rare case that the maxim "law always lags behind reality" was proved to be false. In the question of church ministry for women, reality has been lagging behind law for decades—a shame! Because those responsible in the DBK dioceses have neglected the legal possibilities for women's ministry for so long, women and all those who care about equality have suffered unnecessary anger, frustration, disappointment and rejection, from the Church.

1. https://www.domradio.de/themen/bist%C3%BCmer/2017-07-31/bischof-sieht-erfolge-wegen-mehr-frauen-fuehrungspositionen (30.06.2018); cf. Newsletter Radio Vatican of August 7, 2017: "The employment of women in all areas of the church should be further promoted, said Daniela Engelhard, director of pastoral ministry in the diocese of Osnabrück, in an interview with katholisch.de. When she began her ministry 15 years ago, she was one of the few female theologians to do 'pioneering work.' Today, 40 percent of those working in the pastoral care offices are women, but only 13 percent in management positions."

2. Cf. can. 230 §§2f., according to which only men can be admitted to the ministries of lector and acolyte on a permanent basis (can. 230 §1); women, on the other hand, can be admitted only on a temporary designation (can. 230 §2). This regulation is not tenable, or it has to be evaluated as a relic of the discrimination against women in the old codex.

2. The legal norm preventing women's ordination is not carved in stone.

The legal situation regarding the ordained office for women is on the one hand clear, but on the other hand not irrefutable. First, it should be noted that can. 1024 CIC unmistakably states in a very concise form:

"Only a baptized man (*vir*) validly receives sacred ordination." (can. 1024).

Two aspects are important here:

First, there is no differentiation here between the forms of ordination of bishops, priests, and deacons. Thus, as the law stands, women are banned from receiving all three forms of ordination: episcopal ordination, priestly ordination, diaconal ordination.

Second, there is no reference to "divine commandment," nor to "divine right," so that can. 1024 belongs to human canon law.[3]

Both cases show that can. 1024 is open in several respects to possible reforms and adaptations to the demands of the times, as they result from the interplay between the sense of faith of God's people, the findings of theological science, and the decision-making authority of the magisterium. The basis for this is the fact that the sacraments are "*instituted by Christ the Lord and entrusted to the Church*" so that they are at the same time "*actions of Christ and the Church*," as it is pointedly expressed in can. 840 CIC. Therefore it is explicitly emphasized in the book of canon law as well that the church, represented by the supreme ecclesiastical authority, can and must determine the criteria for the validity of each individual sacrament. It states literally in this context:

3. The following interpretation of can. 1024 is untenable: "The Codex Iuris Canonici says in Canon 1024 that only a baptised man receives the holy consecration validly. The distinction between valid and permitted corresponds exactly to that between divine and human right" (G. L. Müller, Wer hat das letzte Wort? Eine Strategie und ihre Tücken: Zu der endlosen Forderung nach Einführung der Frauenweihe, in: *Die Tagespost* 12, 23 [March 2002] 12f., 12). For the distinction between valid and permissible has nothing to do with the distinction between divine and human law. Rather, the qualifications of a particular case under ecclesiastical law as valid, or as valid and permissible, or as valid but impermissible, or finally as invalid (and thus of course also impermissible) are applied both to divine and to human law.

"Since the sacraments are the same for the whole Church and belong to the divine deposit, it is only for the supreme authority of the Church to approve or define the requirements for their validity" (can. 841).

The form of the sacraments must therefore be determined by the church. Accordingly, the supreme ecclesiastical authority must always reevaluate and determine what is required for the validity of the individual sacraments. Otherwise can. 841 would be invalid and the considerable historical changes that can be ascertained in some cases in the criteria of validity of several sacraments, such as penance, anointing of the sick, and marriage, could not be explained theologically. In other words: in the case of the sacraments just mentioned, no pope has yet claimed that the church has no authority whatsoever to change the criteria of validity. And why should they, when can. 841 states exactly the opposite: that the church has legal authority over the sacraments.

If can. 1024 is therefore not read alone but along with the two canons 840 and 841, one can draw the following theological and legal conclusion: the supreme ecclesiastical authority can—and indeed must—repeatedly reevaluate and determine the requirements for the validity of the sacrament of ordination to the episcopate, presbyterate, and diaconate, naturally without altering the substance of the sacrament.[4]

In the exercise of this task, which has to be supported by the sense of the faith of all believers and the findings of academic theology, the magisterium could reach one of the following conclusions:

> a) The admission of women to the diaconate is theologically viable. Their nonadmission to ordination no longer applies equally to all three forms of ordination (deacon, priest, bishop). The legal norm of can. 1024 should therefore be amended accordingly, for example in this way:
> "§1 Only a baptized man validly receives ordination to the episcopate and presbyterate.

4. The criteria of validity may not be "arbitrarily shaped," as J. Ratzinger rightly emphasizes in Grenzen kirchlicher Vollmacht. Das neue Dokument von Papst Johannes Paul II, zur Frage der Frauenordination, in: *Internationale Katholische Zeitschrift* 23 (1994) 337–45, 338, but must always respect the nature of the sacrament. But that does not mean that can "only be passed on in awestruck fidelity," he adds.

§2 Only a baptized person validly receives ordination to the diaconate."

b) The admission of women is theologically viable not only to the diaconate, but also to the presbyterate, which is why can. 1024 should be amended as follows:
"§1 Only a baptized man validly receives ordination to the episcopate.
§2 Only a baptized person validly receives ordination to the diaconate and the presbyterate."

c) The admission of women to all three forms of ordination is theologically viable, so that can. 1024 reads in future:
"Only a baptized person validly receives holy orders."

3. The doctrine on the exclusion of women from priestly ordination can be changed.

For some experts on canon law and some representatives of other theological disciplines, the admission of women to ordination to the priesthood and thus also to the episcopate[5] has been made impossible for all time, so to speak, since 1994. Even Pope Francis has declared that this door was closed by Pope John Paul II and can no longer be opened. I do not believe that this view is tenable for two reasons, one of which is generally theological and the other specifically ecclesiastical.

From a general theological point of view, one should recall that there is no unilateral duty of obedience to the ecclesiastical magisterium. For as much as it is the duty of every Catholic Christian to recognize and observe the ecclesiastical magisterium and its doctrinal statements, so little can and may this go hand in hand with a prohibition of thought and

5. The admission to priestly ordination also indirectly includes the admission to episcopal ordination, for since the Second Vatican Council it is taught that, on the one hand, "by Episcopal consecration the fullness of the sacrament of Orders is conferred" (LG 21), but on the other hand the priests are nevertheless "united with the bishops in sacerdotal dignity" and "by the power of the sacrament of Orders, in the image of Christ the eternal high Priest, they are consecrated . . . so that they are true priests of the New Testament" (LG 28). On the close connection between priestly and episcopal ordination see S. Demel, Presbyter und Presbyterat, in: Demel, *Handbuch Kirchenrecht. Grundbegriffe für Studium und Praxis* (2nd ed., Freiburg i.Br., 2013) 517–21.

discussion—whether imposed from outside or by oneself. Being a Christian means not only recognition of the magisterium, but also that every Catholic, according to his or her position, should make a contribution serving the mission of the church. Therefore every Catholic is obliged not only to accept and respect the doctrinal proclamation, but also to reflect on the content of faith and doctrine and to engage in dialogue in and with the church community in the search for the truth. Even if the magisterium, after or during a discussion, has made a binding doctrinal decision, the search for the truth can and must continue—because the truth is always greater than its expression in a respective language and is therefore in principle always open for progressive differentiation, expansion, and deepening; every formulation of the truth in language is dependent on the situation and shaped by the respective context. However, the ongoing search for the truth must not be continued as if nothing had yet been clarified by the magisterium, but it must rather be done in such a way that the position of the magisterium is critically considered with respect to the circumstances of its justification. Therefore, the content of every official doctrinal document must be critically examined, and attention must be drawn to problems or errors in a form both appropriate and loyal. In order to fulfill this task in Christian responsibility, the Catholic must observe both the *content-related* criterion of the hierarchy or ranking of the truths and the *formal* element of the level of authority of the respective faith doctrine; he or she may not present his or her *own* views either as indisputable conclusions or as a doctrinal statement.

Regarding specific aspects of canon law, it should be pointed out that the doctrinal proclamation presented by Pope John Paul II in 1994 with *Ordinatio Sacerdotalis* maintaining that the church is not authorized to ordain women as priests is not to be interpreted as infallible doctrinal proclamation. The decisive passage of the pope's letter reads:

"Wherefore, in order that all doubt may be removed regarding a matter of great importance, a matter which pertains to the Church's divine constitution itself, in virtue of my ministry of confirming the brethren (cf. Lk 22:32) I declare that the Church has no authority whatsoever to confer priestly ordination on women and that this judgment is to be definitively held by all the Church's faithful" (OS 4).

There is almost general consensus among theologians and scholars of canon law that this is not an ex-cathedra decision, in other words, that no infallible doctrinal decision has been taken *by virtue of the pontifical office.* The relevant criteria, as set out in can. 749 §1 CIC, are not fulfilled.[6] However, it must be noted that not only the pope, but also the college of bishops together with the Pope, can make an infallible doctrinal decision by virtue of his office. The necessary legal requirements are contained in can. 749 §2. And in the opinion of some theologians and canon lawyers, these requirements are precisely fulfilled in the papal letter about the impossibility of priesthood for women. Most recently, this view was represented by the Freiburg canon lawyer Georg Bier.[7] According to Bier, the pope's statement that the church had no authority to ordain women as priests is an *infallible* doctrinal decision of *the college of bishops* that was not taken, as is the rule, at an ecumenical council, but when the bishops agreed "that a particular proposition is to be held definitively" (can. 749 §2) when they were dispersed throughout the world. Accordingly, the statement about the church's lacking authority with regard to ordaining women is not infallible by a special doctrinal act or by an ex-cathedra decision of the pope according to can. 749 §1, but it is *infallible* because *all* bishops represent *the same* definitively binding judgment (can. 749 §2) that the pope announced publicly in his letter. Georg Bier can indeed refer to the Congregation for the Doctrine of the Faith for his position, which had already expressed this view in a so-called *Responsum* in 1995.[8] However, this *responsum* is problematic

6. Cf. S. Demel, *Frauen und kirchliches Amt. Grundlagen—Grenzen—Möglichkeiten* (Freiburg i.Br., 2012) 181–85.

7. Cf. G. Bier, Frauen weihen?, in: *Herder Korrespondenz* 71 (2017) 45–47. Also W. Aymans, Veritas de fide tenenda. Kanonistische Erwägungen zu dem Apostolischen Schreiben *Ordinatio sacerdotalis* im Lichte des Motu Proprio "Ad tuendam fidem," in: G. L. Müller, ed., *Frauen in der Kirche: Eigensein und Mitverantwortung* (Würzburg, 1999) 380–98, 398; N. Lüdecke, Also doch ein Dogma? Fragen zum Verbindlichkeitsanspruch der Lehre über die Unmöglichkeit der Priesterweihe für Frauen aus kanonistischer Perspektive, in: *Trierer Theologische Zeitschrift* 105 (1996) 161–211, 207f.

8. The decisive passage of the document reads: "This teaching [in *Ordinatio Sacerdotalis*] requires definitive assent, since, founded on the written Word of God, and from the beginning constantly preserved and applied in the Tradition of the Church, it has been set forth infallibly by the ordinary and universal Magisterium (cf. Second Vatican Council, Dogmatic Constitution on the Church *Lumen Gentium*

both formally and in terms of content. For in *formal* terms the view of the CDF expressed therein is irrelevant insofar as the congregation does not have the ecclesiastical competence to determine which doctrine is to be regarded as infallible and which is not. According to the church's Code of Canon Law, only the pope and the college of bishops together with the pope (cf. Canon 749 §1 and §2) can do this, but not the CDF, regardless of whether it makes its statements with or without the approbation (=approval) of the Pope.

In terms of content, the view held by the CDF, and accordingly by Georg Bier as well, stands and falls with the interpretation of the term "proposition" used in can. 749 §2 in the sense of opinion, conviction (Latin: *sententia*). For Georg Bier, a proposition obviously already exists if there is no objection. But a proposition demands more than a passive "noncontradiction" and thus a presumed consent; it demands an active act of expression. In order to be able to assert that all bishops agree on "a particular proposition" in this matter, *all* bishops would therefore have had to *explicitly* represent or *explicitly* agree with the doctrine of the church's lack of authorization with regard to the priesthood of women, either upon request or by a statement made on their own initiative, in order to assert the legal infallibility defined by can. 749 §2. However, this has not yet happened. In other words: a unanimous decision of the entire episcopal college in the sense of can. 749 §2 does not exist with regard to the (im)possibility of women's ordination, because such a unanimous decision cannot simply be presumed, but must be proven. This is all the more true since can. 749 §3 explicitly states: "No doctrine is understood as defined infallibly unless this is manifestly evident." The most cautious conclusion to be drawn from this is: the alleged unanimous judgment of the college of bishops on the inadmissibility of women to ordination to the priesthood is *not manifestly* evident; the most radical conclusion is: this proposition does not exist. In both cases, these conclusions mean

25, 2). Thus, in the present circumstances, the Roman Pontiff, exercising his proper office of confirming the brethren (cf. Lk 22:32), has handed on this same teaching by a formal declaration, explicitly stating what is to be held always, everywhere, and by all, as belonging to the deposit of the faith" (http://www.newadvent.org/library/docs_df95os.htm).

that the doctrinal proclamation concerning the nonadmission of women to priestly ordination is *not infallible* and thus *subject to change* in the face of new theological findings and legal requirements.

<table>
<tr>
<td rowspan="2">Ordinatio sacerdotalis

Wherefore, in order that all doubt may be removed regarding a matter of great importance, a matter which pertains to the Church's divine constitution itself, in virtue of my ministry of confirming the brethren (cf. Lk 22:32) I declare that the Church has no authority whatsoever to confer priestly ordination on women and that this judgment is to be definitively held by all the Church's faithful.

Response of the Congregation for the Doctrine of the Faith

This teaching requires definitive assent, since, founded on the written Word of God, and from the beginning constantly preserved and applied in the Tradition of the Church, it has been set forth infallibly by the ordinary and universal Magisterium.</td>
<td colspan="2">can. 749 CIC/1983

§2. The college of bishops also possesses infallibility in teaching when the bishops gathered together in an ecumenical council exercise the Magisterium as teachers and judges of faith and morals who declare for the universal Church that a doctrine of faith or morals is to be held definitively; or when dispersed throughout the world but preserving the bond of communion among themselves and with the successor of Peter and teaching authentically together with the Roman Pontiff matters of faith or morals, they agree that a particular proposition is to be held definitively.</td>
</tr>
<tr>
<td>not contradicted

presumed consent</td>
<td>explicit consent

statement</td>
</tr>
<tr>
<td>§3. No doctrine is understood as defined infallibly unless this is manifestly evident.</td>
<td colspan="2">§3. No doctrine is understood as defined infallibly unless this is manifestly evident.</td>
</tr>
</table>

Thus, even after *Ordinatio Sacerdotalis,* the way is still open to change the teaching on the gender-specific admission to the sacrament of holy orders—not arbitrarily, but by preserving the substance of the sacrament, and also by including the *sensus fidelium* and the state of theological research. Who knows, perhaps in the wake of revised theological thinking by the magisterium, the reformulation mentioned above will take place much sooner than imagined—canon 1024: *"Only a baptized person validly receives sacred ordination"!*

(Translation from German by Neville Williamson)

V

Broadening the Horizon

Pastoral Perspectives

A Fresh Breeze?

On the Potential of Women Pastors for Renewal in the Protestant Church[1]

Ulrike Link-Wieczorek

Introduction

Let me confess at the outset: I can no longer imagine a church without women pastors—in spite of the fact that I am neither ordained nor a pastor. Looking back on the history of women's ordination in the Protestant churches, I find it quite surprising that this possibility was only opened up in some regional churches at the beginning of my studies in the 1970s. In the whole of my childhood and youth I only knew of male pastors. And looking back, once again, I only know now what I was missing at that time: a more holistic experience of church, in which a balanced representation of men and women existed in the pastorate. That would have conveyed the feeling of understanding and sympathy for one's own experiences, particularly for me as a young girl.

1. "Motherly Types"?

I think most Protestant Christians feel the same way as I do: women pastors have become indispensable, and that actually happened relatively quickly. So it is perhaps not surprising that the academic theological debate occasionally throws a spanner in the works. Where in Roman

1. In this version of my paper I have retained the tone of a lecture.

Catholic and Orthodox churches women who aspire to the priesthood are often considered unbecomingly greedy for power, the wind sometimes blows in the opposite direction in the Protestant Church: there one may speak of "motherly types" who are not "really intellectuals" and who—"mostly coming from a petty bourgeois social background . . . [lived] a form of religiosity with a combination of a cuddly god and bad taste." This sentence was widely quoted in the German press in 2010 and often repeated in private with a tone of spiteful jocularity. It was originally coined by the Protestant theologian Friedrich Wilhelm Graf. He later explained in an interview with the FAZ that his intention was to point provocatively to a structural change in which a formerly male profession—to be precise, "a profession once dominated by men"—would change into a female profession—literally, a "profession for young women."[2]

There can be no question: this still remains a provocation, not just because of its choice of words and images, but also because of the underlying thesis that the profession of pastor is changing from a male to a female one. This is a well-known phenomenon in other areas of cultural work as well: in teaching,[3] cultural work in museums and conference centers, for example, and perhaps even in the lecture halls of the humanities at universities.[4] But beyond that, the examples become more infrequent. At the universities, the proportion of women at the teaching level, especially among professors, is rapidly decreasing in comparison

2. http://www.faz.net/aktuell/feuilleton/geisteswissenschaften/gespraech-mit-friedrich-wilhelm-graf-ein-gott-zum-kuscheln-1610609.html (30.06.2018).

3. According to a study conducted by the Federal Statistical Office in 2016, 90 percent of primary school teachers and 60 percent of secondary school teachers in Germany are female; cf. *Schulen auf einen Blick*, ed. Statistisches Bundesamt (Wiesbaden, 2016) 45; https://www.destatis.de/DE/Themen/Gesellschaft-Umwelt/Bildung-Forschung-Kultur/Schulen/Publikationen/Downloads-Schulen/broschuere-schulen-blick-0110018189004.pdf?__blob=publicationFile (19.06.2018).

4. Cf. D. Hänsel, Frauen im Lehramt—Feminisierung des Lehrberufs?, in: E. Kleinau et al., eds., *Geschichte der Mädchen—und Frauenbildung*, vol. 2, *Vom Vormärz bis zur Gegenwart* (Frankfurt a.M., 1996) 414–33. Women and men have now reached equal numbers in the subjects of business administration, economics, and law, while they tend to go separate ways with regard to languages, educational science, social work, mechanical engineering, computer science, and electrical engineering: cf. https://www.klischee-frei.de/dokumente/pdf/a31_frauen_und_männer_an_hochschulen_in_deutschland_FB06.pdf (19.06.2018).

with the fields just mentioned. However, the thesis of a change from a male to a female profession has already been examined for the teaching profession, and it has been established that young men were influenced in their choice of subject by the consideration of whether they would have to reckon with a majority of males or of females among their fellow students. They did indeed tend to avoid subjects that attracted a large proportion of female students.[5] They did up to now, I hope we can say. For this strategy of avoidance is hopefully a transitional phenomenon as the whole of society moves toward the practice of gender justice. Compared with these developments in cultural sciences and the humanities, things still look good in theology. This has proved to be the case everywhere since Graf came up with his offensive dictum: about 50 percent of males studying for the ministry still dare to go to lectures with the same number of female fellow students. Up to now. It would be a shame if that changed. One has the impression that for some time, at least in Central Europe, there has been among men a noticeable decrease in active religious interest and the corresponding courage to admit to it in public. And fewer of those who still harbor such interests are then prepared to become pastors. Men who still write letters and talk about relationships . . . They are the ones most likely to talk about God. It would be a real shame if their numbers were to continue to dwindle, so that we would become a society of IT professionals, engineers, and chemists instead.

Now, after briefly covering the Protestant theology of the ministry, I will sketch out the situation of women pastors in Protestant churches.

2. Church Ministry from the Protestant Point of View

Even in Protestant churches, the ordination of women into church ministries is a relatively recent phenomenon. As already indicated, the reasons are certainly for the most part cultural and should not be underestimated in their influence. The theological argumentation for the ordination of women was therefore only developed at a late stage and

5. Certainly the argument used in the reform pedagogy of the eighteenth century plays a not insignificant role here, when it was maintained that women were particularly suitable for educational professions because of their "motherliness"; cf. B. Stiegler, *Berufe brauchen kein Geschlecht. Zur Aufwertung sozialer Kompetenzen in Dienstleistungsberufen* (Bonn, 1994) 14f.

was derived from Protestant ecclesiology.[6] The Reformation was actually a struggle against the "overbearing" State Church of that time. In the history of dogma, this means that it was an uprising against the doctrinal and jurisdictional power of the Pope. Breathing the atmosphere of the Renaissance, it held to the conviction that each and every believer could proclaim the Gospel and pass judgment on the right doctrine in his or her own way. All that was necessary was the ability to read the Bible, which all could understand if it was available in their own language. This is what is meant by the doctrine of the priesthood of all believers, which places a great deal of trust and responsibility on every single believer. The Protestant understanding of ministry must be seen within the context of this expectation of responsibility: it is based on the pragmatic insight that the believers must be factually and empirically encouraged, trained, and educated for this task. There was complete rejection of a spiritualistic view of the revelation of the Word of God, for which, as we know, the followers of the Anabaptist movement at that time lost their lives, persecuted as Christians by Lutherans and "Old Believers" (Catholics).[7] In order to be able to exercise the priesthood of all believers, one ought to know the Bible and the relationship among its various parts; one should also be well informed as to how the fundamental convictions of the Christian faith came to be made (that is, knowing above all that God makes us righteous by his grace alone); one should be aware of the Word of God and appreciate its value in one's own life; one should receive assurance and stability in the faith thanks to the regular hearing of sermons and participation in the sacrament. All this is needful for a responsible Christian. How can that be achieved? With the help of a Christian person who has learned to pass on this knowledge and who has been called to do so within the community of believers gathered under the Holy Spirit. That is to say, with the help of a pastor who can preach the Word of God in each specific situation, who can structure the celebration of the sacraments in an appropriate way (in other words, so that their function as representation of Christ's presence at a specific place and time is made clear), to do pastoral work and also teach catechetically or ensure that this happens adequately. I think one should take this broad view of

6. For what follows cf. R. Frieling, *Amt* (Göttingen, 2002).

7. On this cf. *Heilung der Erinnerungen. Die Bedeutung der lutherisch-mennonitischen Versöhnung*, ed. Lutherischer Weltbund (Leipzig, 2017).

the demand that "the Gospel is rightly taught and the Sacraments are rightly administered," which the Protestant confessions apply not just to the pastoral ministry, but also to the church in its entirety.[8] The church, including the pastor, is needed so that believers can live their priesthood. That is why the pastor—in contrast to the members of the priesthood of all believers—should proclaim the Gospel publicly, whether from the pulpit or in other places. That is why the church calls people officially to this service by ordination. Pastors as servants of the church should be properly called and must understand something of the Gospel.

One remark is appropriate here: this description of ministry does not include any indication that Christ is represented by the minister. The long road to the ordination of women in the Protestant churches—which has by no means found an end in all parts of the world[9]—is in no way connected by official theology to the fact that Christ was a man and that therefore the pastor must also be a man. It is much worse than that: it is connected with the fact that for centuries the Protestant churches, despite their strong emphasis on the priesthood of all believers, did not trust women to fulfill this preaching ministry—because they were not as clever and capable as men, and because their place was in the family. This was the Protestant position for a very, very long time, and is still the case in some places in the world down to the present day. In the absence of genuine theological reasons, the Catholic doctrine of representation is often utilized in order to hinder women's ordination (such as in the discussion in Bavaria in the 1960s).[10] But often it is enough to say that women are not yet ready.

3. Gender Characteristics in the Pastorate

So it is not surprising that the professional pastorate is not spared from gender considerations due to socialization either. According to a study undertaken by the three Protestant churches in northern Germany shortly before their merger to form the Nordkirche (Evangelical Lutheran Church in Northern Germany) in 2012, there are definitely noticeable

8. Cf. the Augsburg Confession V, VII, and XIV.
9. Cf. the article by Cordelia Kopsch in this book.
10. Cf. the article by Auguste Zeiß-Horbach in this book.

differences in the professional priorities of male and female pastors.[11] It must be pointed out straightaway, however, that the differences in the respective self-understandings are clearly recognizable but do not play such an important role in the description of their actual activities: here the differences only comprise about 10–15 percent.[12] It would be necessary to do further research on the reasons for this. In any case, both male and female pastors clearly see the priority for their activity in the "core areas" of pastoral ministry (worship, pastoral care, and counseling).[13] However, women pastors would rather have more time to support and encourage other people in their lives, while male pastors, according to the survey, would like more time for further professional training.[14] This means at least that both groups have a guilty conscience, but in different areas: some of them because they had not attended a (theological?) course of further education that had been offered to them, and others, because they had had to cut short the time spent in personal counseling. To be sure, we—just like the people questioned in the survey—do not know whether these answers are the result of gender-specific behavior in connection with questionnaires. It is quite clear that pastors no longer enjoy a unique attribute as men who offer life guidance inside and outside the church, but that they now (have to) accept women as colleagues who have been trained in this field for centuries and who, according to the survey in the churches in northern Germany, do indeed concentrate more strongly on "areas which traditionally have more female connotations."[15] And do women pastors possibly not feel the lack of theological further training so strongly because they usually satisfy this need at women's pastoral conferences or in the women's work of the church? In this regard there

11. Cf. G. Magaard, W. Nethöfel, eds., *Pastorin und Pastor im Norden. Antworten, Fragen, Perspektiven. Ein Arbeitsbuch zur Befragung der Pastorinnen und Pastoren der Evangelisch-Lutherischen Landeskirche Mecklenburgs, der Nordelbischen Evangelisch-Lutherischen Kirche und der Pommerschen Evangelischen Kirche* (Berlin, 2011); cf. also on this topic section 2 of Isolde Karle's article in this book.

12. Cf. Th. Schollas, Selbstbilder im Pfarrberuf und die Gewichtung der pastoralen Tätigkeit aus geschlechtsspezifischer Sicht, in: Magaard, Nethöfel, eds., *Pastorin und Pastor im Norden*, 29–33, esp. 32f.

13. Cf. M. Vetter, Gesellschaft und Kirche im Pfarrberuf, in: Magaard, Nethöfel, eds., *Pastorin und Pastor im Norden*, 25–28, 28.

14. Cf. Schollas, Selbstbilder im Pfarrberuf, 32.

15. Schollas, Selbstbilder im Pfarrberuf, 29, 32.

is another really striking and significant difference between the sexes in the ministry that became obvious in the survey of the North German churches: in their profession, women pastors see themselves much more clearly than their male counterparts as people who accompany *processes of searching*;[16] unlike their male colleagues, they are not so eager to see themselves as "missionaries" or "shepherds."[17] Whatever is exactly meant by these last two designations, they clearly appeal more strongly to the men. A further result of the survey notes that "in offices of church leadership there is more emphasis on representing the church, on being an advocate for the weak and on teamwork, while life guidance and setting a good example withdraw into the background."[18] This assessment could also provide an explanation for the fact that women pastors are less frequently found in positions of church leadership than men. They would have to relinquish their preference for life guidance but would contribute their affinity toward teamwork and advocacy for the weak. It may be assumed that if these qualifications were held in high esteem for positions of church leadership, it would be possible to gain more women pastors to occupy them.

Basically both male and female pastors are, in fact, quite satisfied with their profession despite the decreasing relevance of the church in society, and with regard to the future of the church they expect more from an improvement of communication within the church than from a general change of church structures.

4. Effects of Cultural Change in Society on the Pastorate

Deep down, the problem is probably the result of a cultural change in society as a whole that is not only happening in Germany. But it is happening in the churches as well, in the parishes and gradually also at the level of professional, academically trained ministry, in the pastorate. Even my own children were satisfied with far fewer books than my husband and I owned in our youth and during our studies. They need far fewer trips with furniture vans when they move, and they don't have specialist

16. Cf. Schollas, Selbstbilder im Pfarrberuf, 29, 30f.

17. Cf. Schollas, Selbstbilder im Pfarrberuf, 30f.; M. de Boor, Die Prägungen der Pastorinnen, in: Schollas, Selbstbilder im Pfarrberuf, 91–95, 92.

18. de Boor, Die Prägungen der Pastorinnen, 93.

dictionaries and encyclopedias, because they know very well that educational content becomes obsolete and it is better to rely on electronically accessible, up-to-date information. This also has an impact on the contours of the profession as pastor. Because it must be admitted—mostly with a certain nostalgic sadness—that pastors are no longer perceived primarily as "scholarly" members of the educated bourgeoisie, which was their conventional image in the nineteenth century. Historical exhibitions about life in Protestant vicarages demonstrate this impressively.[19] They show a concept of universal erudition that was socially, culturally, and not least charitably orientated and was transferred into society by the Protestant pastor's household, by his "transparent" family life in the parsonage. Today women pastors are neither willing nor expected to continue the traditional role of the pastor's wife, concentrating on small-scale pastoral care, on children's and women's work, practical assistance in the parish administration, and last but not least on bringing up their own children. Pastors can still embody a symbol for a type of education that is no longer supported by society. The radical change of this role expectation cannot be overestimated in its profundity and its empirical contradiction and ambivalence. It has a particular effect on the pastors. A considerable proportion of pastors are married to pastors, and it is not uncommon for a married couple to share one ministry in the parish.[20] The statistics gathered show that most part-time employees in the church are still female—and this also includes the many part-time positions for pastors, which are mainly taken by women pastors at their own request. It is only the continuation of this phenomenon that ensures that men are still clearly in the majority in the intermediate and higher levels of church management as well as in the many honorary commissions.[21] We are still

19. Cf., e.g., the exhibition in the German Historical Museum Berlin, which was conceived in cooperation with the Evangelical Church in Germany and the International Martin Luther Foundation as part of the Reformation Anniversary 2017; see https://www.dhm.de/archiv/ausstellungen/pfarrhaus/ (19.06.2018) as well as the publication by C. Aschenbrenner, *Das evangelische Pfarrhaus. 300 Jahre Glaube, Geist und Macht. Eine Familiengeschichte* (Munich, 2015).

20. Cf. for what follows the "Gleichstellungsatlas" of the EKD: Studienzentrum der EKD für Genderfragen, ed., *Atlas zur Gleichstellung von Frauen und Männern in der evangelischen Kirche in Deutschland. Eine Bestandsaufnahme* (Hanover, 2015) 23–388.

21. Cf. *Atlas zur Gleichstellung von Frauen und Männern*, 23–388.

in the midst of society's transformation toward truly equal participation. And if the churches show, not least through the ordination of women, that they expect the promises of the Gospel to come into effect with this transformation, then this is also an important proclamation, a sign and instrument of the Word of God.

This proclamatory aspect of women's participation in church ministry now also forces us to consider religious and psychological ambivalences of the yearning for the sacred. Although they often come in the garb of theological argumentation, they nevertheless seem to me to be part of the cultural and philosophical background.

5. Pastorate and Holiness

I have a Polish friend who is not a theologian. She is a good, completely relaxed Catholic, working as a primary school teacher, and she thinks it is good that it's now taken for granted that she can decide, if it's important to her, whether to go to a female or a male doctor. "But when it comes to the church, I see it differently," she says, and she is clearly a bit surprised at herself. She does not approve of female priests. Church is a different reality from the normal world, and it is precisely the gender difference of the priesthood that symbolizes that. This thought explains why there are indeed more than a few women in churches without women's ordination who do not consciously suffer from this situation. It probably does play a role that you cannot choose the sex of the priest as you would when going to the doctor, and that has been the case since time immemorial. For here the question is no more and no less than the longing for the church to represent effectively *holiness* in the proclamation of the Word and above all in the administration of the sacraments. In his book on women's ordination, Klaus Berger develops a (sometimes confusing) line of argument that the priesthood (both Catholic and Orthodox) represents a structure that contrasts with the congregation and thus symbolizes both the difference between God and the world and also their very connection.[22] This confusing picture is presumably what my Polish friend meant by "holiness." Berger also thinks that women are not suitable for this complex representation precisely because they would stand one-sidedly (on account of religious psychology?) for the one pole

22. Cf. K. Berger, *Priesterweihe auch für Frauen*? (Münster, 2012).

of the world.[23] His core thesis is that women can obviously not serve here as bearers of symbols, because their ability to give birth is a special sign of creative humanity as such. (Celibacy would then also have a similar justification from the standpoint of religious psychology.) Women were the perfect symbol of birth and death as good, but not godly creatureliness. The divine grace of consecration would obviously also not be able to remove this. The argumentation seems to lead to the conclusion that it is precisely the exclusion of women from church ministry that demonstrates the creaturely difference between God and humans particularly clearly, thus showing that the church is still on the way to salvation. The latter is also important to my Polish friend, and she prefers to trust in the male priest, whom she can regard as quite different from herself in his desexualized style of life.

The churches of the Reformation have now relinquished the real-life symbol of desexualization for what is holy. They do not really want to locate the profession of a pastor as such in the neighborhood of saintliness. And yet it is not entirely certain whether there are not still traces of the holiness argument here. Verena Hennings, herself a pastor, published a social science study from the Oldenburg Church in 2011.[24] The interviews were not held with the incumbents, but with their wives or husbands in order to gain an impression of "life in the parsonage." Verena Hennings vehemently advocates that pastors' families should no longer have to live and work in a parsonage assigned to them, but should rather be granted the right to a visibly private sphere. This position is supported by a clear result of the survey: more than 80 percent of those questioned believe that the system of official vicarages has a noticeable influence on private life. Many are searching for a "refuge" for the family and their private life.[25] In 2002, the EKD Council published "Recommendations on Questions of the Parsonage" in which it pleaded for the retention of the parsonage rules in order to emphasize the "inseparability of office and person."[26] This is also a great strength of the Protestant side, that

23. Cf. Berger, *Priesterweihe auch für Frauen?*, 89–131.

24. Cf. V. Hennings, *Leben im Pfarrhaus. Eine sozialwissenschaftliche Untersuchung aus der Oldenburgischen Kirche* (Oldenburg, 2011).

25. Cf. Hennings, *Leben im Pfarrhaus*, 38.

26. EKD, Empfehlung zu Fragen des Pfarrhauses, https://www.ekd.de/pfarrhaus_2002.html (19.06.2018), here 5.b) Pfarrhaus als Ausdruck der Untrennbarkeit von

in the parsonage debate there is even an allusion to the doctrine of two natures, claiming that these two aspects should be kept together "undivided" and "unmixed."[27] Is saintliness coming into play after all? In the opinion of Richard Riess, the "fundamental conflict" of the parsonage is the question of "whether and to what extent the 'sacred' really enters into the 'profane', whether—in other words—the parsonage is a 'normal house' or rather not 'of this world' after all."[28] He warns against entering this dilemma in the first place, in order not to "perish in the motifs of omnipotence and redemption."[29] What does this mean but to reject the whole question of holiness and profanity as inapplicable? In the Protestant world, it is certainly possible to reach quick agreement on this. The extent to which this affects the inseparability of the pastor's office from his or her person, and thus life in the parsonage, seems far less clear. It is by no means certain that the expectations placed in the Protestant parsonage up to the present day do not bear traces of hope for a concrete visibility of the presence of the Holy Spirit. Thus, with the abolition of celibacy, the male incumbent would no longer have to symbolize holiness alone, but rather his whole family, which would lead to completely new problems. This means that women are suited to the profession of pastor, because neither they nor their male colleagues have to act as a symbol of holiness, but it makes it increasingly difficult for pastors of both sexes to arrange a family life—at least as difficult as for Catholic or Orthodox priests, who have to symbolize the holiness mediated by the grace of ordination in the midst of the *corpus permixtum.*

6. Concluding Remarks

It is still early days for women ordained into church ministry in the Protestant Church. So it is not surprising that developments in the transi-

---

Amt und Person; cf. Hennings, *Leben im Pfarrhaus*, 38, incl. n. 40.

27. Cf. Hennings, *Leben im Pfarrhaus*, 39, with reference to F. A. Lehnert, V. A. Lehnert, Ehe im Pfarrhaus. Zwischen Kirche, Küche und Kanzelschwalben, in: *Deutsches Pfarrerblatt* (sic) 6 (2006) 304–6.

28. R. Riess, Zur Einstimmung, in: Riess, ed., *Haus in der Zeit. Das evangelische Pfarrhaus heute* (Munich, 1979) 7–16, 13f.; cited from Hennings, *Leben im Pfarrhaus*, 42.

29. Riess, Zur Einstimmung, cited from Hennings, *Leben im Pfarrhaus*, 42.

tion from a "male-dominated profession" to a profession chosen by both men and women are still clearly visible. But at least we have reached the stage in which a male pastor is no longer regarded as a "normal case," but that the parishes consider it pure coincidence whether a pastorate is occupied by a man or a woman. The fact that it is indeed coincidence, and not the result of exclusion, helps both men and women to fill their office of proclamation authentically. It would be a corruption of the Pauline doctrine of charisms if we were to look at it from the perspective of complementary anthropology, assigning different charisms to men and women by gender—even if our social history has obviously (still?!) produced different priorities. All the churches still have to deal with this.

(Translation from German by Neville Williamson)

Women in the Catholic Church—A Look at the Church in the Philippines

Sr. Mary John Mananzan OSB

Introduction

Writing about women in the Catholic Church in the Philippines necessitates a historical background because of the unique experience of women when the church in Spain was transplanted to the Philippines. In most countries, the introduction of Christianity meant an improvement in the status of women. In the Philippines this was not the case.

1. The Domestication of the *Mujer Indígena* by the Spanish Church

In pre-Spanish society the *mujer indígena* enjoyed a singular status not shared by other women from other parts of the world at that time. Though the pre-Spanish society cannot be characterized as matriarchal, elements present equal value given to female offspring. A woman enjoyed equal rights in the family as well as in society. She actively participated in the economic, political, and cultural life of the community and participated in all decision-making processes in all these areas. Moreover, in the religious field, she had the unique role of being the intermediary between the spirit world and the community in her role as the *babaylan* or priestess, an office reserved exclusively for women.

Spain brought Christianity and Western civilization into the islands. This admittedly was an enrichment to the inhabitants, just as the acquaintance with their ways of life and customs was likewise an enrichment for the Western colonizers. Slavery was abolished during this period, which of course affected both men and women. A meaning-giving system was introduced that satisfied many of the peoples' search for an explanation of the different problems of life.

The imposition of a strongly patriarchal system, however, had decidedly negative consequences on the role of women in society. A brief comparison will suffice. Whereas the young girl in pre-Spanish society enjoyed educational opportunities and similar freedom of movement as the young boy, the young girl under the Spanish influence became a sheltered, overprotected, timid maiden who received an education confined to church, kitchen, and children. She who could transact business with anybody, look after the economic welfare of the family, who could bear the responsibility of being a pact holder and even a leader of her tribe was reduced to a helpless creature, like Maria Clara who could never leave the house unaccompanied by an ever present Tia Isabel.

Her freedom of choice in important aspects of her life was curtailed by the imposition of new laws and mores. Confined in her area of action, the woman poured all her innate sensibility and energy into the activities allowed her, developing a religious fervor that would verge on fanaticism. She was constantly reminded of her innate danger to men as the seductive Eve and was relentlessly exhorted to follow an impossible model—the Virgin Mother. She could venerate her but her efforts to emulate her brought her into scrupulous, frustrated efforts that ended up giving her an abiding guilt complex that added to her timidity and lack of self-confidence and, in many cases, reducing her to frigidity. They could still have made Mary a model but one who is strong and courageous and had a social conscience, as shown in her song, the Magnificat.

On the pretext of putting a woman on a pedestal as an object of veneration and adulation, patriarchal society succeeded in alienating her from public life, public decisions, and public significance. She should henceforth be a delicate ornament in the home or the victim soul of the convent.

It is to the credit of the *mujer indígena* that in spite of this inhibiting influence, her innate common sense, wisdom, inner strength, and courage kept on breaking the bonds of her confinement, especially during times of emergency and need. She retained the subversive, "dangerous memory" of her original equality. It is no wonder that even after almost four hundred years of domestication, an American governor-general in the following epoch could exclaim in admiration of her: "In the Philippines, the best man is the Filipino woman."

2. The Role of Religious Women in the Ministry of the Church

During the Spanish era convents and monasteries were not allowed to accept native vocations, because the royal foundations were specifically created for "pious Spanish women and daughters of the conquistadores who cannot marry properly" without mention of native women. This was interpreted as prohibition.[1] The *mujer indígena* could only enter the third order of the religious congregations as a *beata*. It was only in 1632 that a native *beata* of the Third Order of St. Francis from Pampanga was given an exception to join the monastery.

When Spanish rule ended in the Philippines, the church felt threatened by the coming of the Protestant missionaries, the rise of the Indigenous Aglipayan Church, and the prevalence of Masonry. And so church officials appealed to Europe and America to send religious missionaries to counteract these perceived threats. This appeal was heard, and religious congregations sent missionaries to the Philippines.

3. The Contribution of Women Religious to the Church and Society

Religious women are among the most educated women in the Philippines because of the role they play in society.

Whatever the special charisma was of the religious congregations that arrived during the early period of American rule, they were all conscious that they were supposed to inculcate Christian Catholic values and so they all opened schools. The Daughters of Charity established La Concordia College and Sta. Isabel College, the Augustinans La Consolacion College, the St. Paul de Chartres St. Paul College, the Missionary Benedictine Sisters St. Scholastica's College, the Sisters of the Immaculate Heart of Mary St. Theresa's College, the Sister Servants of the Holy Spirit Holy Ghost College, and the Maryknoll Sisters Maryknoll College. They started from the lowest grades and continued to high school, through college, and to graduate school. At first they were all colleges for women. Only very much later on were coeducational branches of some of their flagship schools established all over the islands.

1. L. P. R. Santiago, To Love and to Suffer. The Development of the Religious Congregations for Women in the Spanish Philippines, 1565–1898 (Quezon City, 2005) 66.

The daughters of prominent families were educated by them and prepared not only for being good wives and mothers but for leadership in society. Corazon Aquino, the first woman president of the Philippines, studied at St. Scholastica's College, for example. The second woman president, Gloria Macapagal Arroyo, graduated from the Assumption Convent. In the context of martial law, several of these colleges adopted the motto: Education for justice and for social transformation. At the same time, they were centers of excellence in various disciplines. It is safe to say that many women leaders in all areas of endeavor studied in convent schools run by women religious.

3.1 Health

The congregations of religious women lost no time in also addressing the health problems of the country. They established hospitals: The Holy Spirit Sisters established Lourdes Hospital, the DC Sisters started the San Juan de Dios Hospital, the Missionary Benedictine Sisters the Divine Word Hospital in Tacloban and, more recently, St. Scholastica's Hospital in Pambujan, Northern Samar, the St. Paul Sisters took up the management of the Manila Doctor's Hospital, and many other health centers and clinics all over the country.

Religious women who established the Rural Missionaries of the Philippines initiated the Community Based Health Program and held responsible positions in it. This worthwhile project is described thus:

> People's participation is the core principle of the community-based health program (CBHP) in the Philippines that differentiates it from the other health programs' approaches. Without people's participation, a CBHP would be just another "band-aid solution." CBHPs give primacy to the organization of the local people before they are implemented. Organizing the people would include activities such as education or consciousness-raising and leadership formation. It ensures people's participation in the planning, implementation and evaluation of the program. Thus, the success of any undertaking that aims at serving the people is dependent on the people's participation at all levels.[2]

Community-based health programs are found all over the Philippines.

2. Martin Khor and Lim Li Lin, eds., *Good Practices and Innovative Experiences in the South* (UNDP; New York, 2001) 2.

3.2 Socio-pastoral Work

Without religious women, parishes would be very limited in their services. Usually one or two communities of sisters take charge of activities in the parish such as parochial schools, organizing and training catechists and fielding them in different parts of the parish, and building basic ecclesial communities. They also arrange the liturgical services and some even take care of the housekeeping of the priest's house and of the seminary where there is one. They also take care of orphanages that are attached to the parish or diocese.

There are many social issues that have become the focus of the commitment of religious women.

Current Issues Affecting Women

Women religious are particularly sensitive to the many issues that disempower women—the prevailing inequality in a patriarchal society, subordination of women in the homes, different forms of exploitation, many forms of violence against women, and trafficking of women.

With regard to *violence against women*, religious congregations have set up shelters for female victims of violence with psychological and spiritual counseling, legal and medical advocacy, and organization and economic empowerment of survivors. Two such organizations in which religious women have been active as founders or administrators are the Women Crisis (Care) Center and the Office of Women and Gender Concerns of the Association of Major Religious Superiors of the Philippines.

Religious women are also active with regard to *human trafficking*, especially involving women and children. A campaign called TALITHA KUM was spearheaded by a Filipino Salesian Sister, Sr. Estrella Castelone, when she worked at the English Section of the UISG (Union of Superior Generals in Rome). The program includes conscientization seminars and various forms of advocacy against human trafficking. The campaign has spread to countries all over the world. The first center for migrant workers, called Tipanan, was established by the Missionary Benedictine Sisters in Madrid, Spain in 1984. It was transferred to Barcelona and renamed Tuluyan San Benito. The center, which the sisters helped to set up, has been given over to the organization of migrant workers.

A school for women run by the Missionary Benedictine Sisters, St. Scholastica's College, was also the first school to *mainstream gender in the academe*. Sr. Mary John Mananzan established an Institute of Women's

Studies to *empower women through alternative feminist education*. It has given seminars to thousands of women not only in the Philippines but in other Asian countries that send participants to their long-term courses.

3.3 Environmental Advocacy

Religious women have been very active at the very onset of ecological advocacy in the Philippines. Sr. Aida Velasquez spearheaded the campaign against the nuclear power plant in the 1970s, educating a whole village in which it was supposed to be built. This became a national campaign that succeeded in the mothballing of the nuclear power plant built in Bataan, which has never operated even as to this writing. Sisters were also involved in the organizing of the Nuclear Free Philippines Coalition.

Many congregations of sisters have acquired farms to propagate organic farming and sustainable agriculture. Their schools have included environmental protection in the curriculum in all levels and encourage environmentally friendly practices with regard to waste management, anti-pollution, energy conservation, and reforestation.

3.4 The Role of Cloistered Nuns

The main orders of cloistered nuns in the Philippines are the Carmelites, the Adoration Sisters (Pink Sisters), the Contemplative Branch of the Good Shepherd Sisters, and the La Consolacion Sisters, the Poor Clares, the Benedictine Nuns of the Eucharistic King, and lately the Trappistines. Cloistered nuns believe that their vocation is to witness to the primacy of prayer in the church, to serve as a reminder of the contemplative dimension in all lives, and to intervene for others before God. Besides being available to individual persons who seek their help and counsel, they bring the needs and sorrows of the world to God in their life of prayer. In spite of being cloistered, many contemplative communities have shown interest in and concern for the burning issues of society. They sometimes also serve as sanctuary for endangered people. An example was when Cory Aquino sought sanctuary among the Carmelite nuns when she ran against the dictator Ferdinand Marcos and became the first woman president of the Philippines.

3.5 Filipino Religious Women as Missionaries to Foreign Lands

With the decline of vocations in the mother houses of religious women congregations, Filipino nuns and sisters are now being sent to staff their mother houses and other mission houses all over the world. They are not only sent in a kind of reverse missionary activity to Europe and the United States, they are also sent to mission houses in Africa, India, and Latin America, especially in such leadership positions as prioresses, mother provincials, novice directresses, and principals of schools.

3.6 The Special Prophetic Role of Filipino Religious

During the martial law years 1972–1986, many religious women became aware of the injustices and oppression of the people and became actively involved in the struggle of the basic masses: peasants, workers, urban poor, and Indigenous people.

In the 1970s a movie entitled *Sister Stella L* was shown in many theaters in the Philippines. It was all about a young sister who typified the religious women who became aware of the social issues and her commitment and involvement in the national liberation movement. The scriptwriter, Jose Lacaba, said that he based his character on the interviews he conducted with three religious women: Sr. Christine Tan, RGS (Good Shepherd Sister), Sr. Marianni Dimaranan, SFIC (Franciscan Sister of the Immaculate Concepcion, more popularly known as St. Joseph's Sisters), and Sr. Mary John Mananzan, OSB (Missionary Benedictine Sister).

In summary, Mina Roces, in her article "Militant Nuns as Political Activist and Feminist in Martial Law," writes:

> The fictionalised story of Sister Stella L. depicted the militant nun's metamorphosis into political activist. It was the nuns' exposure to the victims of martial law that inspired them to speak out for political detainees, support labour strikes, report on the abuses of the regime and later act as human barricades in the front lines that faced the military . . . The nuns were transformed into political activists almost immediately after martial law was declared in 1972. The plight of a vast number of political prisoners or detainees (many of whom were tortured and killed or savaged) first attracted the attention of these women, who—because of their Christian vocation—staunchly believed in the causes of social justice. Eventually, the problems of labourers who participated in illegal strikes against low salaries and inappropriate working conditions, and the evictions of tribal groups from their lands compelled the progressive nuns to come out of their convents, braving arrest and military force . . . the militant nuns consistently took to the streets to champion human rights. . . .

> They became the first women to challenge cultural constructions of the feminine. . . . The nuns became the first women's group to challenge traditional cultural constructions of the feminine, form feminist organizations and then focus on trying to alter these traditional definitions of the feminine by teaching women's studies courses and supporting research on women.[3]

4. The Role of Lay Women in the Church

The most significant event in the Catholic Church in contemporary times is the Second Vatican Council, convened in 1962. This introduced radical changes in the life of the church. Among the most significant is the change in the perspective of the church as a church in the world. This is the context of the rise of the laity in the church.

In the Philippines, the event that actually gave impetus to the rise of the laity was the PCP II, the Second Plenary Council of the Philippines. In his address to the assembly of SAC directors in 2006, Cardinal Quevedo emphasized the role of the laity and especially women in the church:

> **Empowerment of the Laity toward Social Transformation.** We shall promote and support the exercise of the God-given gifts and charisms of lay people. Lay people must take the lead in social transformation. In particular we shall consult a wide range of women's experiences in different life situations and explore new possible roles of women in Church and society.[4]

Lay people became very involved and were the main actors in the basic ecclesial community movement that spread to all parishes of the country.

The Filipinos are a church-going people. It is safe to say that among churchgoers about 80 percent are women. So the first role of the lay woman in the church is that of a *worshiper.* And perhaps in the eyes of God that is the most important role. But we live in a human society and therefore there is a need of developing the active role of lay women in the pursuit of the church's vision/mission. But before Vatican II the role of the lay woman consisted of being in the choir (manangs), arranging the flowers on the altar, passing the collection bags after the offertory, and leading the rosary or novena prayers before or after Mass. After Vatican

3. *Portal* 1, no. 1 (2004) 1, 2, 5, 7, 8.
4. Orlando Quevedo, "Behold I Make All Things New," *NPCCR* 7, no. 2.

II, she could read the first and second readings and she could distribute Holy Communion and act as commentator during the Mass. Girls could be sacristans and mass servers.

After PCPII, women started to join church organizations that gave them opportunities for leadership and decision-making. They are not only active in church-mandated women's organizations such as the Catholic Women's League and Mother Butler's Guild but also in mixed organizations such as Couples for Christ, the Christian Family Movement, Christian Life Community, and others. But leadership in this mixed group is still mainly in the hands of the men. There were some prominent women who played a big role in the church such as Henrietta de Villa, who spearheaded the calling of PCPII and later on founded the PPCRV, which became the official watchdog on elections within the church. She also became the first woman ambassador to the Vatican and was succeeded by two other women.

5. The Phenomenon of Reverse Mission

With the rise of migration and migrant labor abroad, a new task for the laity, especially the women migrant workers, emerged: Reverend Canon Marx Oxbrow quotes Samuel Escobar in his article, "Recovering Mission":

> Another missionary force is also at work today, although it does not appear in the records of missionary activity or the databanks of specialists. It is the transcultural witnessing for Christ that takes place as people move around as migrants or refugees, just as in New Testament days. . . . They are missionaries 'from below' who do not have the power, the prestige, or the money from a developed nation, and are not part of a missionary organisation. They are vulnerable in many ways, but have learnt the art of survival, supported by their faith in Jesus Christ.[5]

In our Center for Migrant Workers in Spain—the Tuluyan San Benito—a nanny once proudly shared with us how she "converted" the whole family she was working with. It seems that when she would go

5. Quoted in Rev. Canon Mark Oxbrow, Recovering Mission: Majority World Mission—A Return to Mission for the Majority, Lausanne World Pulse, January 2009, https://www.lausanneworldpulse.com/themedarticles-php/1071/01-2009.

to Mass every Sunday, she would always bring her ward, a young boy, along with her. The boy later on began to ask his parents why they were not going to church. The parents then started accompanying them and are now regular churchgoers.

When one goes to church in Europe and some non-Christian countries in Asia, one is at once impressed by the fact that almost 80 percent of the faithful are Filipinos. One European said, "Without them, our churches are dead." And of course they bring with them their devotions, such as the Novena to the Perpetual Help, and even organize branches of Couples for Christ, El Shaddai, and other groups.

6. Current Women's Issues in the Church

6.1 Reproductive Health Law—Contemporary Women's Issue in the Philippine Church

A recent controversy highlights a contemporary women's issue in the church. This has to do with the introduction of a bill that, after considerable controversy, was passed as *Republic* Act No. 10354, otherwise known as the "Responsible Parenthood and Reproductive Health Act of 2012." In general, it guarantees universal access to methods of contraception, fertility control, sexual education, and maternal care.

The bishops launched a massive campaign against the bill, objecting mainly to the provision regarding contraceptives and sex education. Women's organizations lobbied for it. Outstanding is the group led by lay women who called themselves Catholics for Reproductive Health. It is amazing that in spite of massive opposition the bill was passed in 2012. But the fight is far from over. There is still the budget allocation, without which the law will be inoperative. Because of the pro-life (*sic*) lawmakers and government officials, full funding is not yet available.

This issue, I believe, will be a continuing bone of contention between women and the hierarchy in the Philippines.

6.2 Sexual Abuse by the Clergy

A serious problem in the church that affects women and girls and, in some instances, young boys is the sexual harassment and abuse by the clergy. Since the priests cannot or will not assume any responsibility for the children they cause to be brought into the world, the responsibility and burden falls on the shoulders of the victims—the unwed, single mothers. They and their children also bear the brunt of the scorn of society and the shame of being victims of sexual abuse or being "children of priests." In the Philippines, no priest has ever been imprisoned for his crime and is often just simply transferred to another parish where often the offenses are repeated.

6.3 Continuing Gender Inequality in the Church

Although this is a universal fact, it has to be addressed in the context of the Philippines. There has been great progress in gender consciousness in the Philippines due to the strong women's movement. In fact, many woman-friendly laws have been passed, including a Magna Carta for women. In 2015 the first Memorandum of the year passed by CHED (Commission on Higher Education) is gender mainstreaming in all tertiary educational institution. There has not been corresponding progress in the church. In fact, to counteract the influence of the militant secular women's organization, Gabriela, the church formed its own women's organization called Teodora. When one recalls that in Philippine history, Gabriela was the woman hero who fought against the Spaniards and Teodora was the middle-class mother of Jose Rizal, one recognizes the intention of the creation of this group.

The Catholic Church still holds a conservative view of women. Church teachings on family life still emphasize the "obey your husband" dictum. Battered women are advised to stay in such a marriage so as not to have a "broken family."

Its moral theology still focuses on the "sins of the flesh" with a certain bias against women as "Eve the temptress." The cult of virginity that prevails makes women who lose their virginity, even not through their fault, feel like garbage. Many prostitutes make a plunge into prostitution because they lost their virginity through either rape or incest. The portrayal of the ideal woman as one who is self-sacrificing, long-suffering, patient, meek, and so forth is actually a conditioning of a victim consciousness in women. No wonder there are so many women victims of violence.

In the liturgy, there is still a sexist tone addressing the assembly as "brethren," praying for the salvation of "mankind," and exhorting to love one's "fellowmen." The women are given minor roles in the liturgy, but they shoulder the more burdensome preparations behind the scenes and the "making order" after each celebration

Although women are the most active in church service functions and activities, they are deprived of participation in the major decision-making processes and are denied full ministry in the church. Celibate priests continue, in fact, to make the rules and prescriptions governing marriage and family life. The structure is hierarchical and clerical, and women have no part in either.

6.4 Feminist Theology of Liberation

The women in the Philippines, both lay and religious, conscious of the continuing gender inequality in the church, participated in the development of a feminist theology of liberation from the perspective of Asian women within the Ecumenical Association of Third World Theologians (EATWOT). Their avowed task is to deconstruct what is oppressive in religion and to reconstruct what is liberating. They have participated in national, regional, and international conferences on feminist theology, delineating its methodology, defining its hermeneutic, and embarking on such concrete projects as a feminist journal entitled *In God's Image*, and writing books on the gender aspects of theologizing—God-talk, Christology, Mariology, ecclesiology, missiology, and so forth. A new development is the establishment of a Catholic feminist theologians organization called Ecclesia.

7. Conclusion

Talking about the ministry of women in the church brings us to the perplexing situation that women actually do the great part of ministering to the needs of people in the church and yet are not given the title of ministers, nor do they participate in the decision-making processes in the church. In all parishes, women constitute the majority in the organizations and groups that actually alleviate the material and spiritual needs of the people short of administering the sacraments. We have also seen how religious women minister to society in general by their work in education, health, social activism, and their solidarity with the struggle of the poor, oppressed, and marginalized.

However, it must be said that there is still a virtual inequality of women in the Catholic Church in spite of the theoretical acceptance of their equality. The practice in the church has not kept up with the progress of women's empowerment in the larger society. There is no possibility of her ever enjoying full ministry in the church. This has given impetus to the development of a feminist theology from an Asian perspective determined to see to it that the liberating factors in Christianity will somehow neutralize its oppressive aspects.

Osnabrück Theses

A scientific congress under the title "Women in Church Ministries. Reform Movements in Ecumenism" was held in Osnabrück, Germany from December 6 to 9, 2017, as a joint ecumenical cooperation between theological institutions of the Universities of Osnabrück, Oldenburg, and Münster, together with German Roman Catholic and Protestant associations and institutions. After lectures, discussions, and intensive consultations, a majority of over 120 participants to the congress, who came from multilateral ecumenical contexts in Germany and other countries, adopted the following theses:

(1)

The declared goal of the ecumenical movement, the visible unity of the churches, cannot be achieved without an agreement on the presence of women in all ecclesiastical ministries.

(2)

Women in church ministries make a profound difference to the way each religious community is perceived by itself and by others.

(3)

It is necessary to find reasons not for women's access to offices and ministries of the church, but rather for their exclusion.

(4)

The discussion can and must remain open as to whether God has given an immutable instruction as to how and by whom he/she is to be witnessed through the church's ministry.

(5)

The distinction between specific offices within the one (sacramental) ministry (episcopate, priesthood, and diaconate) has developed historically and can be further developed in an ecumenical perspective. All forms of office should be opened for women. It is important to ensure that no gender-specific determination is made.

(6)
Critical inquiries into the church's teaching on the exclusion of women from church offices and ministries are a manifestation of women's readiness to exercise their vocation to serve the proclamation of the Gospel in word and deed.

(7)
The Spirit of Jesus Christ obliges us always to approach the various theological convictions regarding ecclesiastical ministries with argumentative cooperation, appreciation, and readiness to reconciliation.

Self-commitment

(1)
We will ensure that gender equality in the assumption and exercise of ecclesiastical ministries is the touchstone for credibility in the proclamation of the Gospel. This is indispensable for the apostolic mission of the churches. Beyond the question of the ordination of women, other forms of insensitivity toward gender equality in the churches should be recognized and overcome.

(2)
We will continue the theological discussions on the presence of women in all ecclesiastical ministries with the goal of reaching an understanding in the remaining controversies. Depending on the denominational situation, we will not shun critical discussion with the responsible church leaders about all forms of ordained ministry. In ecumenical fellowship, we strive for the ordination of women as deaconesses, presbyters (pastors, priests), and bishops.

(3)
We will continue to make theological contributions to the necessary differentiation between the opening to women of the diaconate and of other ministries within the one (sacramental) *ordo*. As a ministry for men and women, the diaconate strengthens the basic diaconal orientation of the church.

(4)

Within the bounds of our responsibility, we will strive for the increasing participation of women in leadership positions and ministries. We seek a culture of partnership in all churches.

Osnabrück, December 9, 2017

Prof. Dr. Margit Eckholt, University of Osnabrück
Prof. Dr. Ulrike Link-Wieczorek, University of Oldenburg
Prof. Dr. Dorothea Sattler, University of Münster
Prof. Dr. Andrea Strübind, University of Oldenburg

Explanatory Notes on the Theses

(1)

The declared goal of the ecumenical movement, the visible unity of the churches, cannot be achieved without an agreement on the presence of women in all ecclesiastical ministries.

The joint ecumenical commemoration of the Reformation in 2017 invites discussion of the issue of the presence of women in all ecclesiastical ministries. This ecumenical event has been an encouragement to strive constantly for reform movements in all Christian churches as a common path to renewal.

After a long internal struggle in the twentieth century, many churches of the Reformation as well as the Old Catholic Church introduced the practice of ordaining women with prayer and laying on of hands. In Protestant churches, women preach the Gospel and lead the celebration of Holy Communion. Since the middle of the twentieth century, in a process of several stages involving painful discrimination, women have come to assume various ecclesiastical ministries, offices, and functions in many churches of the Reformation. In numerous church ordinances the equality of women and men in the service of the church has, meanwhile, been explicitly defined. In recent decades, women have been able to form and shape not only the pastorate but also many other areas of the Protestant churches. This includes the office of bishop. The participation of women in church offices is therefore part of the profile of the churches of the Reformation and thus also influences ecumenical relations.

The question of women in church ministries is therefore of central importance in the search for the visible unity of the churches.

(2)

Women in church ministries make a profound difference to the way each religious community is perceived by itself and by others.

Nowadays, the way in which women exercise ecclesiastical ministries is perceived as one of the primary features distinguishing churches from one another. Society expects women and men to be equal in professional life, and this forms the backdrop for a critical examination of gender roles in the churches. Gender equality is an essential criterion in today's society in order to test the legitimacy of institutions claiming universal representation.

The consideration of the official roles of women in the churches is closely connected to the general question of upcoming reforms in the exercise of ecclesiastical ministries by men and women. The outward appearance of the church community influences the credibility of the proclamation of the Gospel of Jesus Christ.

In the Roman Catholic tradition, the legacy of the Second Vatican Council with its normative doctrines on the understanding of the mission of the church is of the utmost importance. The council drew attention to the fact that the nature of the church is its mission to proclaim Jesus Christ. Closely related to this is the concept of a prophetic dimension to which all believers are called, at first by baptism and later strengthened by confirmation. Accordingly, all baptized persons are entrusted with a prophetic, royal, and priestly ministry by Jesus Christ (cf. 1 Pet 2:9-10; *Lumen Gentium* 34; *Apostolicam Actuositatem* 3), and a new breadth of the representation of Christ is established in this common priesthood. In view of the council's new perception of the church's global horizon, combined with the recollection of the basic diaconal determination of the church's mission in solidarity with the poor and the marginalized, there is now—in the subsequent period in which we stand—no excuse for any kind of activity that excludes or discriminates against women.

In all churches, women have increasingly taken on leadership positions at local, regional, and national levels in recent decades. Women are responsible for training women and men for the preaching ministry in parishes, schools, and universities. Women are now heading departments for personnel, pastoral care, finance, or public relations. They act as legal advisors, directors of academies, human resource developers, or as leaders in Caritas and Diakonie. Many academically educated women are engaged in research and teaching of scientific theology with a social mandate.

For the churches of the Reformation, it is desirable that the number of women in church leadership functions continues to increase despite the equality of women and men in the ecclesiastical ministries that has already been achieved. All churches need to review the history of discrimination against women with regard to exclusionary practices.

(3)

It is necessary to find reasons not for women's access to offices and ministries of the church, but rather for their exclusion.

From a theological point of view, the mere reference to social changes in the description of gender roles is not sufficient to justify women's access to ecclesiastical ministries. Theological reasons must be given if charismatically gifted women are still excluded today from the public preaching of the Gospel in most churches, especially in the Roman Catholic and Orthodox Churches and even in some of the Reformed churches. According to common ecumenical conviction, biblical testimonies are normative for doctrine when justifying a decision. Tradition should preserve what the canon of the Scriptures teaches.

In the controversial discourses on this subject, it was and is undisputed that women and men enjoy the same dignity before God in the order of creation and redemption. God created humankind as man and woman in his image (see Gen 1:26f.). The affiliation to Jesus Christ by baptism overcomes the socially or religiously based boundaries between Jews and Greeks, slaves and the free, male and female (Gal 3:28). In the light of this theological-anthropological insight, the question arises whether there are sufficient arguments to allow only men into the circle of possible ministers. Such arguments would have to be equivalent to a divine directive for the institutional form of the church.

The development of ecclesiastical ministries reflected in biblical texts leaves open the possibility of women's participation in such ministries. Many women belonged to the group of people who were open to Jesus' proclamation of the kingdom of God and joined in his mission (Luke 8:1-3). They were the first witnesses to the resurrection. In the biblical and postbiblical Christian tradition, there were longer periods in which it was a matter of course that women exercised ecclesiastical ministries. In the Pauline communities, women and men had missionary duties and were locally the leaders of the first small congregations. Women were also charged with regional services and even recognized as apostles (cf.

Rom 16:7). As Christian congregations emerged in the first centuries, women were officially involved as deaconesses in the baptism of women.

Thus there is a very ancient tradition of women's participation in various church offices and ministries. In this context, it is particularly important to remember the ministry of deaconesses, who were indeed ordained in the first millennium by prayer and the laying on of hands, as can be verified by reference to the sources. The alteration of this practice, which led to the exclusion of women from church ministries—first of all in the West and later in the East—is in need of justification.

(4)

The discussion can and must remain open as to whether God has given an immutable instruction as to how and by whom God is to be witnessed through the church's ministry.

Bible texts repeatedly emphasize that God moves in a mysterious way, and in scientific theology it is an open question whether humans can possibly discern the will of God as he/she directs the course of the world. In controversial discussions about the ecclesiastical ministries, the recognition of this fact is not always confessed.

In the Christian tradition, the question has often been considered whether Jesus may have appointed twelve (male) disciples in order to predetermine the divinely intended future shape of the community that was to preserve his memory. Exegetical commentaries on the relevant biblical passages mostly hold the opinion that the calling of the twelve members of his inner circle was supposed to symbolize Jesus Christ's enduring mission to Israel until his death, to one nation in twelve tribes. At that time, in a patriarchal society, it would not have been possible to convey this theological concern if women had been allowed to belong to the Twelve.

It was only the New Testament author Luke who identified the twelve disciples with the apostles in his Gospel and in Acts, and this only for a certain period as a sign of continuity with Israel's history of salvation. Later in Acts, this group is replaced by other authorities such as James, the brother of Jesus, and Paul. All the other authors understand witness to an encounter with the risen Christ as the foundation of the apostolate. From ancient times, Mary of Magdala therefore bore the honorable title of *apostola apostolorum*—the apostle sent to the apostles with the Easter message (cf. John 20:17ff.).

The discovery that women held responsibility in the early Christian communities (Rom 16) and that their charismatic equality was thus recognized renders the idea of exclusively male representation particularly dubious. In addition, this teaching is an affront to the churches of the Reformation, in which women work in all areas of service and bring blessing by their activity.

The interpretation of the texts of the Second Vatican Council together with differentiations in systematic theology and church law lead to the realization that the existing Roman Catholic doctrinal texts have not come to an ultimately binding decision on the access of women to all ecclesiastical ministries.

(5)

The distinction between specific offices within the one (sacramental) ministry (episcopate, priesthood, and diaconate) has developed historically and can be further developed in an ecumenical perspective. All forms of office should be opened for women. It is important to ensure that no gender-specific determination is made.

At the institutional level, the Christian denominations have chosen different models of differentiation between the official ministries up to the present time, which is also due to the variety of concepts of ministry in the New Testament. In many Christian churches there is presently a renewed attention to the question of whether there may indeed be theological reasons for making a distinction between the ministry of supervision over many parishes (episkopé), the leadership of the local congregation (presbyterate), and the leadership of missionary-social services (diaconate).

After the sixteenth century, the churches of the Reformation tradition tended to focus on church ministry in the local pastorate. The ecumenical dialogue, especially with churches of the Anglican, Old Catholic, and Orthodox traditions, has led worldwide to a reconsideration of the biblical tradition of three differentiated ministries. For Roman Catholic theology, Vatican II was formative for doctrine. Since the fullness of the sacrament of orders is given in the episcopate, whose primary task is the preaching of the Gospel (see LG 25), diaconate and presbyterate can be assigned to the episcopate in a complementary fashion, that is to say, as additional and autonomous ministries: the diaconal ministry as a mission directed to the margins of the church, while the priestly ministry acts from the center of the parish.

As understood ecumenically, a sacrament is a divinely endowed symbolic action that reveals God's being in time and history. God made human in Jesus Christ is the most evident sign of God's presence in the world. According to biblical terminology (see Col 2:2), Jesus Christ is God's sacrament (*mysterion*). A person who follows Jesus Christ as a leader in ministry to his neighbor is Christ's representative in the social context. The ordained deacons and deaconesses are especially entrusted with the charitable administration of care for the poor, the weak, the sick, and the marginalized. In this way they share with the other church ministries the missionary task of proclaiming the Gospel, as well as in celebrating the Eucharist and baptism in the sense of personal representation of Christ Jesus the servant. The argumentation of Roman Catholic scientific theology thus reinforces the position that the diaconate of men and women should be positioned in one single sacramental *ordo*.

The form and practice of ecclesiastical ministries as well as their relationship to one another serve the proclamation of the Gospel. Thus, constant reform and examination should be inspired by impulses from Holy Scripture. At just this point, ecumenical fellowship in reconciled diversity can be revealed as a space for renewal and inspiration. The recent ordination of deaconesses in the Patriarchate of Alexandria and in the Patriarchate of Jerusalem is a sign of hope.

(6)

Critical inquiries into the church's teaching on the exclusion of women from church offices and ministries are a manifestation of women's readiness to exercise their vocation to serve the proclamation of the Gospel in word and deed.

All offices and ministries must always be directed toward the glorification of God and the proclamation of his Good News. The impetus for the recognition of women in church offices and ministries was caused by the calling of women to the preaching ministry. They set out to develop structures and functions in the church corresponding to their mission. Women who see themselves called into the discipleship of Jesus Christ suffer from the disregard of their spiritual experience in those churches which continue to reject the ordination of women to this day. At the present time, people are aware that the categorical exclusion of women from church ministries (in the denominations concerned) limits both the effectiveness of the proclamation of the Gospel and the diversity of the charisms. As long as the respective churches do not seriously examine the vocation of women to the ministry, they deny that God also calls women.

It is not the *zeitgeist* that determines the debate about women's access to ecclesiastical ministries, but the recognition of the mission of Jesus Christ to proclaim God in all ages. In ecumenical solidarity we jointly pose the question: How can we convey to people today the significance of following Jesus Christ in the search for a life filled with meaning? Many people think that church leaders today are disregarding the gifts of God's Spirit when they fail to offer women an official vocation so that they may use their calling and their talents to testify publicly to the Gospel in word and deed.

(7)

The Spirit of Jesus Christ obliges us always to approach the various theological convictions regarding ecclesiastical ministries with argumentative cooperation, appreciation, and readiness to reconciliation.

The history of the discussions on the issue of women's access to church offices and ministries is highly charged in all Christian churches. In all traditions, many wounds have been inflicted and continue to cause pain today. When this unsettled question is brought up, fears of imminent sanctions accompany the discussion down to our own day.

From a scientific point of view, it is necessary to present the arguments to the public dispassionately and not to conceal the personal interests that always play a role in the findings. There can be no impartial opinion on the matter. Every insight is limited. In the scientific discussion, the conditions leading to the arguments are considered critically.

Osnabrück, December 9, 2017

(Translation from German by Neville Williamson)

Authors

Thomai Chouvarda, Dr. theol., Lecturer at the Faculty of Theology, Aristotle University of Thessaloniki.

Sabine Demel, Dr. theol., Professor of Canon Law at the Faculty of Catholic Theology, University of Regensburg.

Margit Eckholt, Dr. theol., Dr. h.c., Professor of Dogmatics (with Fundamental Theology) at the Institute of Catholic Theology, University of Osnabrück.

Eva-Maria Faber, Dr. theol., Professor of Dogmatics and Fundamental Theology at the Theological University of Chur/Switzerland.

Sr. Makrina Finlay, OSB, Dr. theol., Benedictine Abbey of St. Scholastica, Dinklage.

Theresia Hainthaler, Dr. theol., Dr. h.c., Professor emerita of Christology of the Early Church and Theology of the Christian East at Sankt Georgen Graduate School of Philosophy and Theology.

Peter Hünermann, Dr. theol., Dr. h.c. mult., Professor emeritus of Dogmatics at the Faculty of Catholic Theology, University of Tübingen.

Isolde Karle, Dr. theol., Professor of Practical Theology at the Faculty of Protestant Theology, University of Bochum.

Ulrike Link-Wieczorek, Dr. theol., Professor of Systematic Theology and Religious Education at the Institute of Protestant Theology and Religious Education, University of Oldenburg.

Sr. Mary John Mananzan, OSB, Dr. theol., Vice-President of St. Scholastica's College, a Catholic girls' school in Manila/Philippines, and Director of the College's Institute of Women's Studies as well as Research and Development Foundation.

Dorothea Sattler, Dr. theol., Professor of Ecumenical Theology and Dogmatics at the Faculty of Catholic Theology, University of Münster.

Andrea Strübind, Dr. theol., Professor of Church History and Historical Theology at the Institute of Protestant Theology and Religious Education, University of Oldenburg.

Michael Theobald, Dr. theol., Professor emeritus of New Testament Studies at the Faculty of Catholic Theology, University of Tübingen.

Saskia Wendel, Dr. theol., Professor of Systematic Theology at the Institute of Catholic Theology, University of Cologne.